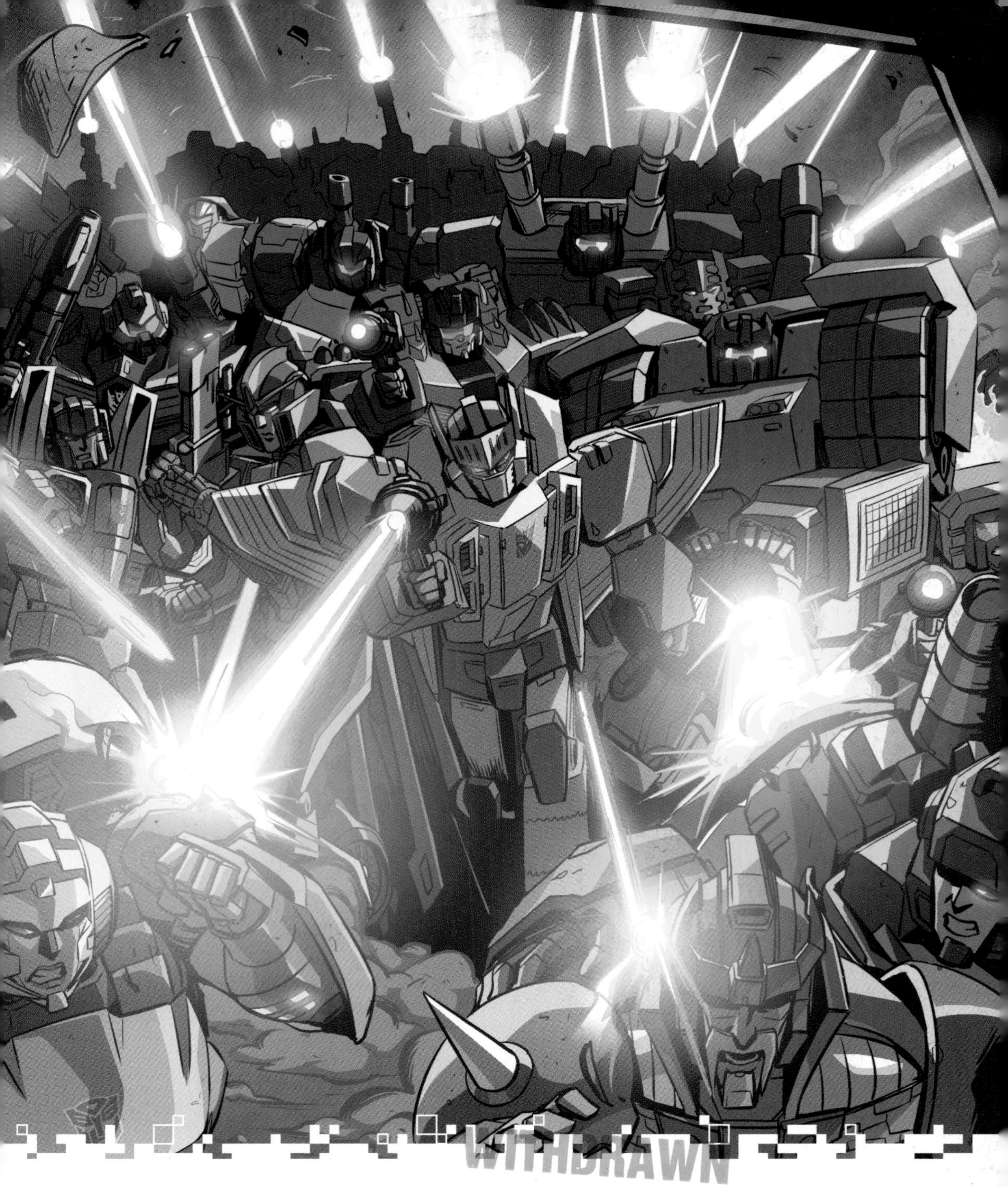

TRANSFORMERS

THE TRANSFORMERS
VOLUME 9

Collection Cover by Andrew Griffith
Series Edits by Carlos Guzman
Collection Edits by Justin Eisinger and Alonzo Simon
Collection Design by Claudia Chong
Publisher: Ted Adams

Special thanks to Hasbro's Clint Chapman, Heather Hopkins, Jerry Jivoin, Joshua Lamb, Ed Lane, Mark Weber, and Michael Kelly for their invaluable assistance.   For international rights, contact licensing@idwpublishing.com

ISBN: 978-1-63140-668-3   19 18 17 16   1 2 3 4

Ted Adams, CEO & Publisher
Greg Goldstein, President & COO
Robbie Robbins, EVP/Sr. Graphic Artist
Chris Ryall, Chief Creative Officer/Editor-in-Chief
Matthew Ruzicka, CPA, Chief Financial Officer
Dirk Wood, VP of Marketing
Lorelei Bunjes, VP of Digital Services
Jeff Webber, VP of Licensing, Digital and Subsidiary Rights
Jerry Bennington, VP of New Product Development

www.IDWPUBLISHING.com

Facebook: **facebook.com/idwpublishing**
Twitter: **@idwpublishing**
YouTube: **youtube.com/idwpublishing**
Tumblr: **tumblr.idwpublishing.com**
Instagram: **instagram.com/idwpublishing**

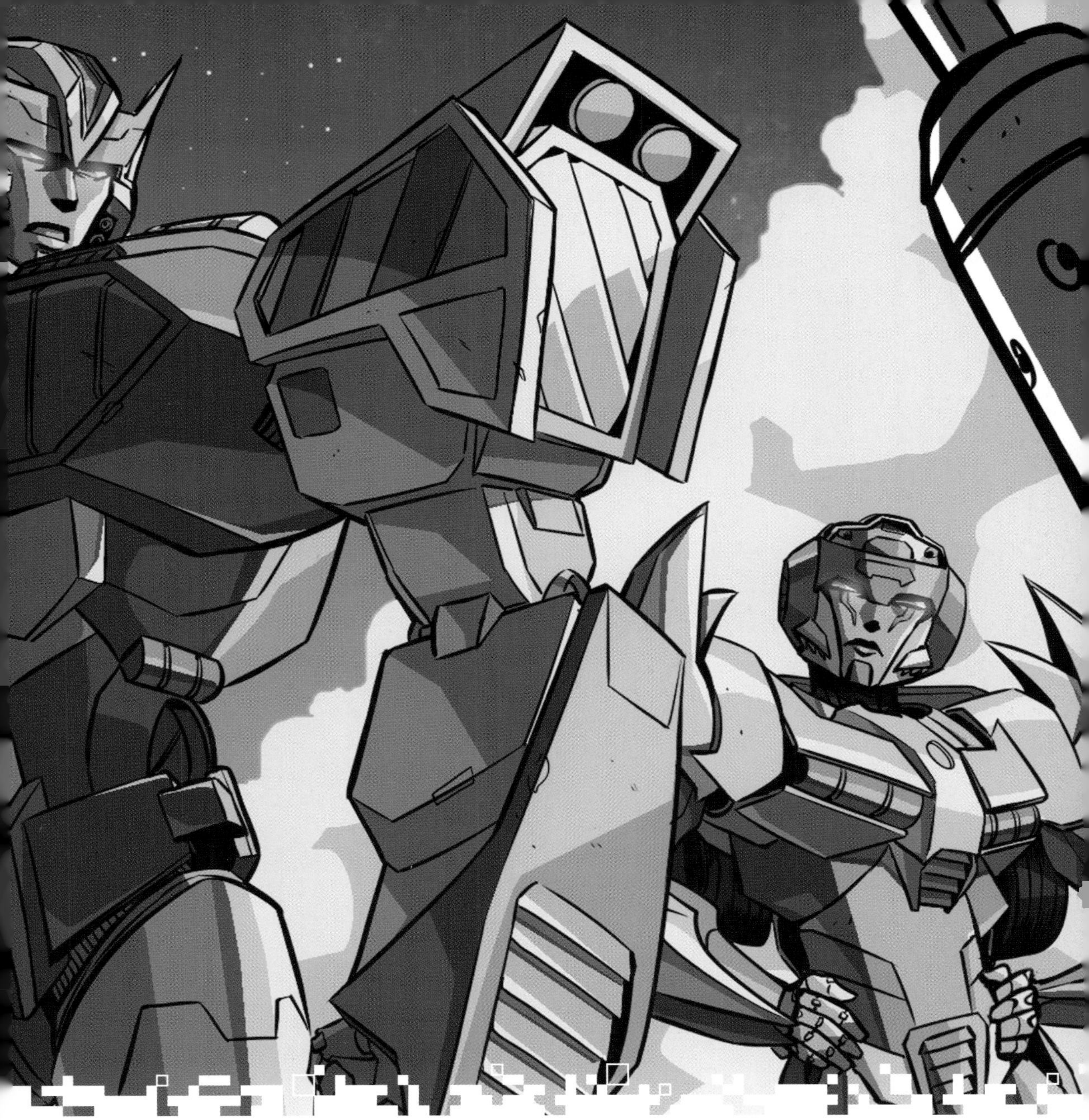

WRITTEN BY **JOHN BARBER**

ART BY **SARA PITRE-DUROCHER** AND **ANDREW GRIFFITH** (ISSUE #49)

COLORS BY **JOSH PEREZ** ADDITIONAL COLORS BY **JOSH BURCHAM**

LETTERS BY **TOM B. LONG**

PREVIOUSLY

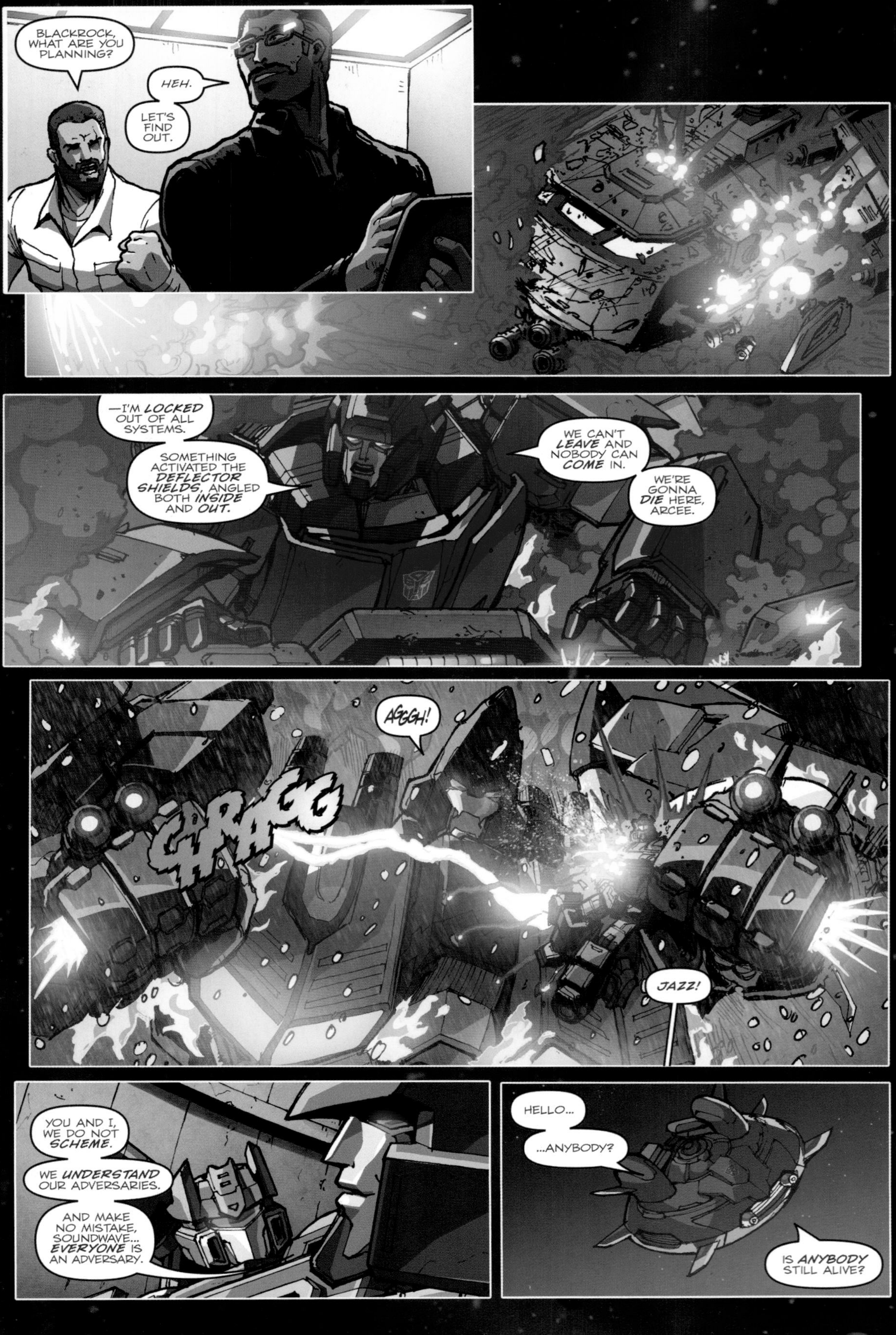
BLACKROCK, WHAT ARE YOU PLANNING?
HEH.
LET'S FIND OUT.
—I'M LOCKED OUT OF ALL SYSTEMS.
SOMETHING ACTIVATED THE DEFLECTOR SHIELDS, ANGLED BOTH INSIDE AND OUT.
WE CAN'T LEAVE AND NOBODY CAN COME IN.
WE'RE GONNA DIE HERE, ARCEE.
AGGGH!
CHRAGG
JAZZ!
YOU AND I, WE DO NOT SCHEME.
WE UNDERSTAND OUR ADVERSARIES.
AND MAKE NO MISTAKE, SOUNDWAVE... EVERYONE IS AN ADVERSARY.
HELLO...
...ANYBODY?
IS ANYBODY STILL ALIVE?

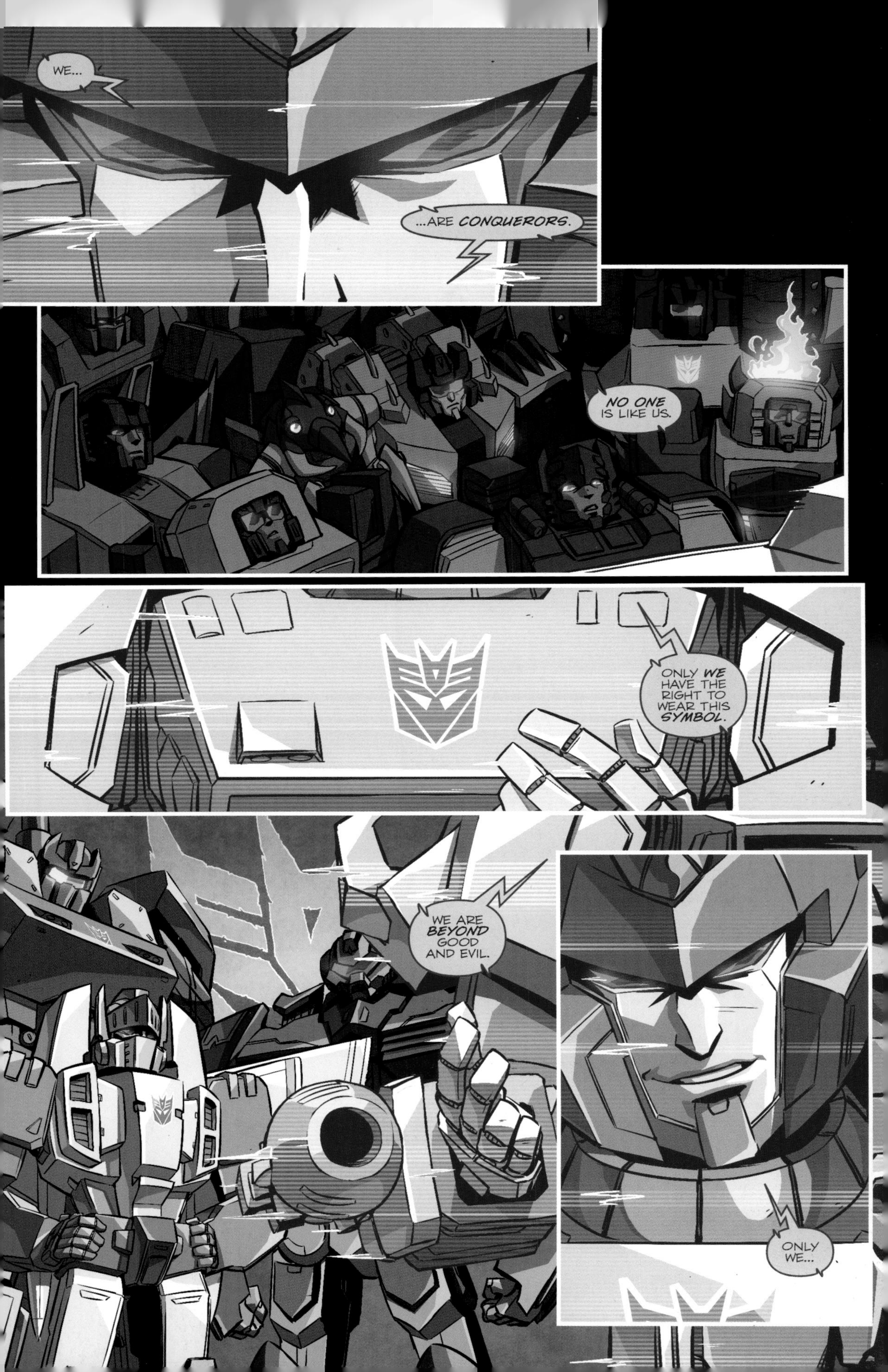
WE...
...ARE CONQUERORS.
NO ONE IS LIKE US.
ONLY WE HAVE THE RIGHT TO WEAR THIS SYMBOL.
WE ARE BEYOND GOOD AND EVIL.
ONLY WE...

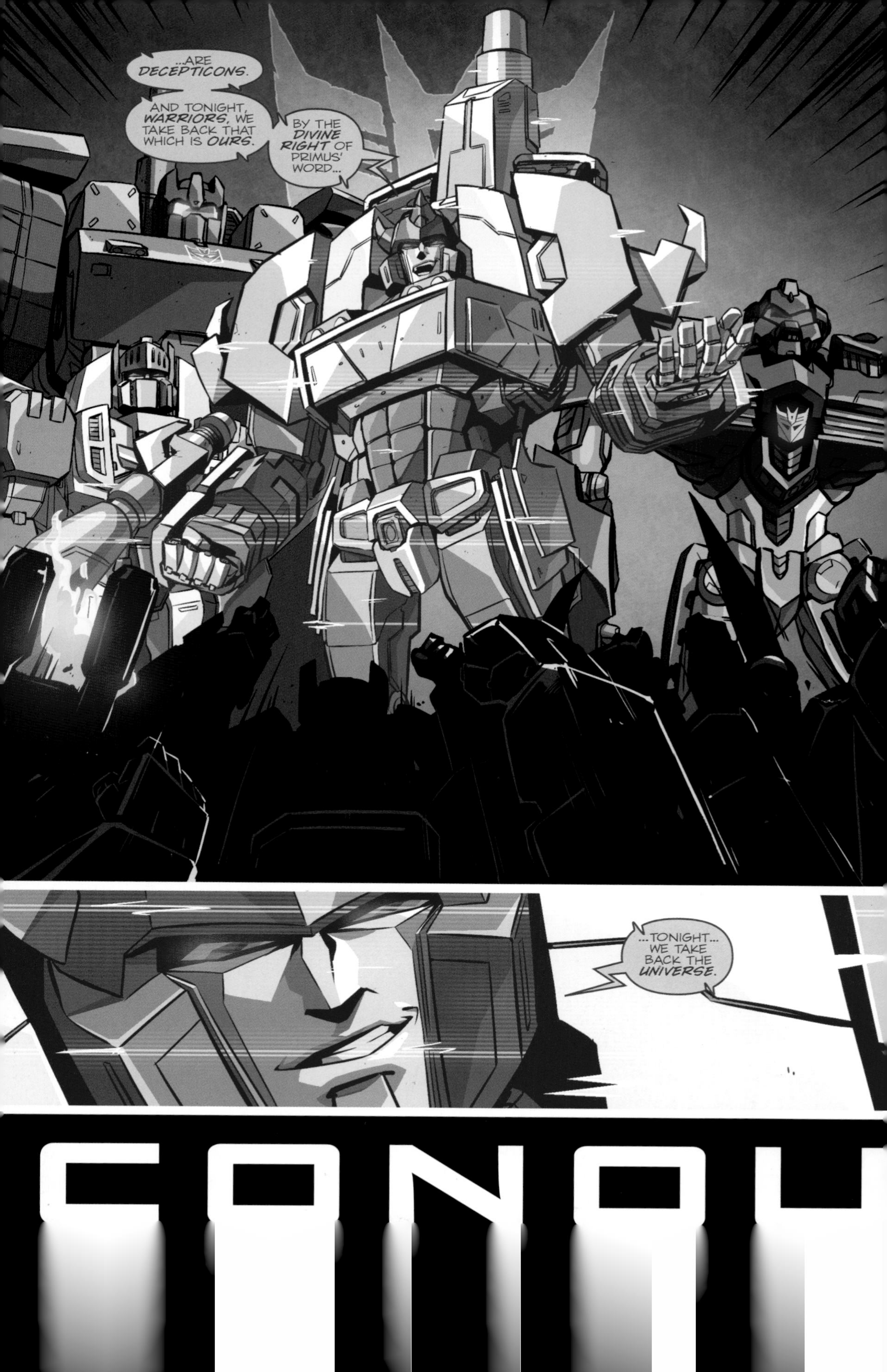
...ARE DECEPTICONS.
AND TONIGHT, WARRIORS, WE TAKE BACK THAT WHICH IS OURS.
BY THE DIVINE RIGHT OF PRIMUS' WORD...
...TONIGHT... WE TAKE BACK THE UNIVERSE.

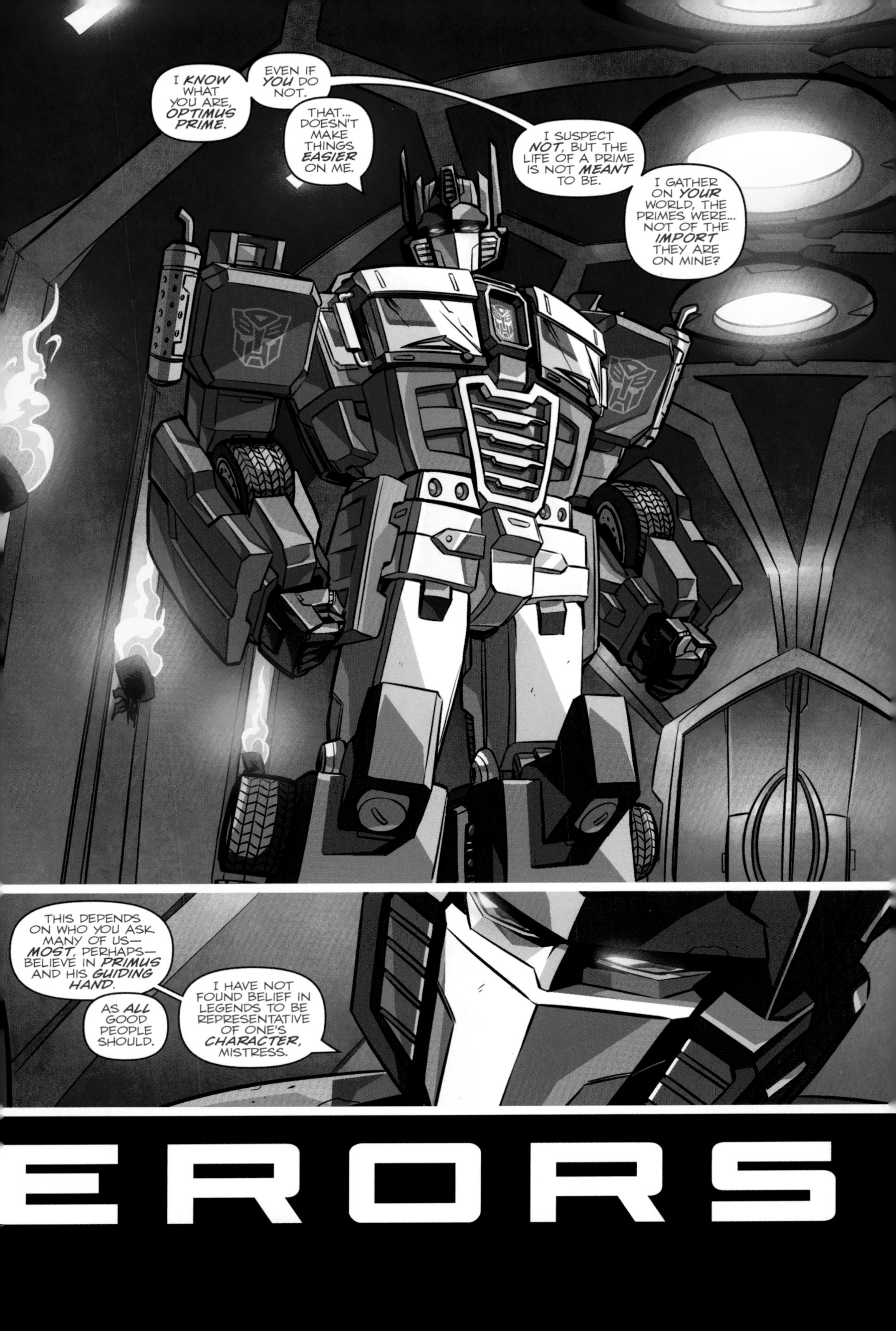

I KNOW WHAT YOU ARE, OPTIMUS PRIME.
EVEN IF YOU DO NOT.
THAT... DOESN'T MAKE THINGS EASIER ON ME.
I SUSPECT NOT, BUT THE LIFE OF A PRIME IS NOT MEANT TO BE.
I GATHER ON YOUR WORLD, THE PRIMES WERE... NOT OF THE IMPORT THEY ARE ON MINE?
THIS DEPENDS ON WHO YOU ASK. MANY OF US— MOST, PERHAPS— BELIEVE IN PRIMUS AND HIS GUIDING HAND.
AS ALL GOOD PEOPLE SHOULD.
I HAVE NOT FOUND BELIEF IN LEGENDS TO BE REPRESENTATIVE OF ONE'S CHARACTER, MISTRESS.
ERORS

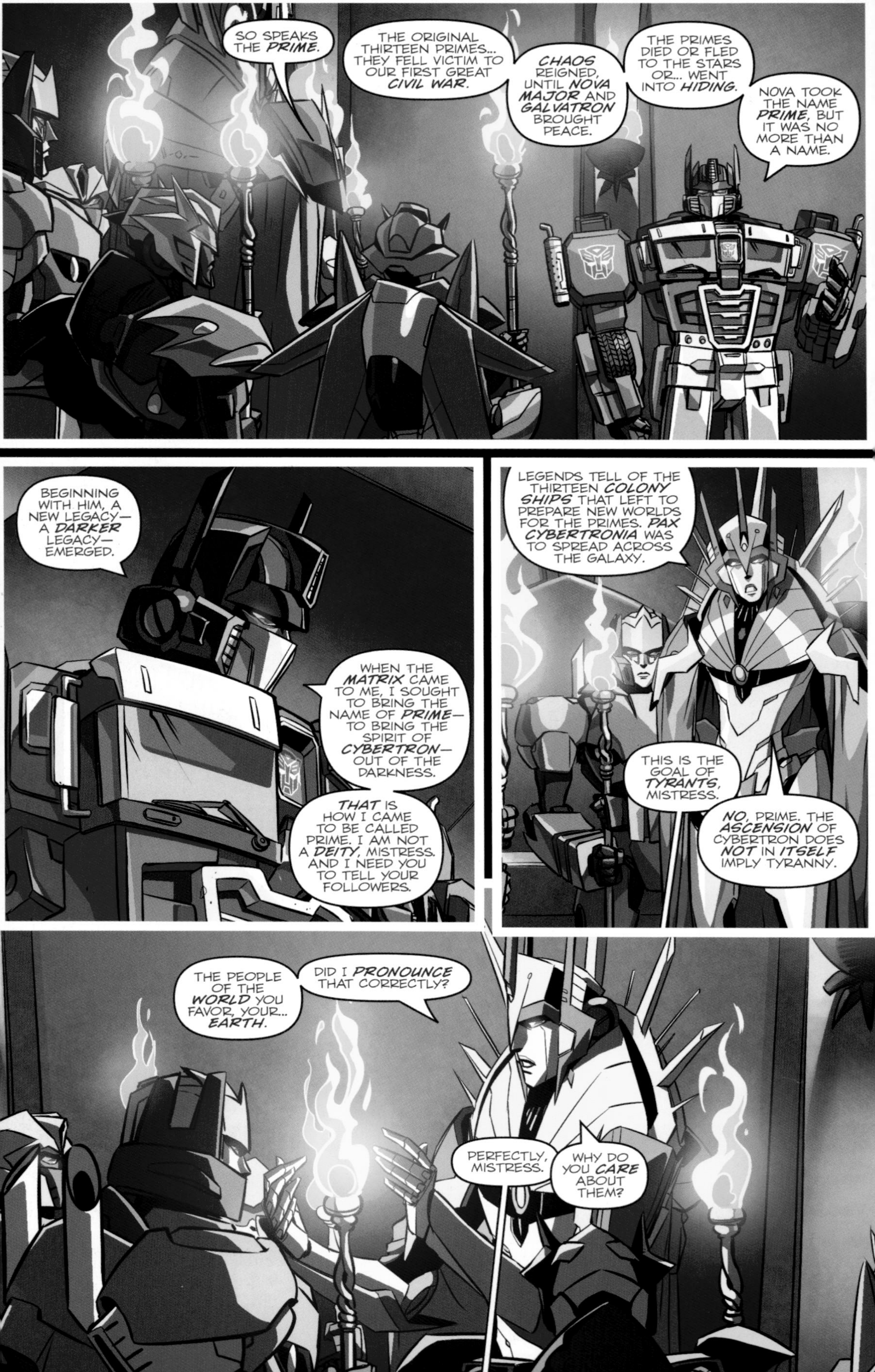
SO SPEAKS THE PRIME.
THE ORIGINAL THIRTEEN PRIMES... THEY FELL VICTIM TO OUR FIRST GREAT CIVIL WAR.
CHAOS REIGNED, UNTIL NOVA MAJOR AND GALVATRON BROUGHT PEACE.
THE PRIMES DIED OR FLED TO THE STARS OR... WENT INTO HIDING.
NOVA TOOK THE NAME PRIME, BUT IT WAS NO MORE THAN A NAME.
BEGINNING WITH HIM, A NEW LEGACY— A DARKER LEGACY— EMERGED.
WHEN THE MATRIX CAME TO ME, I SOUGHT TO BRING THE NAME OF PRIME— TO BRING THE SPIRIT OF CYBERTRON— OUT OF THE DARKNESS.
THAT IS HOW I CAME TO BE CALLED PRIME. I AM NOT A DEITY, MISTRESS. AND I NEED YOU TO TELL YOUR FOLLOWERS.
LEGENDS TELL OF THE THIRTEEN COLONY SHIPS THAT LEFT TO PREPARE NEW WORLDS FOR THE PRIMES. PAX CYBERTRONIA WAS TO SPREAD ACROSS THE GALAXY.
THIS IS THE GOAL OF TYRANTS, MISTRESS.
NO, PRIME. THE ASCENSION OF CYBERTRON DOES NOT IN ITSELF IMPLY TYRANNY.
THE PEOPLE OF THE WORLD YOU FAVOR, YOUR... EARTH.
DID I PRONOUNCE THAT CORRECTLY?
PERFECTLY, MISTRESS.
WHY DO YOU CARE ABOUT THEM?

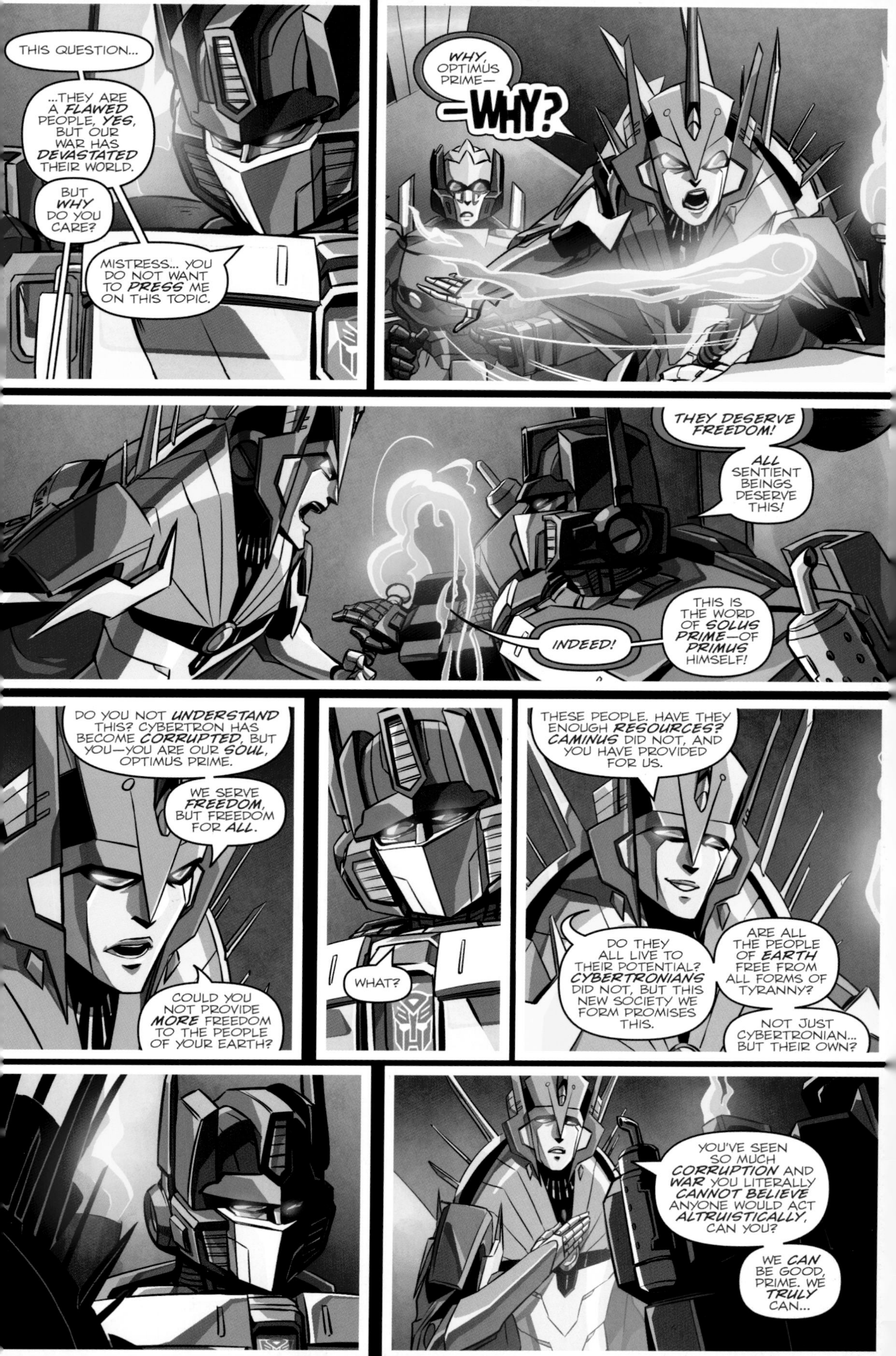

THIS QUESTION...
...THEY ARE A FLAWED PEOPLE, YES, BUT OUR WAR HAS DEVASTATED THEIR WORLD.
BUT WHY DO YOU CARE?
MISTRESS... YOU DO NOT WANT TO PRESS ME ON THIS TOPIC.
WHY, OPTIMUS PRIME—
—WHY?
THEY DESERVE FREEDOM!
ALL SENTIENT BEINGS DESERVE THIS!
THIS IS THE WORD OF SOLUS PRIME—OF PRIMUS HIMSELF!
INDEED!
DO YOU NOT UNDERSTAND THIS? CYBERTRON HAS BECOME CORRUPTED, BUT YOU—YOU ARE OUR SOUL, OPTIMUS PRIME.
WE SERVE FREEDOM, BUT FREEDOM FOR ALL.
COULD YOU NOT PROVIDE MORE FREEDOM TO THE PEOPLE OF YOUR EARTH?
WHAT?
THESE PEOPLE. HAVE THEY ENOUGH RESOURCES? CAMINUS DID NOT, AND YOU HAVE PROVIDED FOR US.
DO THEY ALL LIVE TO THEIR POTENTIAL? CYBERTRONIANS DID NOT, BUT THIS NEW SOCIETY WE FORM PROMISES THIS.
ARE ALL THE PEOPLE OF EARTH FREE FROM ALL FORMS OF TYRANNY?
NOT JUST CYBERTRONIAN... BUT THEIR OWN?
YOU'VE SEEN SO MUCH CORRUPTION AND WAR YOU LITERALLY CANNOT BELIEVE ANYONE WOULD ACT ALTRUISTICALLY, CAN YOU?
WE CAN BE GOOD, PRIME. WE TRULY CAN...

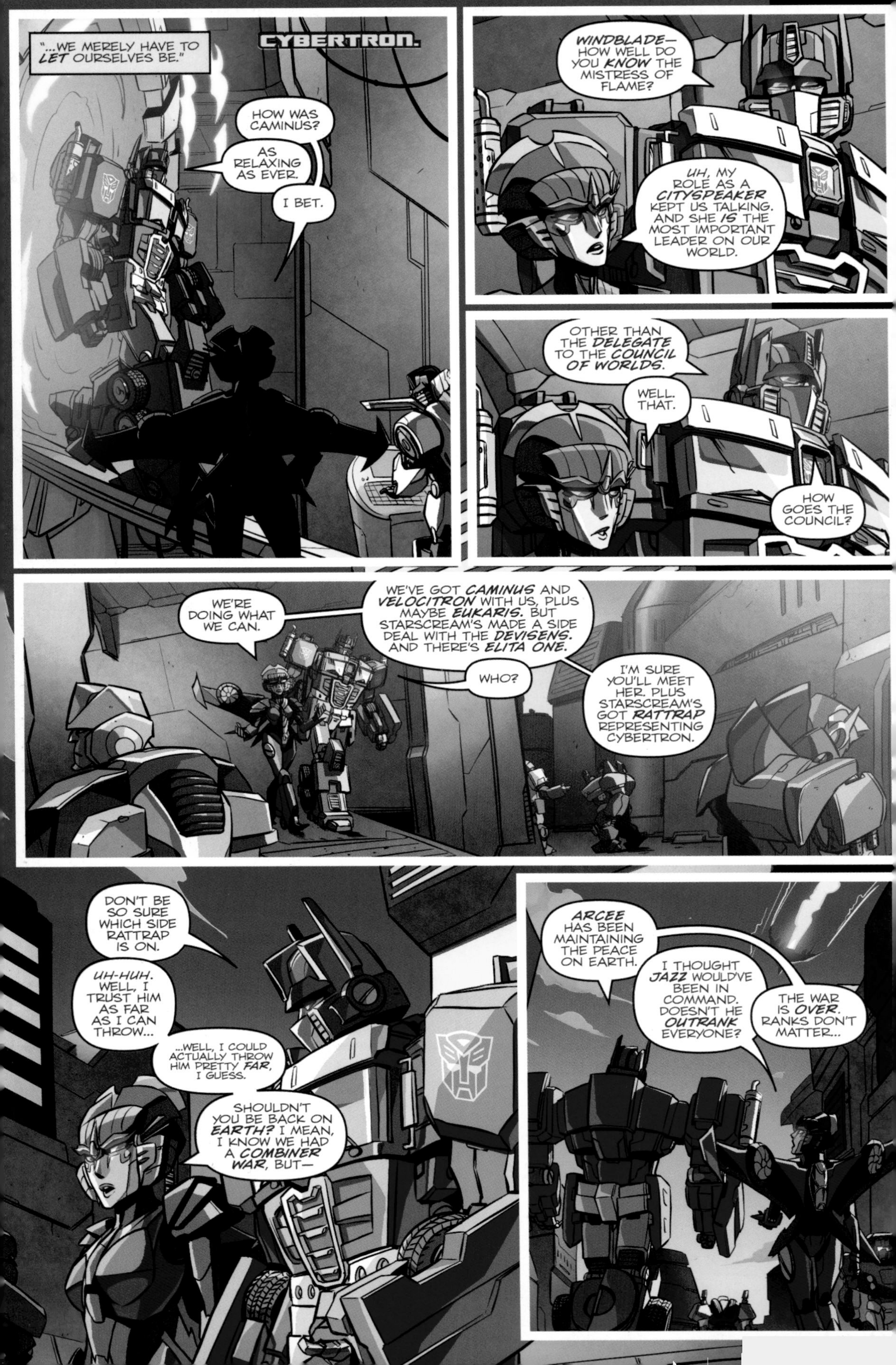
"...WE MERELY HAVE TO LET OURSELVES BE."
CYBERTRON.
HOW WAS CAMINUS?
AS RELAXING AS EVER.
I BET.
WINDBLADE— HOW WELL DO YOU KNOW THE MISTRESS OF FLAME?
UH, MY ROLE AS A CITYSPEAKER KEPT US TALKING. AND SHE IS THE MOST IMPORTANT LEADER ON OUR WORLD.
OTHER THAN THE DELEGATE TO THE COUNCIL OF WORLDS.
WELL. THAT.
HOW GOES THE COUNCIL?
WE'RE DOING WHAT WE CAN.
WE'VE GOT CAMINUS AND VELOCITRON WITH US, PLUS MAYBE EUKARIS. BUT STARSCREAM'S MADE A SIDE DEAL WITH THE DEVISENS. AND THERE'S ELITA ONE.
WHO?
I'M SURE YOU'LL MEET HER. PLUS STARSCREAM'S GOT RATTRAP REPRESENTING CYBERTRON.
DON'T BE SO SURE WHICH SIDE RATTRAP IS ON.
UH-HUH. WELL, I TRUST HIM AS FAR AS I CAN THROW...
...WELL, I COULD ACTUALLY THROW HIM PRETTY FAR, I GUESS.
SHOULDN'T YOU BE BACK ON EARTH? I MEAN, I KNOW WE HAD A COMBINER WAR, BUT—
ARCEE HAS BEEN MAINTAINING THE PEACE ON EARTH.
I THOUGHT JAZZ WOULD'VE BEEN IN COMMAND. DOESN'T HE OUTRANK EVERYONE?
THE WAR IS OVER. RANKS DON'T MATTER...

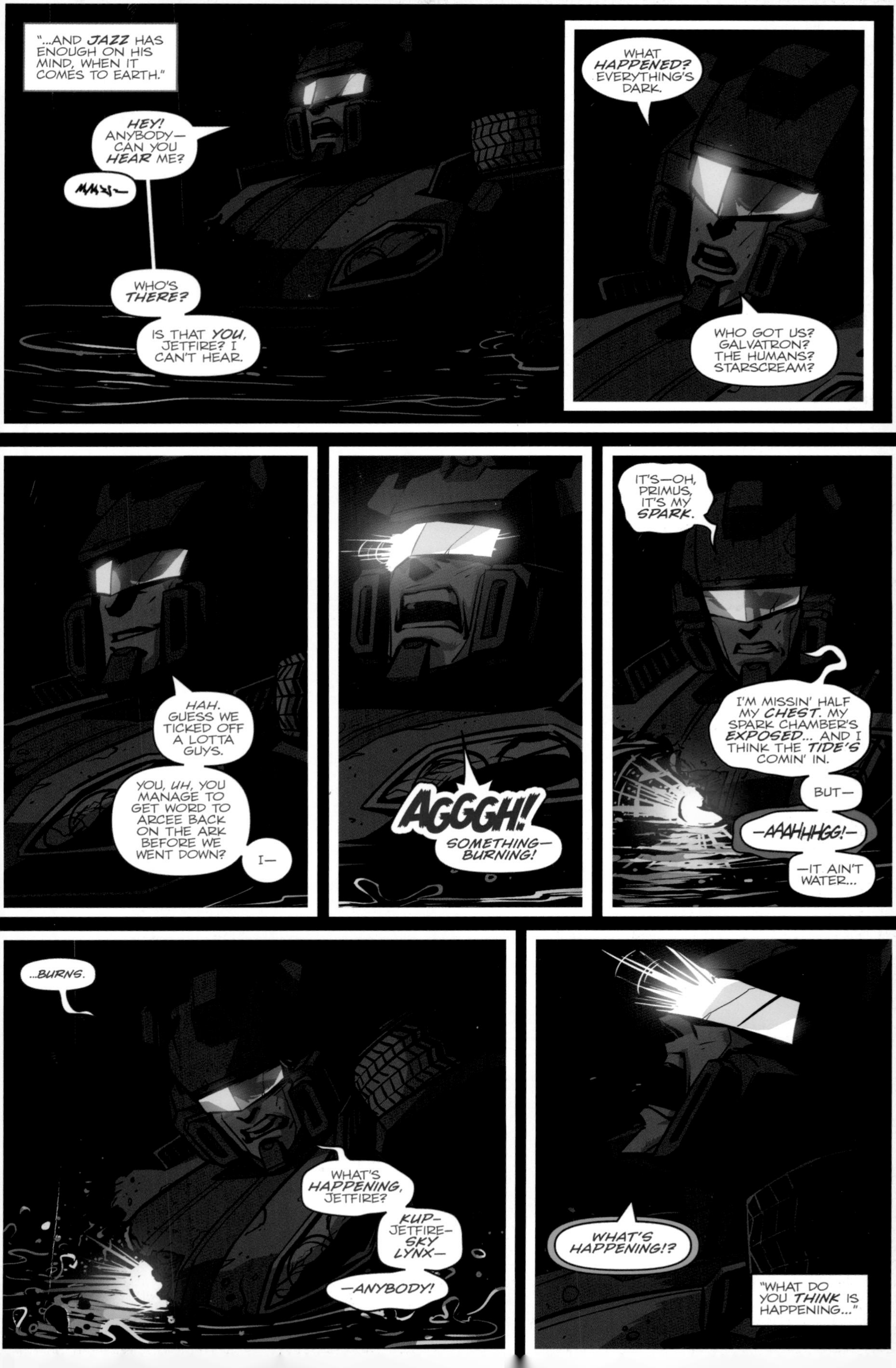
"...AND JAZZ HAS ENOUGH ON HIS MIND, WHEN IT COMES TO EARTH."
HEY! ANYBODY— CAN YOU HEAR ME?
WHO'S THERE?
IS THAT YOU, JETFIRE? I CAN'T HEAR.
WHAT HAPPENED? EVERYTHING'S DARK.
WHO GOT US? GALVATRON? THE HUMANS? STARSCREAM?
HAH. GUESS WE TICKED OFF A LOTTA GUYS.
YOU, UH, YOU MANAGE TO GET WORD TO ARCEE BACK ON THE ARK BEFORE WE WENT DOWN?
I—
AGGGH!
SOMETHING— BURNING!
IT'S—OH, PRIMUS, IT'S MY SPARK.
I'M MISSIN' HALF MY CHEST. MY SPARK CHAMBER'S EXPOSED... AND I THINK THE TIDE'S COMIN' IN.
BUT—
—AAAHHHGG!—
—IT AIN'T WATER...
...BURNS.
WHAT'S HAPPENING, JETFIRE?
KUP— JETFIRE— SKY LYNX—
—ANYBODY!
WHAT'S HAPPENING!?
"WHAT DO YOU THINK IS HAPPENING..."

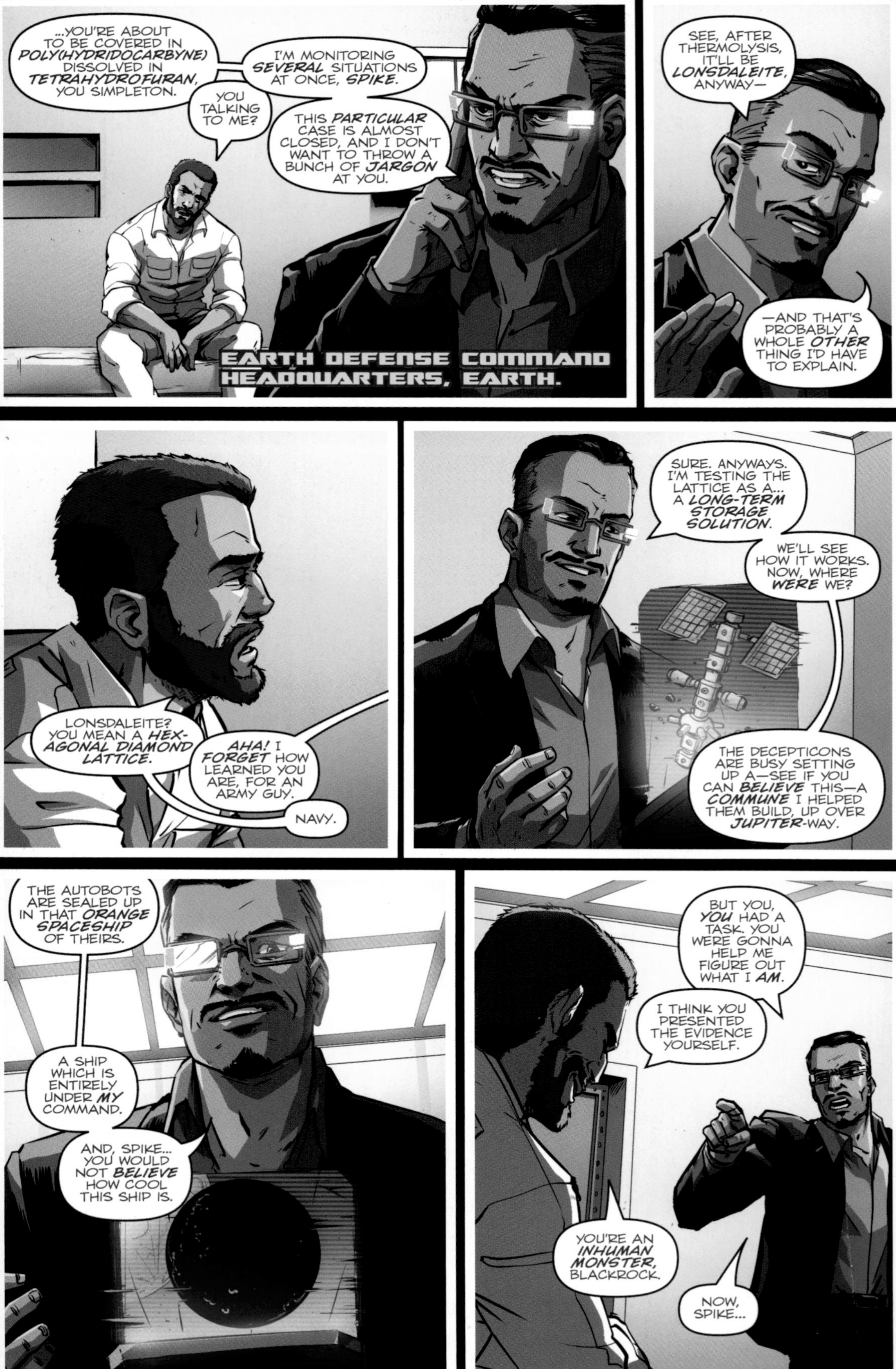
...YOU'RE ABOUT TO BE COVERED IN POLY(HYDRIDOCARBYNE) DISSOLVED IN TETRAHYDROFURAN, YOU SIMPLETON.
YOU TALKING TO ME?
I'M MONITORING SEVERAL SITUATIONS AT ONCE, SPIKE.
THIS PARTICULAR CASE IS ALMOST CLOSED, AND I DON'T WANT TO THROW A BUNCH OF JARGON AT YOU.
EARTH DEFENSE COMMAND HEADQUARTERS, EARTH.
SEE, AFTER THERMOLYSIS, IT'LL BE LONSDALEITE, ANYWAY—
—AND THAT'S PROBABLY A WHOLE OTHER THING I'D HAVE TO EXPLAIN.
LONSDALEITE? YOU MEAN A HEX-AGONAL DIAMOND LATTICE.
AHA! I FORGET HOW LEARNED YOU ARE, FOR AN ARMY GUY.
NAVY.
SURE. ANYWAYS. I'M TESTING THE LATTICE AS A... A LONG-TERM STORAGE SOLUTION.
WE'LL SEE HOW IT WORKS. NOW, WHERE WERE WE?
THE DECEPTICONS ARE BUSY SETTING UP A—SEE IF YOU CAN BELIEVE THIS—A COMMUNE I HELPED THEM BUILD, UP OVER JUPITER-WAY.
THE AUTOBOTS ARE SEALED UP IN THAT ORANGE SPACESHIP OF THEIRS.
A SHIP WHICH IS ENTIRELY UNDER MY COMMAND.
AND, SPIKE... YOU WOULD NOT BELIEVE HOW COOL THIS SHIP IS.
BUT YOU, YOU HAD A TASK. YOU WERE GONNA HELP ME FIGURE OUT WHAT I AM.
I THINK YOU PRESENTED THE EVIDENCE YOURSELF.
YOU'RE AN INHUMAN MONSTER, BLACKROCK.
NOW, SPIKE...

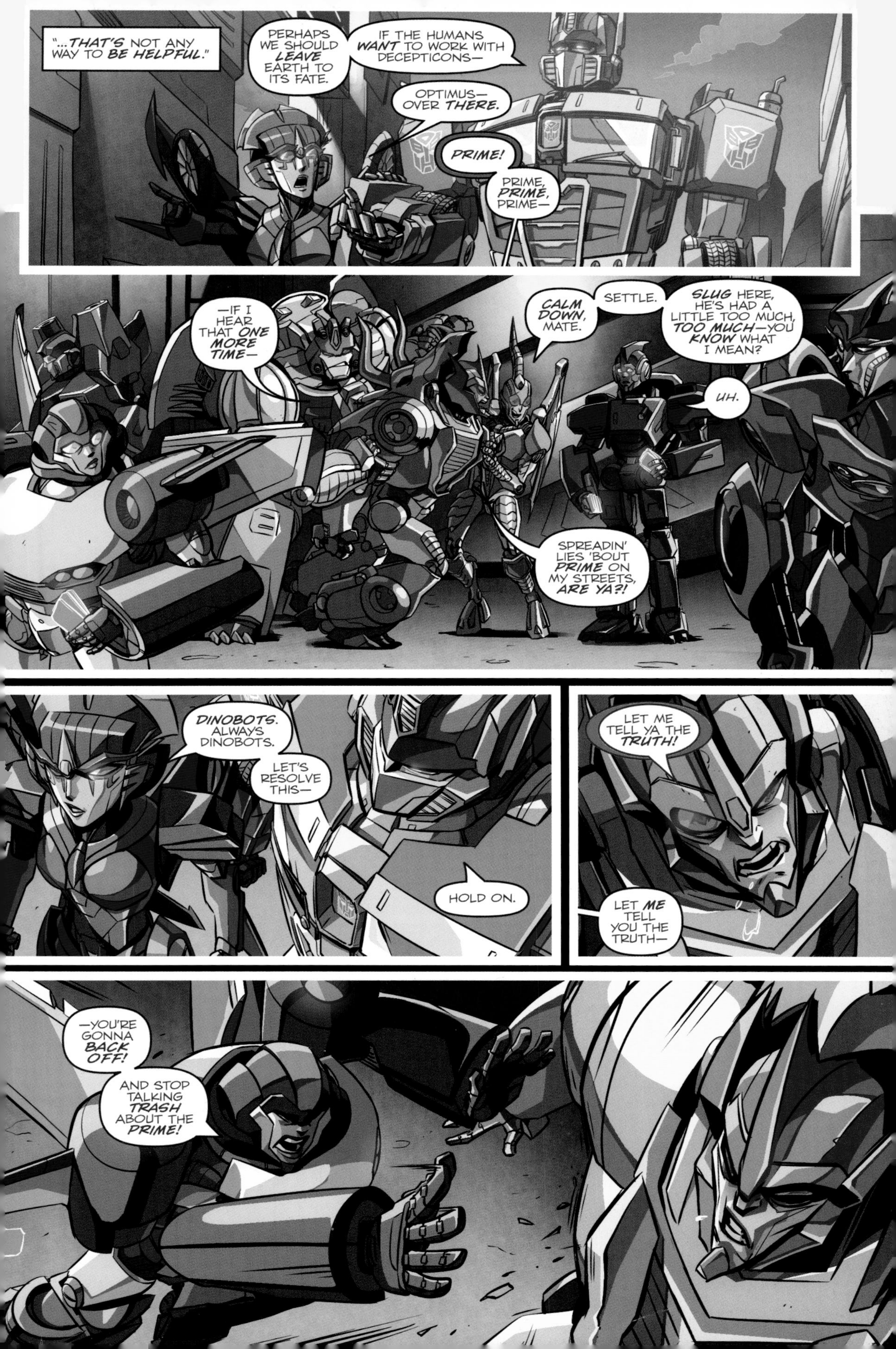
"...THAT'S NOT ANY WAY TO BE HELPFUL."
PERHAPS WE SHOULD LEAVE EARTH TO ITS FATE.
IF THE HUMANS WANT TO WORK WITH DECEPTICONS—
OPTIMUS— OVER THERE.
PRIME!
PRIME, PRIME, PRIME—
—IF I HEAR THAT ONE MORE TIME—
CALM DOWN, MATE.
SETTLE.
SLUG HERE, HE'S HAD A LITTLE TOO MUCH, TOO MUCH—YOU KNOW WHAT I MEAN?
UH.
SPREADIN' LIES 'BOUT PRIME ON MY STREETS, ARE YA?!
DINOBOTS. ALWAYS DINOBOTS.
LET'S RESOLVE THIS—
HOLD ON.
LET ME TELL YA THE TRUTH!
LET ME TELL YOU THE TRUTH—
—YOU'RE GONNA BACK OFF!
AND STOP TALKING TRASH ABOUT THE PRIME!

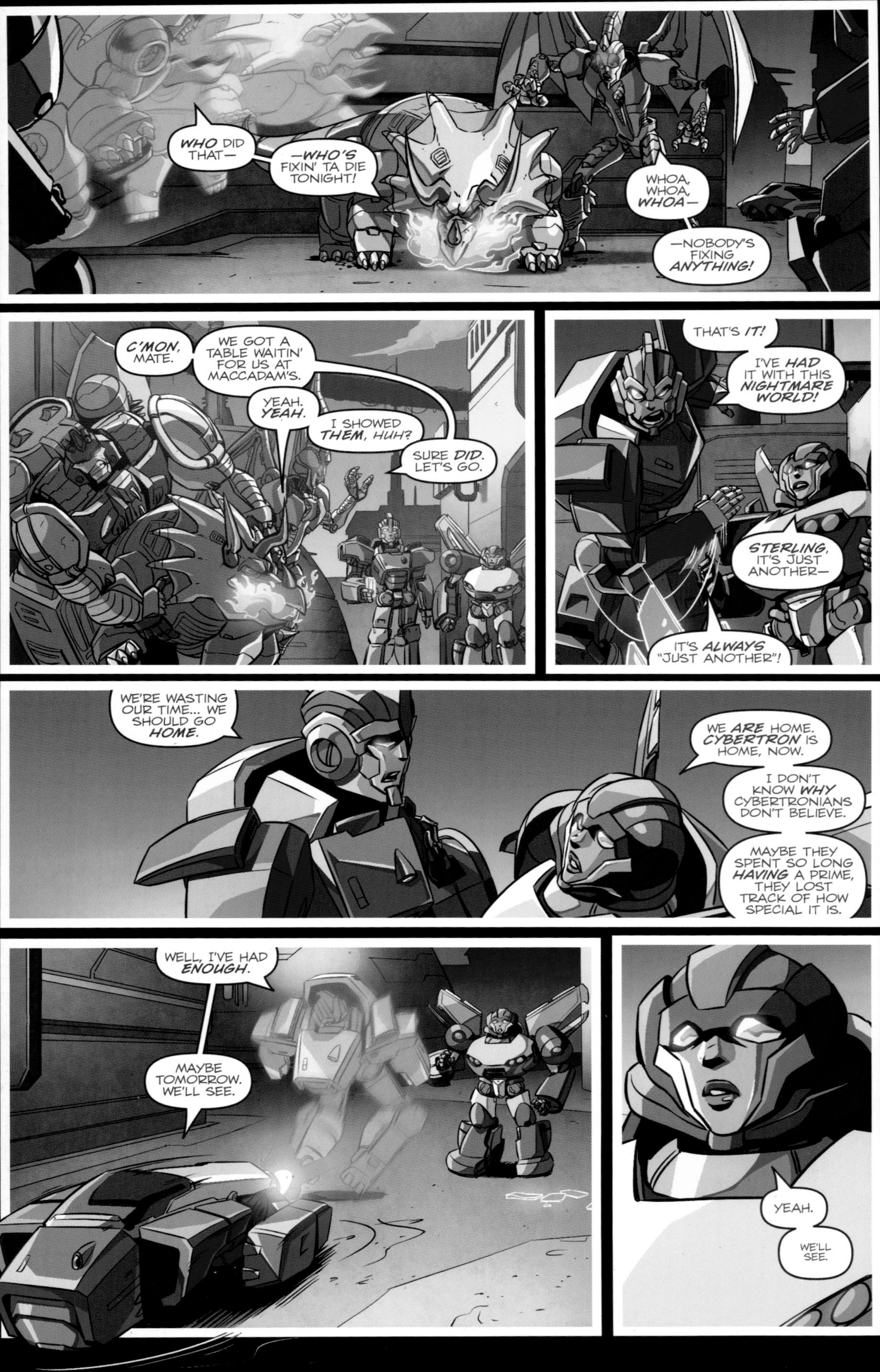

WHO DID THAT—
—WHO'S FIXIN' TA DIE TONIGHT!
WHOA, WHOA, WHOA—
—NOBODY'S FIXING ANYTHING!
C'MON, MATE.
WE GOT A TABLE WAITIN' FOR US AT MACCADAM'S.
YEAH. YEAH.
I SHOWED THEM, HUH?
SURE DID. LET'S GO.
THAT'S IT!
I'VE HAD IT WITH THIS NIGHTMARE WORLD!
STERLING, IT'S JUST ANOTHER—
IT'S ALWAYS "JUST ANOTHER"!
WE'RE WASTING OUR TIME... WE SHOULD GO HOME.
WE ARE HOME. CYBERTRON IS HOME, NOW.
I DON'T KNOW WHY CYBERTRONIANS DON'T BELIEVE.
MAYBE THEY SPENT SO LONG HAVING A PRIME, THEY LOST TRACK OF HOW SPECIAL IT IS.
WELL, I'VE HAD ENOUGH.
MAYBE TOMORROW. WE'LL SEE.
YEAH.
WE'LL SEE.

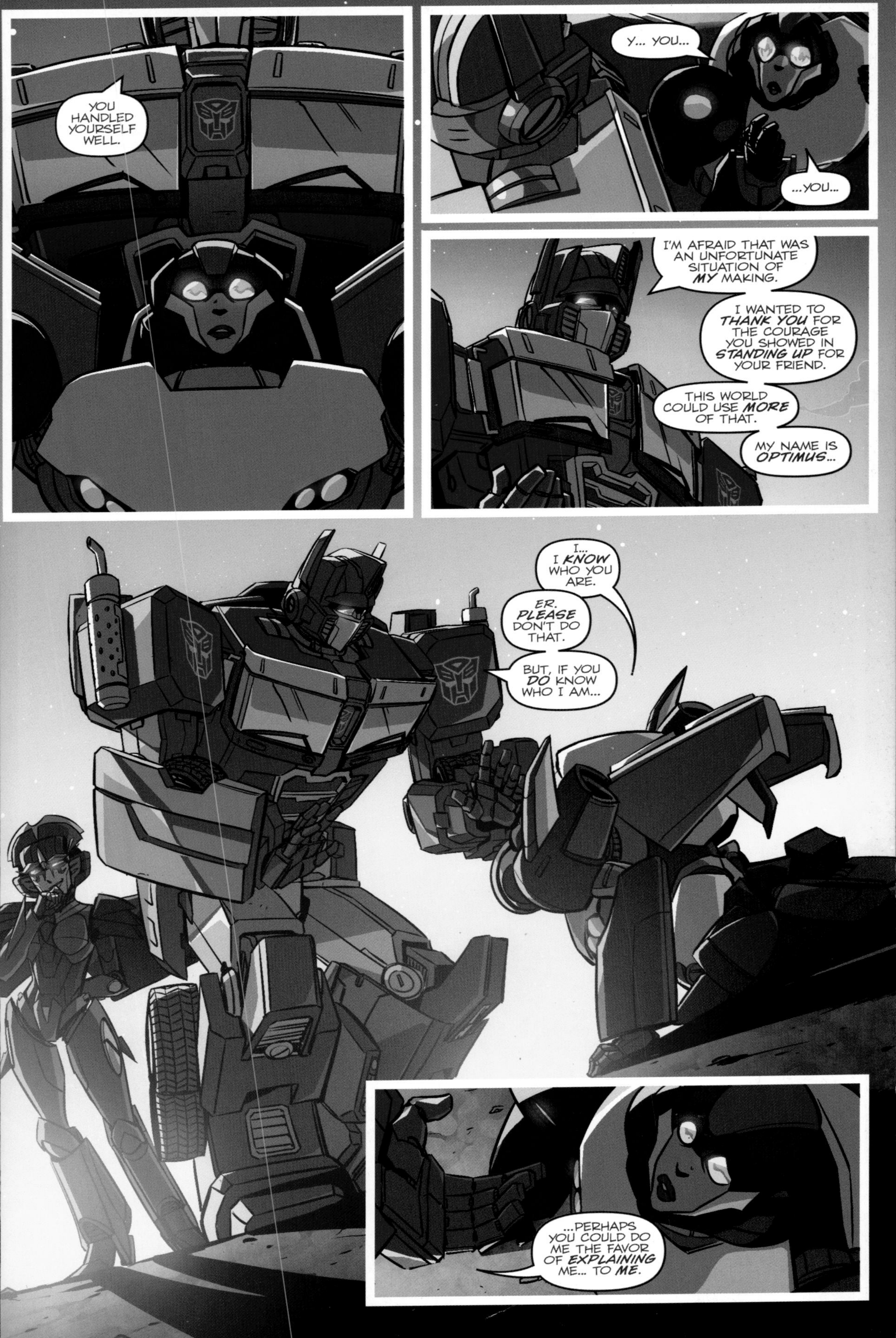
YOU HANDLED YOURSELF WELL.
Y... YOU...
...YOU...
I'M AFRAID THAT WAS AN UNFORTUNATE SITUATION OF MY MAKING.
I WANTED TO THANK YOU FOR THE COURAGE YOU SHOWED IN STANDING UP FOR YOUR FRIEND.
THIS WORLD COULD USE MORE OF THAT.
MY NAME IS OPTIMUS...
I... I KNOW WHO YOU ARE.
ER. PLEASE DON'T DO THAT.
BUT, IF YOU DO KNOW WHO I AM...
...PERHAPS YOU COULD DO ME THE FAVOR OF EXPLAINING ME... TO ME.

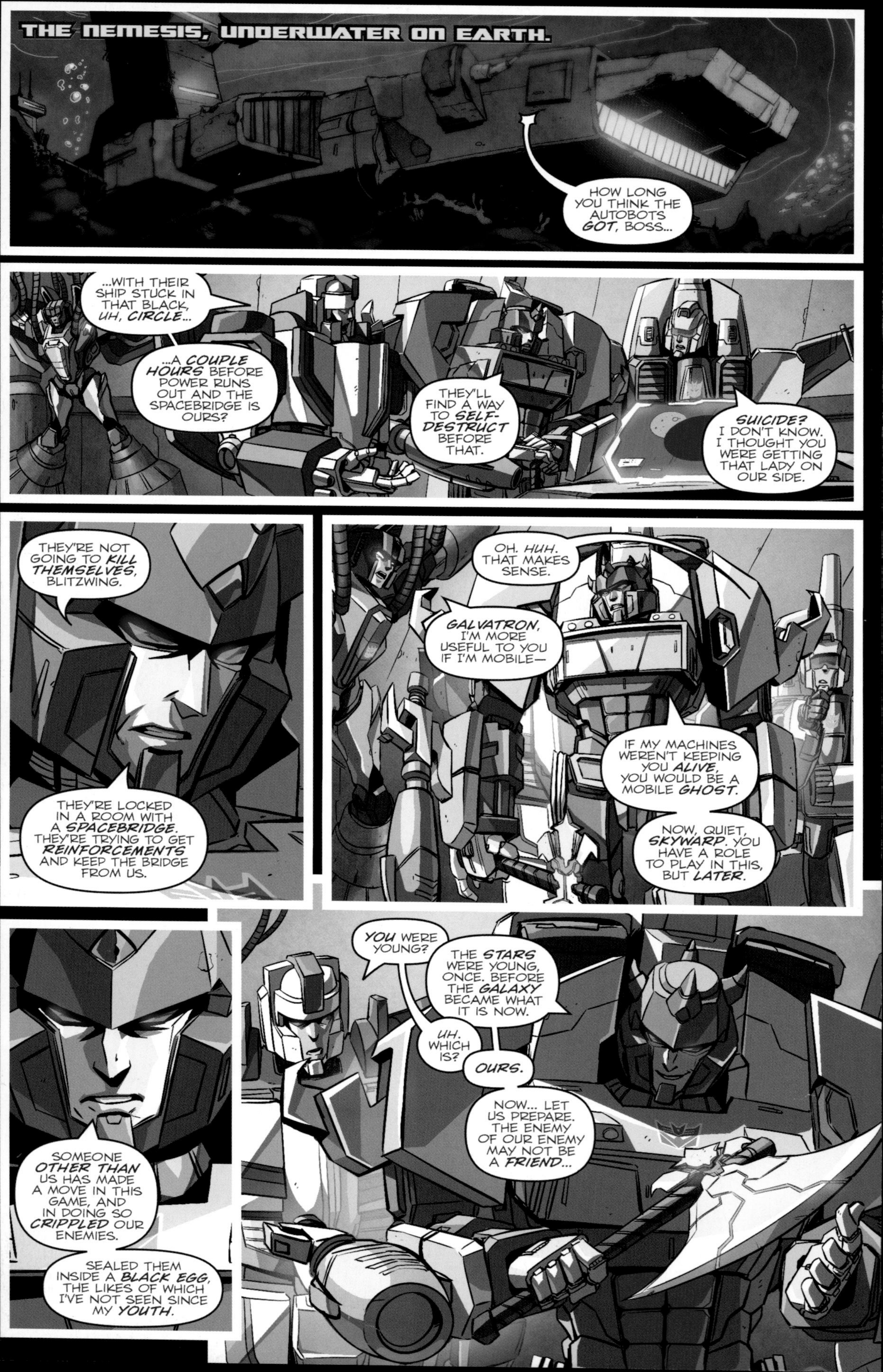
THE NEMESIS, UNDERWATER ON EARTH.
HOW LONG YOU THINK THE AUTOBOTS GOT, BOSS...
...WITH THEIR SHIP STUCK IN THAT BLACK, UH, CIRCLE...
...A COUPLE HOURS BEFORE POWER RUNS OUT AND THE SPACEBRIDGE IS OURS?
THEY'LL FIND A WAY TO SELF-DESTRUCT BEFORE THAT.
SUICIDE? I DON'T KNOW. I THOUGHT YOU WERE GETTING THAT LADY ON OUR SIDE.
THEY'RE NOT GOING TO KILL THEMSELVES, BLITZWING.
THEY'RE LOCKED IN A ROOM WITH A SPACEBRIDGE. THEY'RE TRYING TO GET REINFORCEMENTS AND KEEP THE BRIDGE FROM US.
OH. HUH. THAT MAKES SENSE.
GALVATRON, I'M MORE USEFUL TO YOU IF I'M MOBILE—
IF MY MACHINES WEREN'T KEEPING YOU ALIVE, YOU WOULD BE A MOBILE GHOST.
NOW, QUIET, SKYWARP. YOU HAVE A ROLE TO PLAY IN THIS, BUT LATER.
SOMEONE OTHER THAN US HAS MADE A MOVE IN THIS GAME, AND IN DOING SO CRIPPLED OUR ENEMIES.
SEALED THEM INSIDE A BLACK EGG, THE LIKES OF WHICH I'VE NOT SEEN SINCE MY YOUTH.
YOU WERE YOUNG?
THE STARS WERE YOUNG, ONCE. BEFORE THE GALAXY BECAME WHAT IT IS NOW.
UH. WHICH IS?
OURS.
NOW... LET US PREPARE. THE ENEMY OF OUR ENEMY MAY NOT BE A FRIEND...

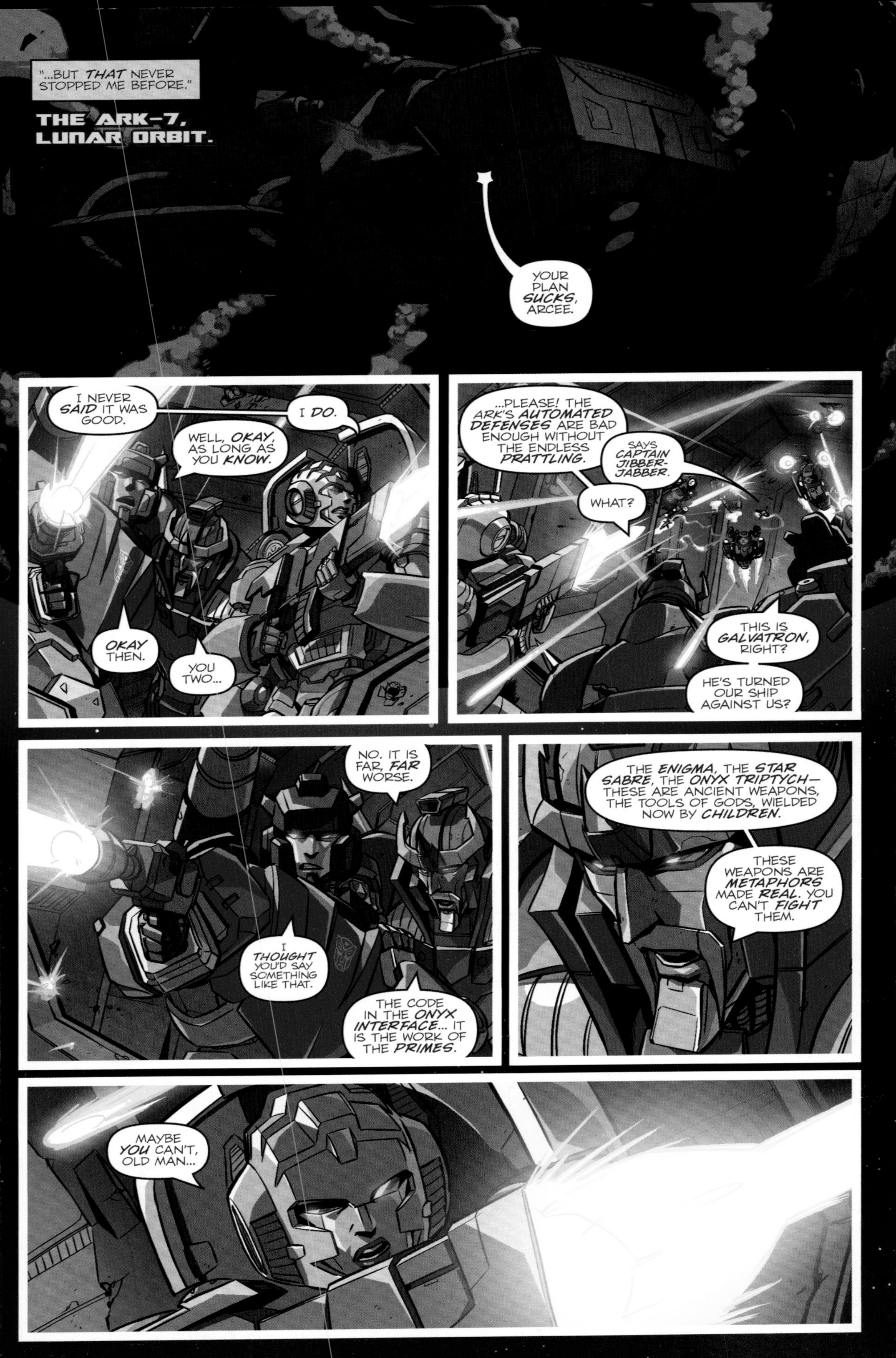

"...BUT THAT NEVER STOPPED ME BEFORE."
THE ARK-7, LUNAR ORBIT.
YOUR PLAN SUCKS, ARCEE.
I NEVER SAID IT WAS GOOD.
I DO.
WELL, OKAY, AS LONG AS YOU KNOW.
OKAY THEN.
YOU TWO...
...PLEASE! THE ARK'S AUTOMATED DEFENSES ARE BAD ENOUGH WITHOUT THE ENDLESS PRATTLING.
SAYS CAPTAIN JIBBER-JABBER.
WHAT?
THIS IS GALVATRON, RIGHT?
HE'S TURNED OUR SHIP AGAINST US?
NO. IT IS FAR, FAR WORSE.
I THOUGHT YOU'D SAY SOMETHING LIKE THAT.
THE CODE IN THE ONYX INTERFACE... IT IS THE WORK OF THE PRIMES.
THE ENIGMA, THE STAR SABRE, THE ONYX TRIPTYCH— THESE ARE ANCIENT WEAPONS, THE TOOLS OF GODS, WIELDED NOW BY CHILDREN.
THESE WEAPONS ARE METAPHORS MADE REAL. YOU CAN'T FIGHT THEM.
MAYBE YOU CAN'T, OLD MAN...

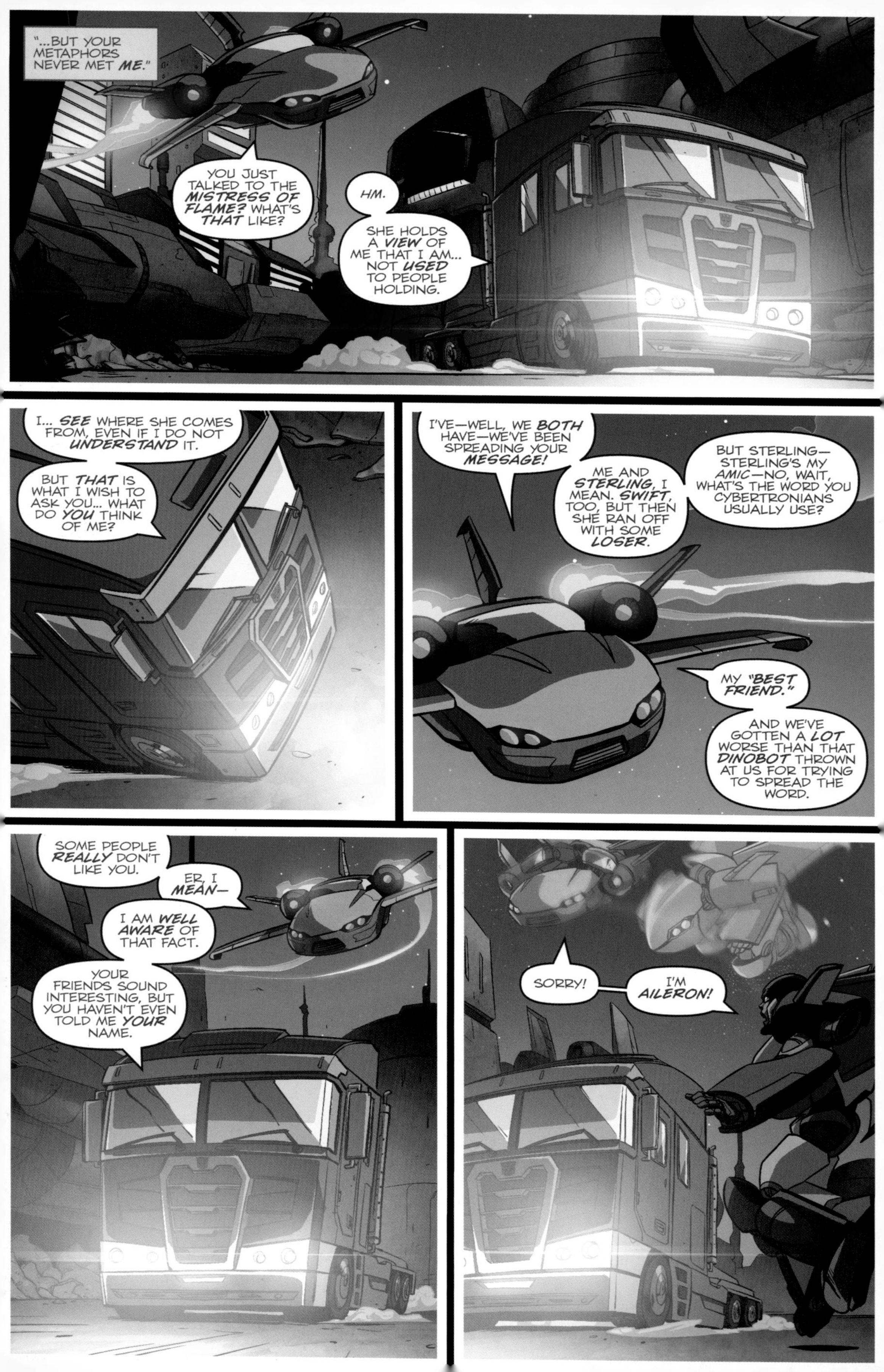
"...BUT YOUR METAPHORS NEVER MET ME."
YOU JUST TALKED TO THE MISTRESS OF FLAME? WHAT'S THAT LIKE?
HM.
SHE HOLDS A VIEW OF ME THAT I AM... NOT USED TO PEOPLE HOLDING.
I... SEE WHERE SHE COMES FROM, EVEN IF I DO NOT UNDERSTAND IT.
BUT THAT IS WHAT I WISH TO ASK YOU... WHAT DO YOU THINK OF ME?
I'VE—WELL, WE BOTH HAVE—WE'VE BEEN SPREADING YOUR MESSAGE!
ME AND STERLING, I MEAN. SWIFT, TOO, BUT THEN SHE RAN OFF WITH SOME LOSER.
BUT STERLING—STERLING'S MY AMIC—NO, WAIT, WHAT'S THE WORD YOU CYBERTRONIANS USUALLY USE?
MY "BEST FRIEND."
AND WE'VE GOTTEN A LOT WORSE THAN THAT DINOBOT THROWN AT US FOR TRYING TO SPREAD THE WORD.
SOME PEOPLE REALLY DON'T LIKE YOU.
ER, I MEAN—
I AM WELL AWARE OF THAT FACT.
YOUR FRIENDS SOUND INTERESTING, BUT YOU HAVEN'T EVEN TOLD ME YOUR NAME.
SORRY!
I'M AILERON!

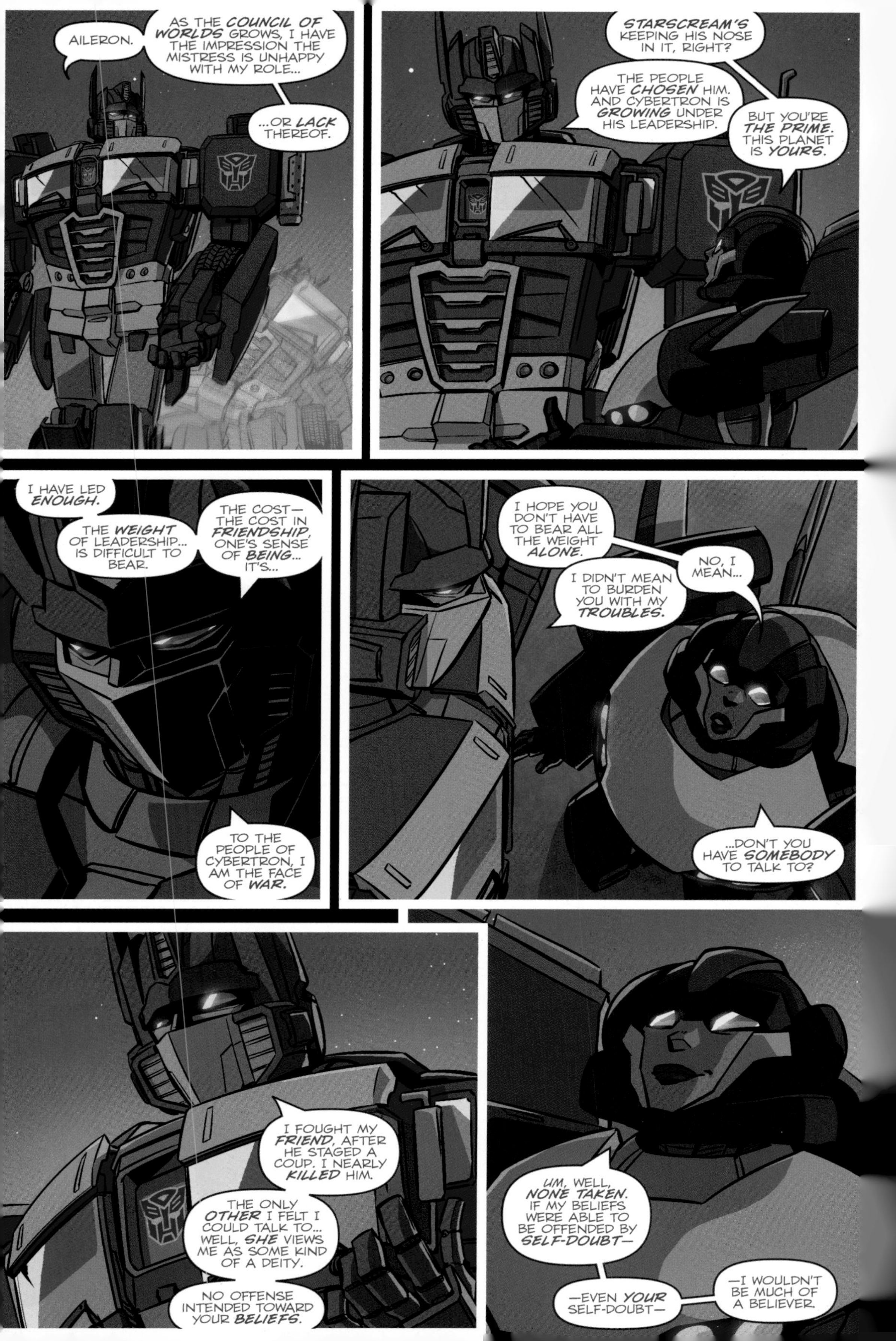
AILERON.
AS THE COUNCIL OF WORLDS GROWS, I HAVE THE IMPRESSION THE MISTRESS IS UNHAPPY WITH MY ROLE...
...OR LACK THEREOF.
STARSCREAM'S KEEPING HIS NOSE IN IT, RIGHT?
THE PEOPLE HAVE CHOSEN HIM. AND CYBERTRON IS GROWING UNDER HIS LEADERSHIP.
BUT YOU'RE THE PRIME. THIS PLANET IS YOURS.
I HAVE LED ENOUGH.
THE WEIGHT OF LEADERSHIP... IS DIFFICULT TO BEAR.
THE COST— THE COST IN FRIENDSHIP, ONE'S SENSE OF BEING... IT'S...
TO THE PEOPLE OF CYBERTRON, I AM THE FACE OF WAR.
I HOPE YOU DON'T HAVE TO BEAR ALL THE WEIGHT ALONE.
NO, I MEAN...
I DIDN'T MEAN TO BURDEN YOU WITH MY TROUBLES.
...DON'T YOU HAVE SOMEBODY TO TALK TO?
I FOUGHT MY FRIEND, AFTER HE STAGED A COUP. I NEARLY KILLED HIM.
THE ONLY OTHER I FELT I COULD TALK TO... WELL, SHE VIEWS ME AS SOME KIND OF A DEITY.
NO OFFENSE INTENDED TOWARD YOUR BELIEFS.
UM, WELL, NONE TAKEN. IF MY BELIEFS WERE ABLE TO BE OFFENDED BY SELF-DOUBT—
—EVEN YOUR SELF-DOUBT—
—I WOULDN'T BE MUCH OF A BELIEVER.

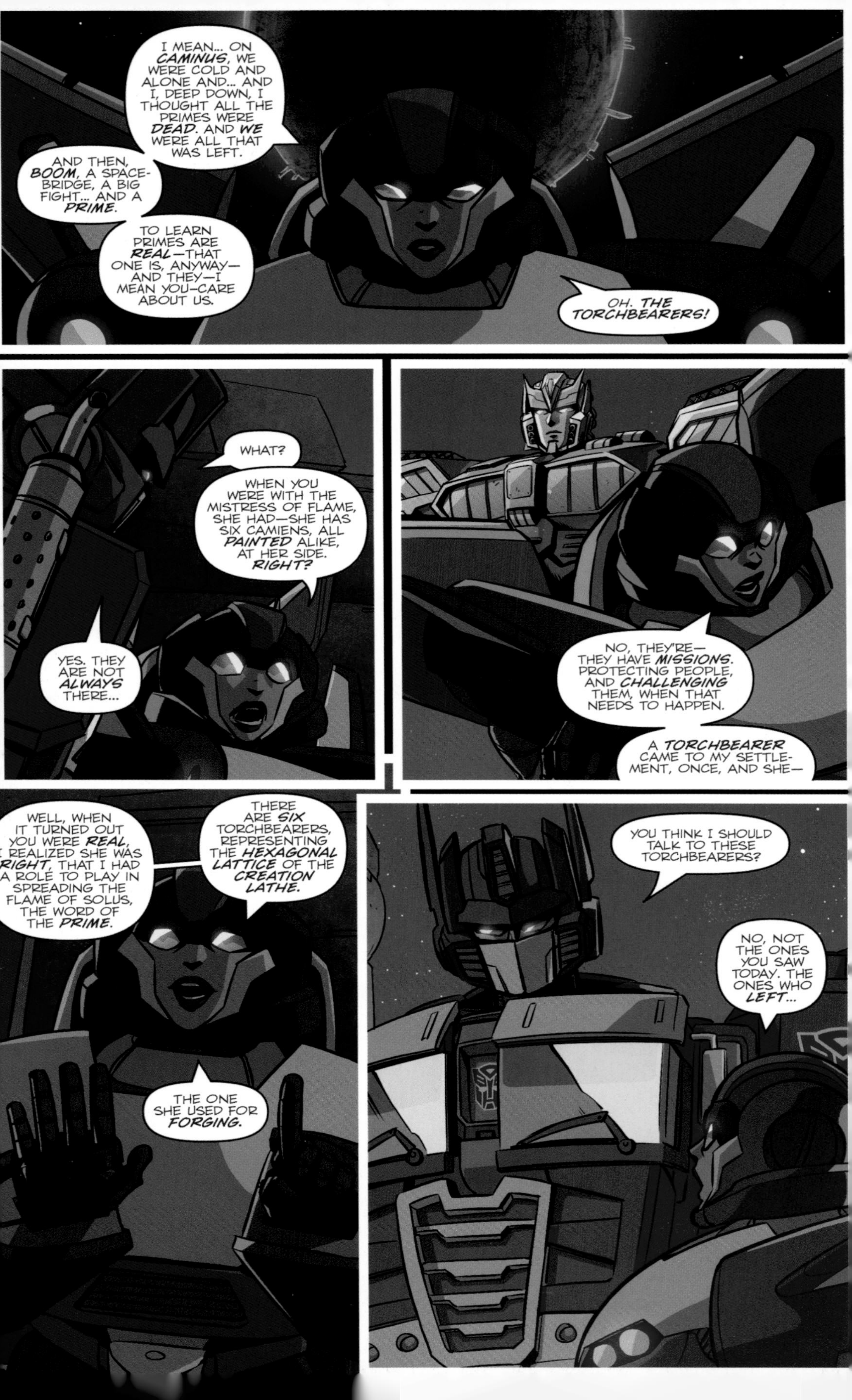
I MEAN... ON CAMINUS, WE WERE COLD AND ALONE AND... AND I, DEEP DOWN, I THOUGHT ALL THE PRIMES WERE DEAD. AND WE WERE ALL THAT WAS LEFT.
AND THEN, BOOM, A SPACE-BRIDGE, A BIG FIGHT... AND A PRIME.
TO LEARN PRIMES ARE REAL—THAT ONE IS, ANYWAY—AND THEY—I MEAN YOU—CARE ABOUT US.
OH. THE TORCHBEARERS!
WHAT?
WHEN YOU WERE WITH THE MISTRESS OF FLAME, SHE HAD—SHE HAS SIX CAMIENS, ALL PAINTED ALIKE, AT HER SIDE. RIGHT?
YES. THEY ARE NOT ALWAYS THERE...
NO, THEY'RE—THEY HAVE MISSIONS. PROTECTING PEOPLE, AND CHALLENGING THEM, WHEN THAT NEEDS TO HAPPEN.
A TORCHBEARER CAME TO MY SETTLE-MENT, ONCE, AND SHE—
WELL, WHEN IT TURNED OUT YOU WERE REAL, I REALIZED SHE WAS RIGHT, THAT I HAD A ROLE TO PLAY IN SPREADING THE FLAME OF SOLUS, THE WORD OF THE PRIME.
THERE ARE SIX TORCHBEARERS, REPRESENTING THE HEXAGONAL LATTICE OF THE CREATION LATHE.
THE ONE SHE USED FOR FORGING.
YOU THINK I SHOULD TALK TO THESE TORCHBEARERS?
NO, NOT THE ONES YOU SAW TODAY. THE ONES WHO LEFT...

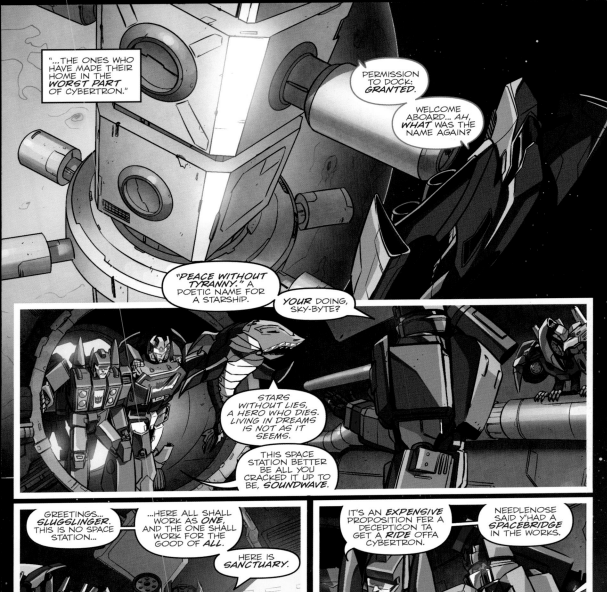

"...THE ONES WHO HAVE MADE THEIR HOME IN THE *WORST PART* OF CYBERTRON."

PERMISSION TO DOCK: *GRANTED.*

WELCOME ABOARD... *AH, WHAT* WAS THE NAME AGAIN?

"PEACE WITHOUT TYRANNY." A POETIC NAME FOR A STARSHIP.

YOUR DOING, SKY-BYTE?

STARS WITHOUT LIES, A HERO WHO DIES. LIVING IN DREAMS IS NOT AS IT SEEMS.

THIS SPACE STATION BETTER BE ALL YOU CRACKED IT UP TO BE, *SOUNDWAVE.*

GREETINGS... *SLUGSLINGER.* THIS IS NO SPACE STATION...

...HERE ALL SHALL WORK AS *ONE,* AND THE ONE SHALL WORK FOR THE GOOD OF *ALL.*

HERE IS SANCTUARY.

SLUGSLINGER AND THE *FLYING SHARK?* I FEEL UNDERDRESSED.

SQUAK! WHY START AT THE *TOP* WHEN THE *BOTTOM'S* SO MUCH CLOSER.

IT'S AN *EXPENSIVE* PROPOSITION FER A *DECEPTICON* TA GET A *RIDE* OFFA CYBERTRON.

NEEDLENOSE SAID Y'HAD A *SPACEBRIDGE* IN THE WORKS.

GALVATRON HAS A PLAN IN PLAY.

SOON, ACCESS TO *CYBERTRON,* AND THE *CYBERTRONIAN COUNCIL WORLDS,* WILL BE BUT A STEP—

WHAT?

I DIDN'T SAY NOTHIN'.

SOMEWHERE... SOMEONE IS *CALLING.*

SOUNDWAVE...

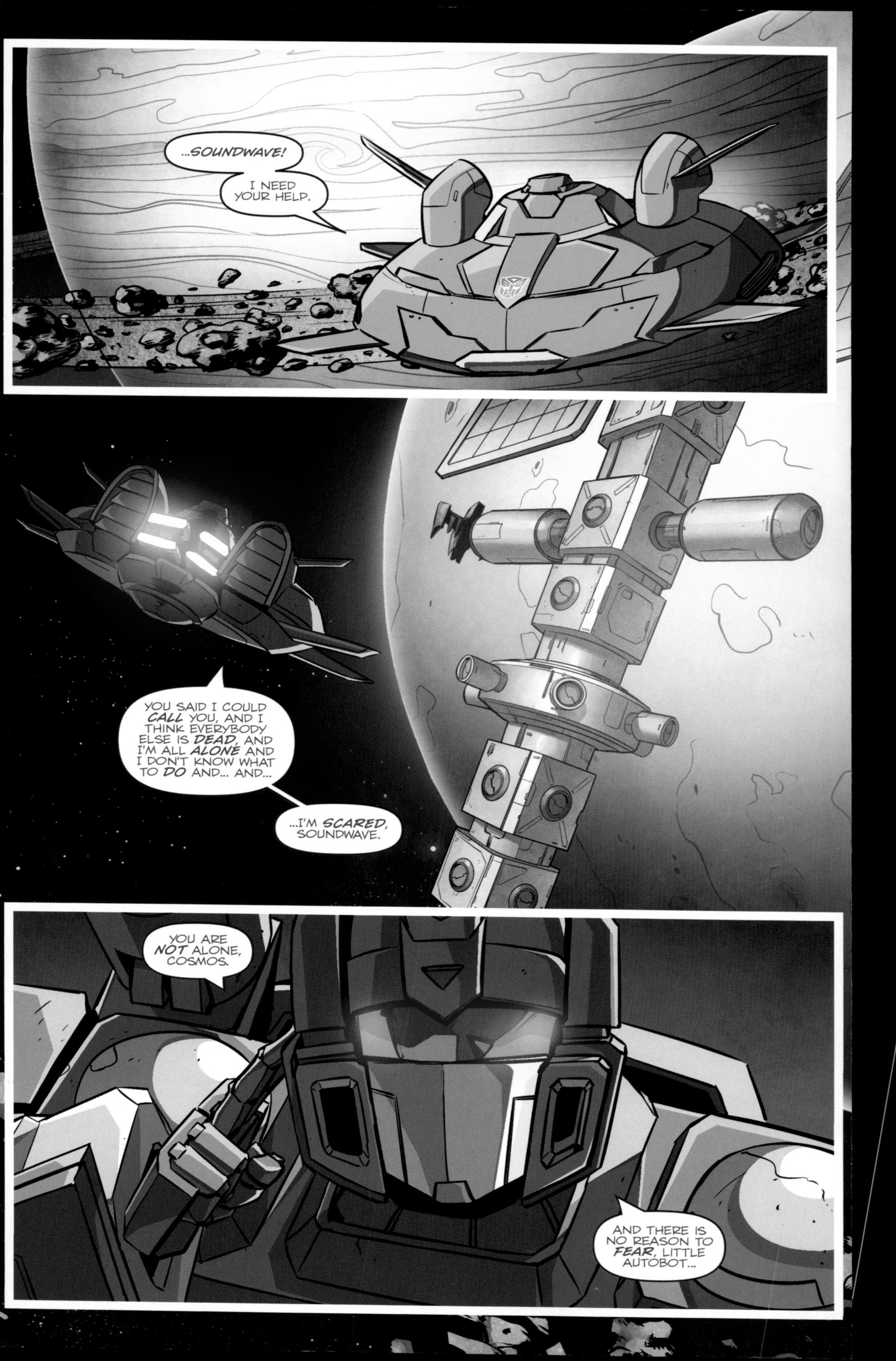
...SOUNDWAVE!
I NEED YOUR HELP.
YOU SAID I COULD CALL YOU, AND I THINK EVERYBODY ELSE IS DEAD, AND I'M ALL ALONE AND I DON'T KNOW WHAT TO DO AND... AND...
...I'M SCARED, SOUNDWAVE.
YOU ARE NOT ALONE, COSMOS.
AND THERE IS NO REASON TO FEAR, LITTLE AUTOBOT...

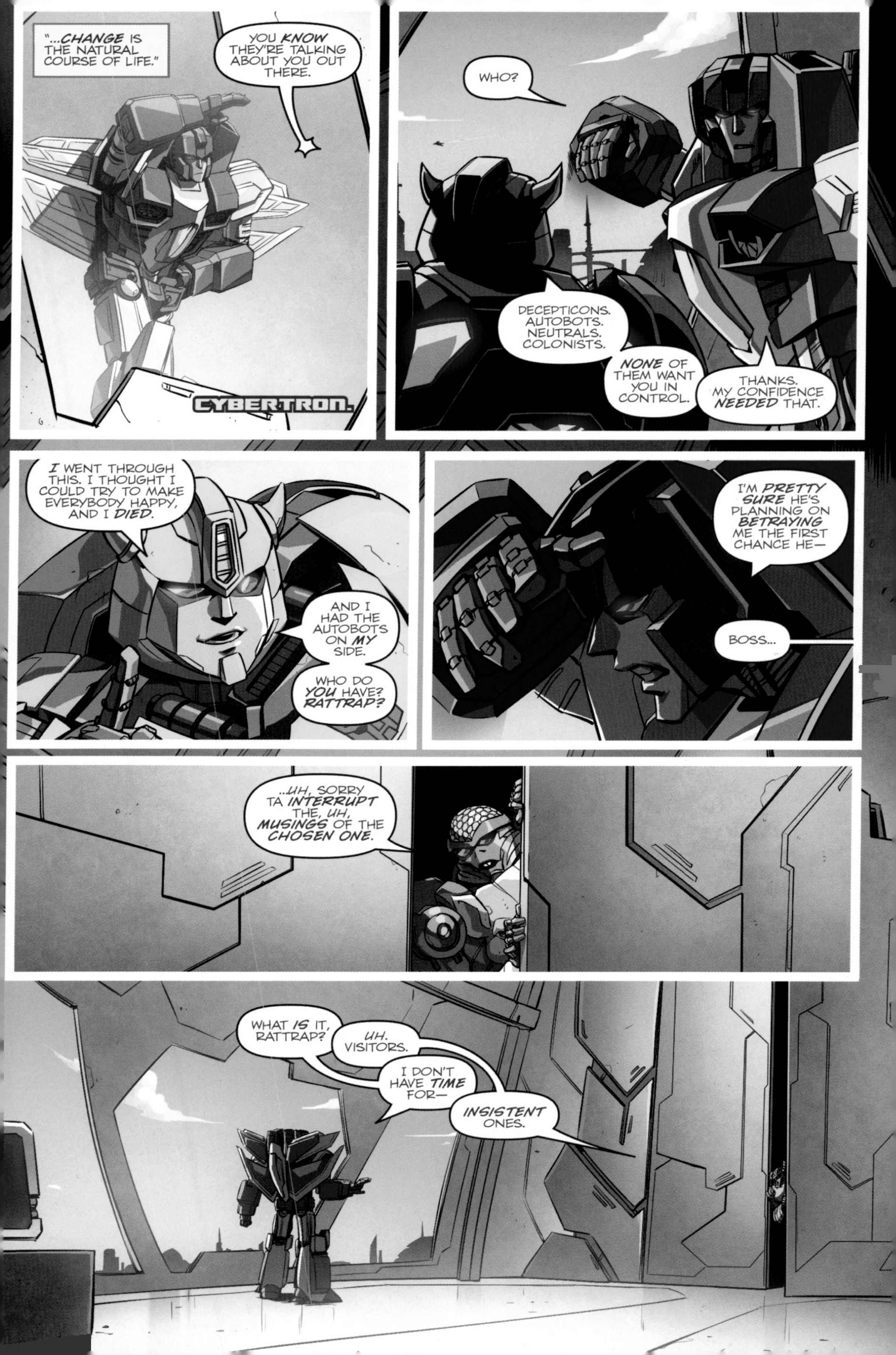
"...CHANGE IS THE NATURAL COURSE OF LIFE."
YOU KNOW THEY'RE TALKING ABOUT YOU OUT THERE.
CYBERTRON.
WHO?
DECEPTICONS. AUTOBOTS. NEUTRALS. COLONISTS.
NONE OF THEM WANT YOU IN CONTROL.
THANKS. MY CONFIDENCE NEEDED THAT.
I WENT THROUGH THIS. I THOUGHT I COULD TRY TO MAKE EVERYBODY HAPPY, AND I DIED.
AND I HAD THE AUTOBOTS ON MY SIDE.
WHO DO YOU HAVE? RATTRAP?
I'M PRETTY SURE HE'S PLANNING ON BETRAYING ME THE FIRST CHANCE HE—
BOSS...
...UH, SORRY TA INTERRUPT THE, UH, MUSINGS OF THE CHOSEN ONE.
WHAT IS IT, RATTRAP?
UH. VISITORS.
I DON'T HAVE TIME FOR—
INSISTENT ONES.

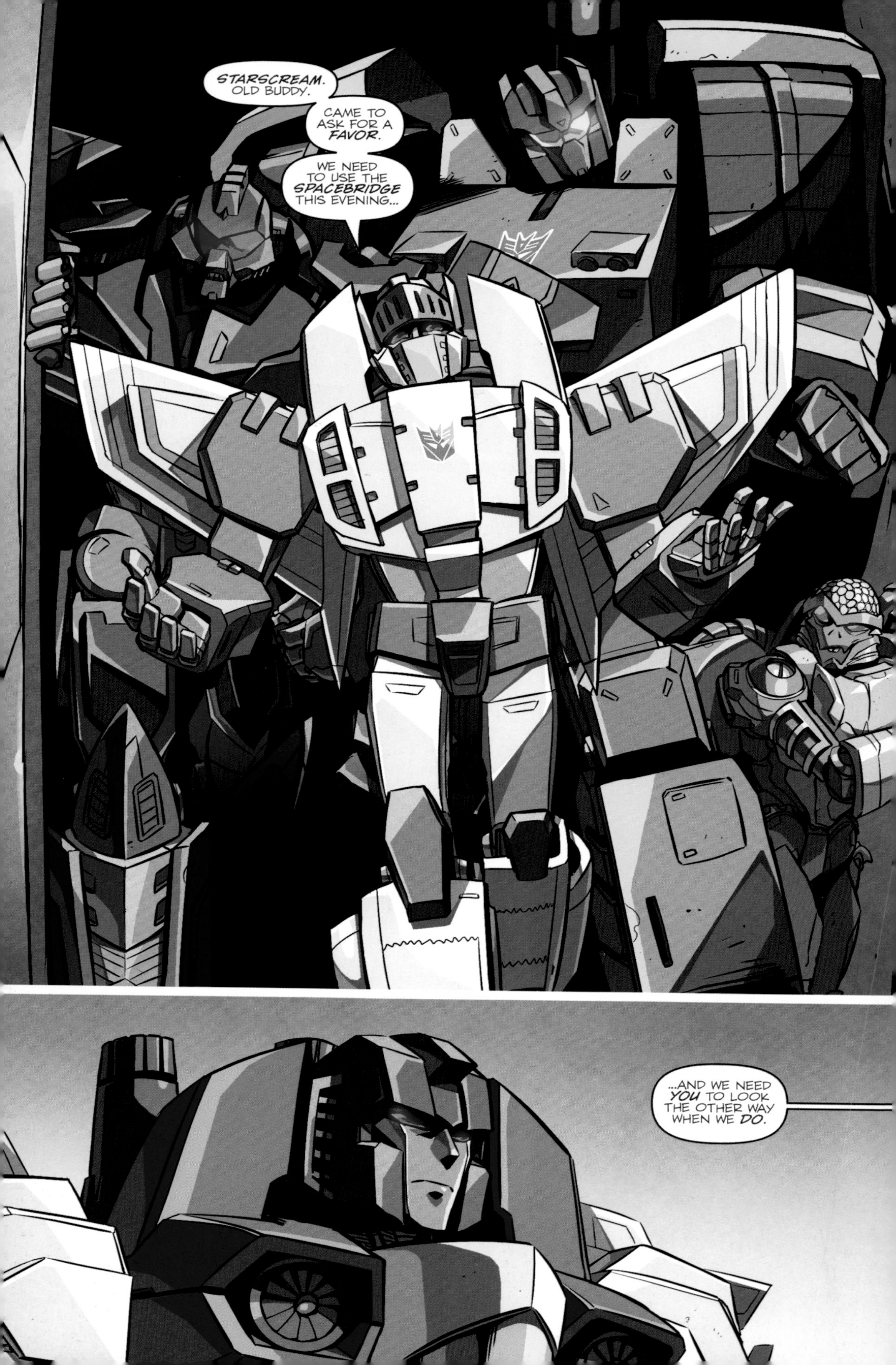
STARSCREAM. OLD BUDDY.
CAME TO ASK FOR A FAVOR.
WE NEED TO USE THE SPACEBRIDGE THIS EVENING...
...AND WE NEED YOU TO LOOK THE OTHER WAY WHEN WE DO.

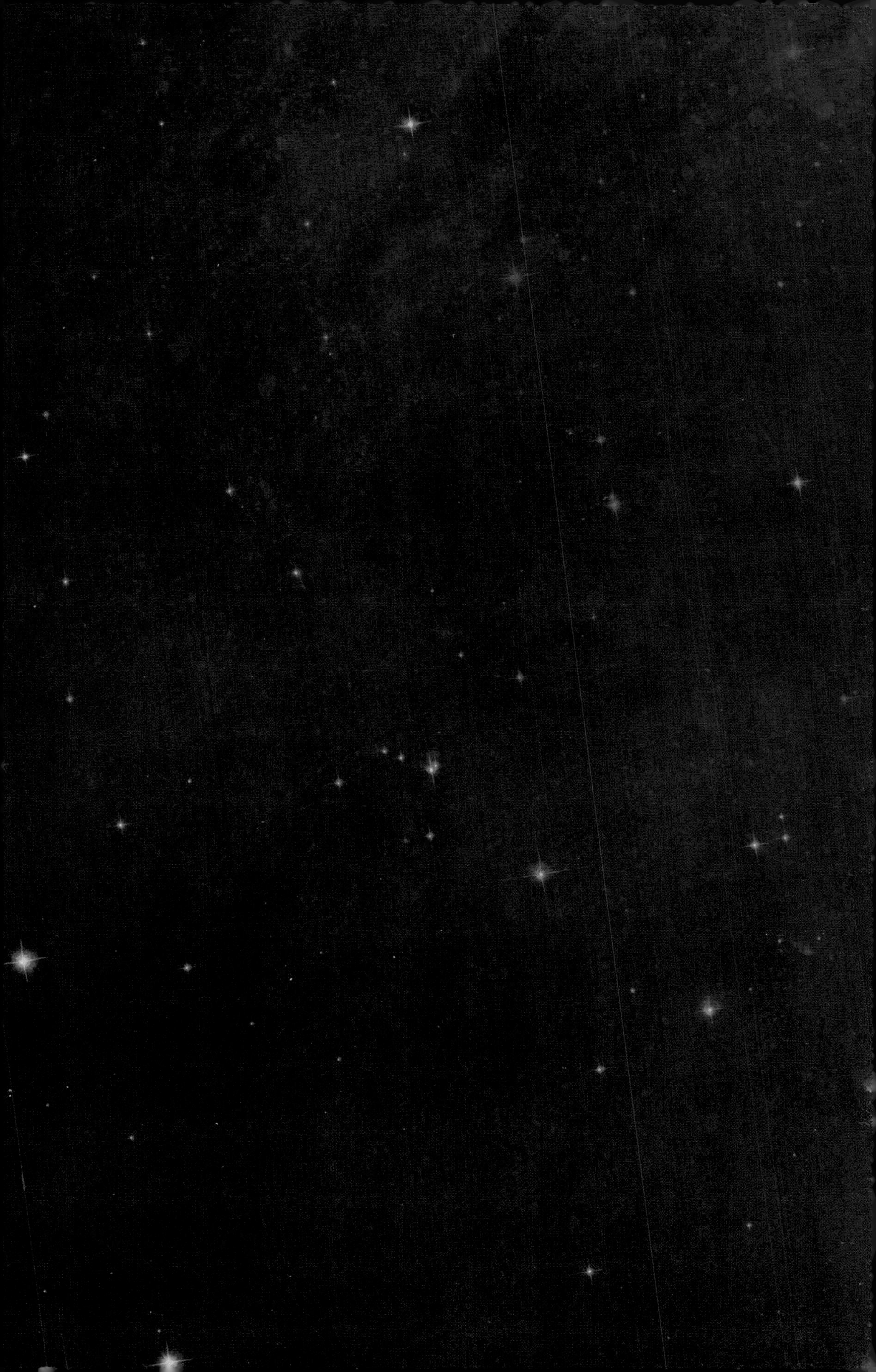

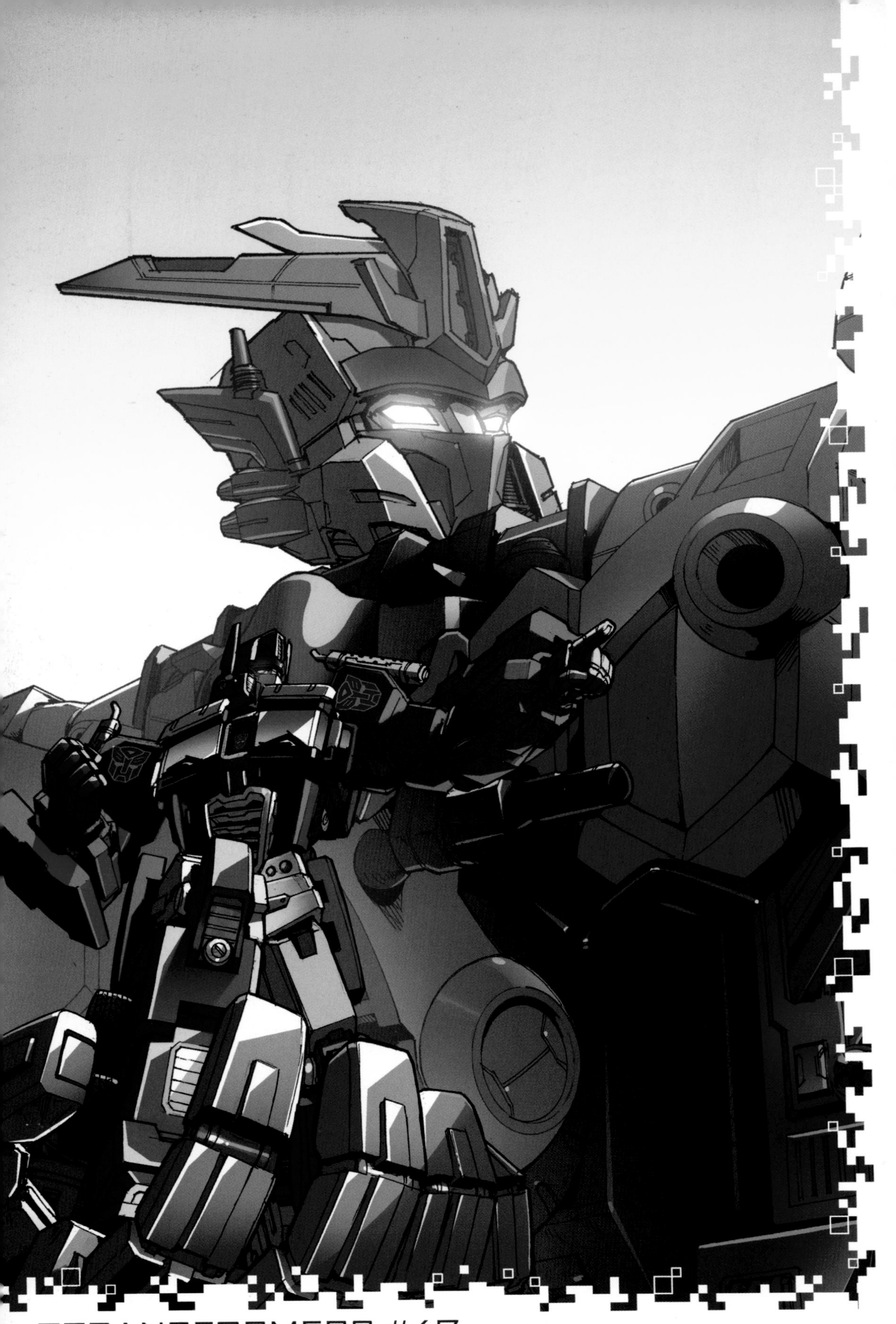

□TRANSFORMERS #47 COVER A

by **ANDREW GRIFFITH** Colors by **JOSH PEREZ**

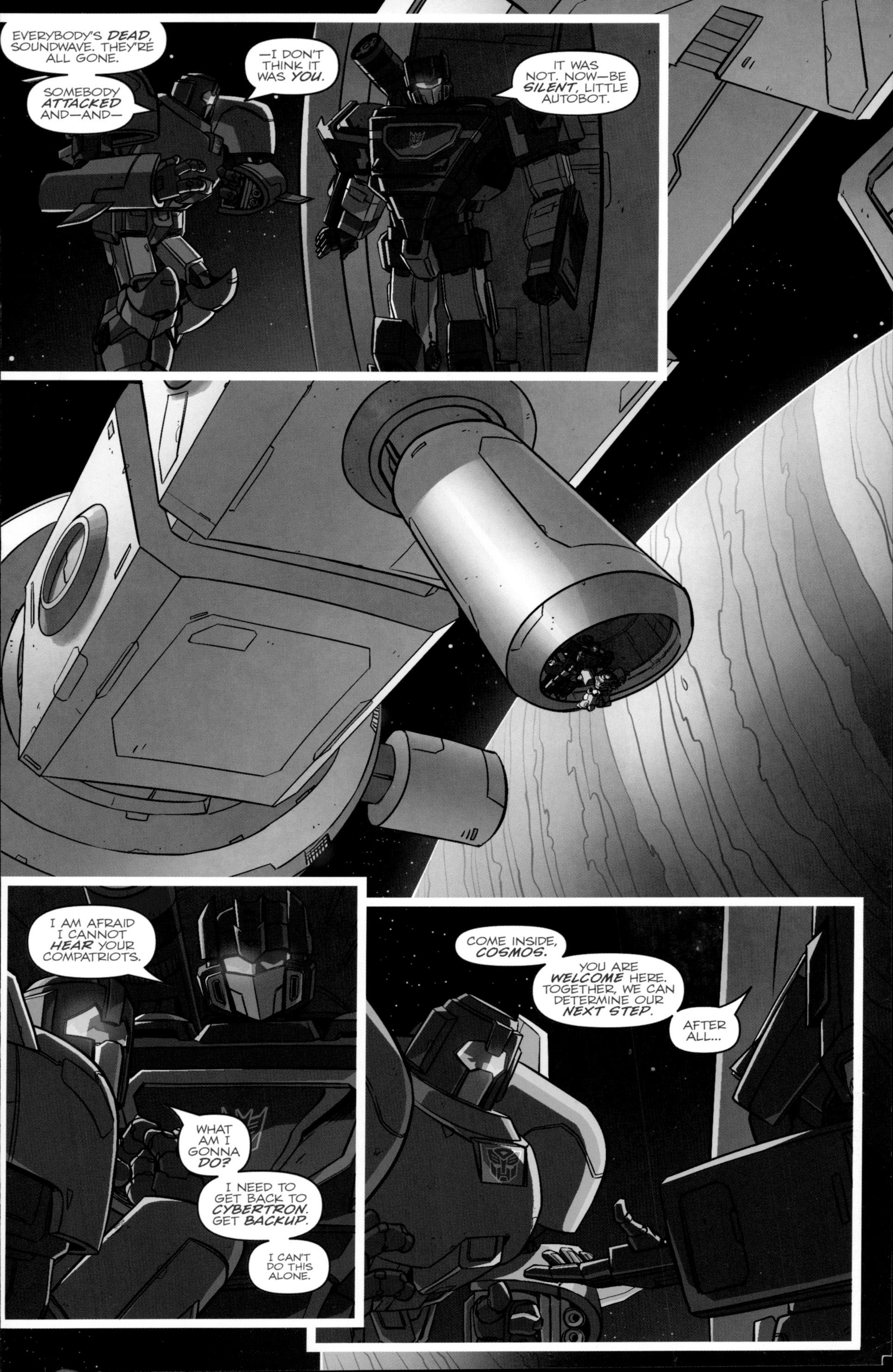
EVERYBODY'S DEAD, SOUNDWAVE. THEY'RE ALL GONE.
SOMEBODY ATTACKED AND—AND—
—I DON'T THINK IT WAS YOU.
IT WAS NOT. NOW—BE SILENT, LITTLE AUTOBOT.
I AM AFRAID I CANNOT HEAR YOUR COMPATRIOTS.
WHAT AM I GONNA DO?
I NEED TO GET BACK TO CYBERTRON. GET BACKUP.
I CAN'T DO THIS ALONE.
COME INSIDE, COSMOS.
YOU ARE WELCOME HERE. TOGETHER, WE CAN DETERMINE OUR NEXT STEP.
AFTER ALL...

"...WE ARE ALL *ONE* IN THE EYES OF *PRIMUS*."

WOOF.

THAT'S *RIGHT*, BUSTER. THEY WON'T EVEN LET ME *TALK* TO HIM, AND THEY GIVE THAT *BLACKROCK* GUY *FULL ACCESS*.

HRRRRR.

BETWEEN *YOU* AND *ME*? I THINK HE'S FLIPPED A *DIODE*...

"...OR *WHATEVER* HUMANS HAVE."

WHEN I WAS A CHILD, A *BLACK ANGEL* APPEARED BEFORE ME.

IT SPOKE IN A LANGUAGE I HAD NEVER HEARD, BUT I *UNDERSTOOD*.

IT SHOWED ME A WORLD OF *RUST DESERTS* ORBITING AN *INFINITE DARKNESS*.

SO I GOT *THAT* GOING FOR ME. WHICH IS NICE.

WELL, YOU'RE *HALF-RIGHT*. MAYBE *TWO THIRDS*.

BLACKROCK... THERE'S NO ANSWER FOR ME TO *GIVE*. YOU NEED *PSYCHOLOGICAL HELP*.

YOU KNOW THE AUTOBOT'S SHIP?

THIS ONE—ONE OF A *FLEET*—CARRIES THE SAME *DESTRUCTIVE POTENTIAL* AS THE SUM TOTAL OF *HUMANKIND*.

UP UNTIL THE CYBERTRONIANS *INVADED* US, I MEAN.

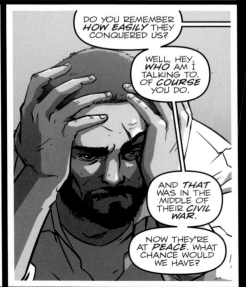

DO YOU REMEMBER *HOW EASILY* THEY CONQUERED US?

WELL, HEY, *WHO* AM I TALKING TO. OF *COURSE* YOU DO.

AND *THAT* WAS IN THE MIDDLE OF THEIR *CIVIL WAR*.

NOW THEY'RE AT *PEACE*. WHAT CHANCE WOULD WE HAVE?

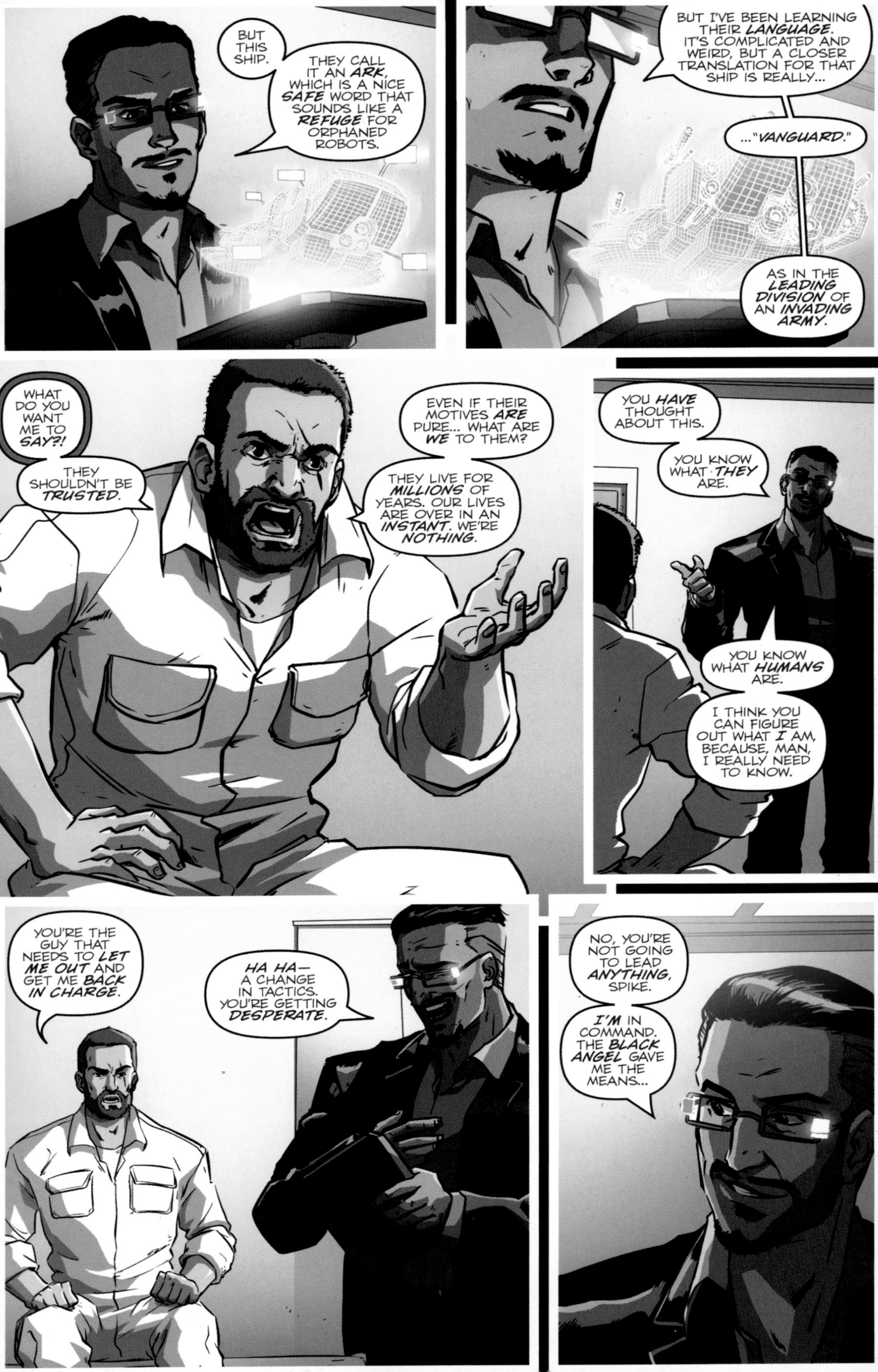

BUT THIS SHIP.
THEY CALL IT AN ARK, WHICH IS A NICE SAFE WORD THAT SOUNDS LIKE A REFUGE FOR ORPHANED ROBOTS.
BUT I'VE BEEN LEARNING THEIR LANGUAGE. IT'S COMPLICATED AND WEIRD, BUT A CLOSER TRANSLATION FOR THAT SHIP IS REALLY...
..."VANGUARD."
AS IN THE LEADING DIVISION OF AN INVADING ARMY.
WHAT DO YOU WANT ME TO SAY?!
THEY SHOULDN'T BE TRUSTED.
EVEN IF THEIR MOTIVES ARE PURE... WHAT ARE WE TO THEM?
THEY LIVE FOR MILLIONS OF YEARS. OUR LIVES ARE OVER IN AN INSTANT. WE'RE NOTHING.
YOU HAVE THOUGHT ABOUT THIS.
YOU KNOW WHAT THEY ARE.
YOU KNOW WHAT HUMANS ARE.
I THINK YOU CAN FIGURE OUT WHAT I AM, BECAUSE, MAN, I REALLY NEED TO KNOW.
YOU'RE THE GUY THAT NEEDS TO LET ME OUT AND GET ME BACK IN CHARGE.
HA HA— A CHANGE IN TACTICS. YOU'RE GETTING DESPERATE.
NO, YOU'RE NOT GOING TO LEAD ANYTHING, SPIKE.
I'M IN COMMAND. THE BLACK ANGEL GAVE ME THE MEANS...

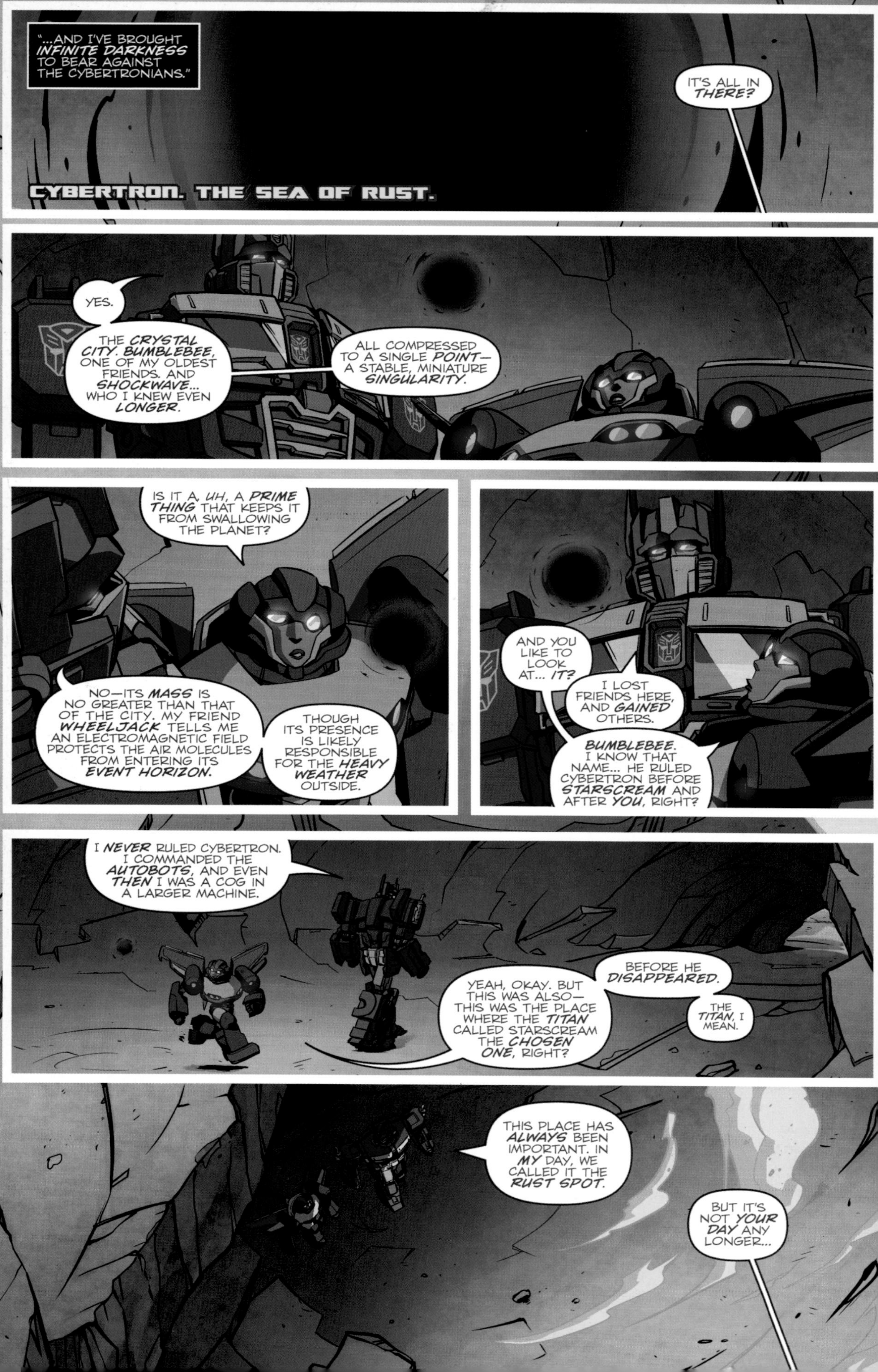
"...AND I'VE BROUGHT INFINITE DARKNESS TO BEAR AGAINST THE CYBERTRONIANS."
IT'S ALL IN THERE?
CYBERTRON. THE SEA OF RUST.
YES.
THE CRYSTAL CITY. BUMBLEBEE, ONE OF MY OLDEST FRIENDS. AND SHOCKWAVE... WHO I KNEW EVEN LONGER.
ALL COMPRESSED TO A SINGLE POINT—A STABLE, MINIATURE SINGULARITY.
IS IT A, UH, A PRIME THING THAT KEEPS IT FROM SWALLOWING THE PLANET?
NO—ITS MASS IS NO GREATER THAN THAT OF THE CITY. MY FRIEND WHEELJACK TELLS ME AN ELECTROMAGNETIC FIELD PROTECTS THE AIR MOLECULES FROM ENTERING ITS EVENT HORIZON.
THOUGH ITS PRESENCE IS LIKELY RESPONSIBLE FOR THE HEAVY WEATHER OUTSIDE.
AND YOU LIKE TO LOOK AT... IT?
I LOST FRIENDS HERE, AND GAINED OTHERS.
BUMBLEBEE. I KNOW THAT NAME... HE RULED CYBERTRON BEFORE STARSCREAM AND AFTER YOU, RIGHT?
I NEVER RULED CYBERTRON. I COMMANDED THE AUTOBOTS, AND EVEN THEN I WAS A COG IN A LARGER MACHINE.
YEAH, OKAY. BUT THIS WAS ALSO—THIS WAS THE PLACE WHERE THE TITAN CALLED STARSCREAM THE CHOSEN ONE, RIGHT?
BEFORE HE DISAPPEARED.
THE TITAN, I MEAN.
THIS PLACE HAS ALWAYS BEEN IMPORTANT. IN MY DAY, WE CALLED IT THE RUST SPOT.
BUT IT'S NOT YOUR DAY ANY LONGER...

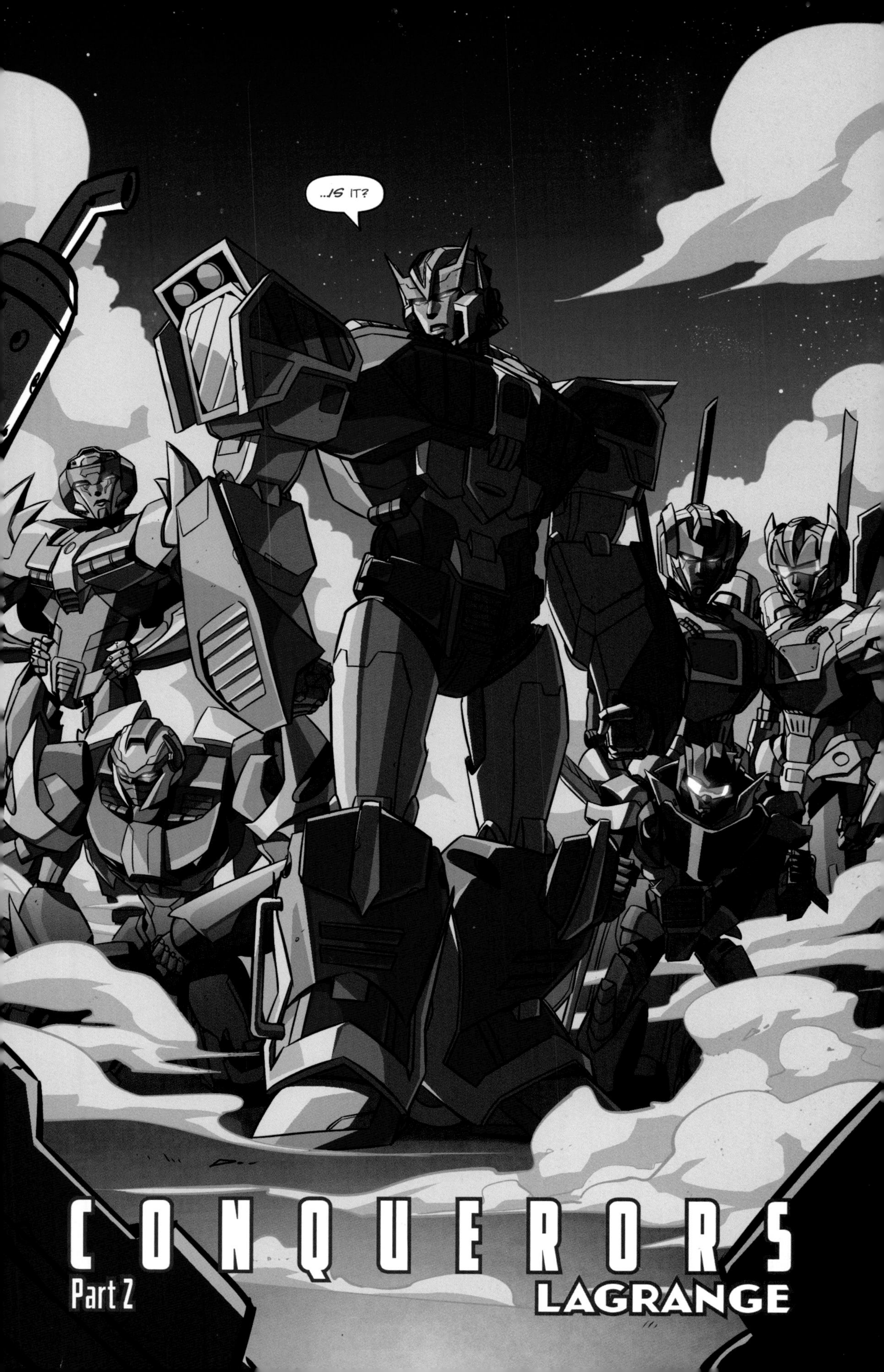

..IS IT?
CONQUERORS
Part 2
LAGRANGE

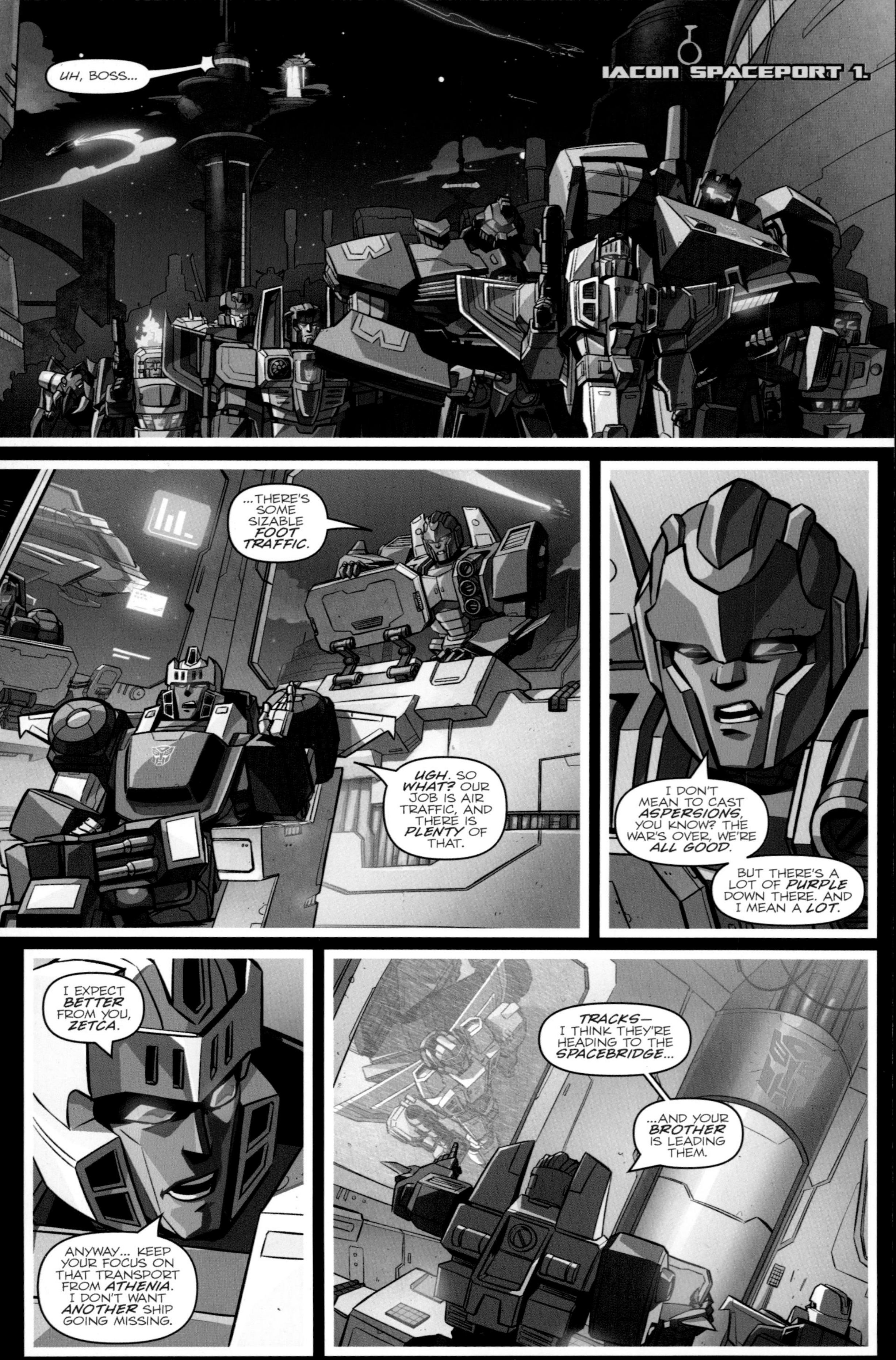
UH, BOSS...
IACON SPACEPORT 1.
...THERE'S SOME SIZABLE FOOT TRAFFIC.
UGH. SO WHAT? OUR JOB IS AIR TRAFFIC, AND THERE IS PLENTY OF THAT.
I DON'T MEAN TO CAST ASPERSIONS, YOU KNOW? THE WAR'S OVER, WE'RE ALL GOOD.
BUT THERE'S A LOT OF PURPLE DOWN THERE. AND I MEAN A LOT.
I EXPECT BETTER FROM YOU, ZETCA.
ANYWAY... KEEP YOUR FOCUS ON THAT TRANSPORT FROM ATHENIA. I DON'T WANT ANOTHER SHIP GOING MISSING.
TRACKS— I THINK THEY'RE HEADING TO THE SPACEBRIDGE...
...AND YOUR BROTHER IS LEADING THEM.

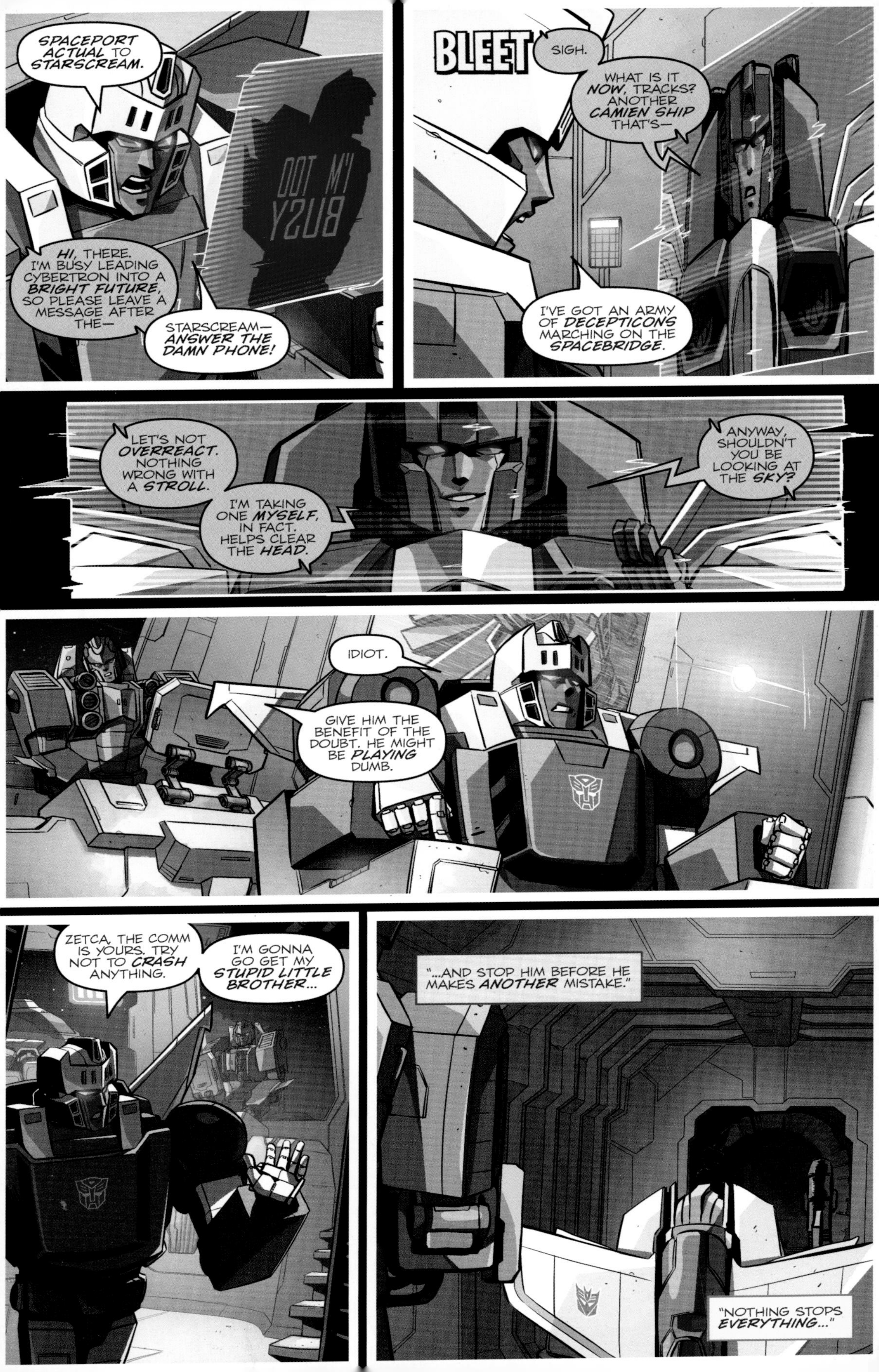
SPACEPORT ACTUAL TO STARSCREAM.
I'M TOO BUSY
HI, THERE. I'M BUSY LEADING CYBERTRON INTO A BRIGHT FUTURE, SO PLEASE LEAVE A MESSAGE AFTER THE—
STARSCREAM— ANSWER THE DAMN PHONE!
BLEET
SIGH.
WHAT IS IT NOW, TRACKS? ANOTHER CAMIEN SHIP THAT'S—
I'VE GOT AN ARMY OF DECEPTICONS MARCHING ON THE SPACEBRIDGE.
LET'S NOT OVERREACT. NOTHING WRONG WITH A STROLL.
I'M TAKING ONE MYSELF, IN FACT. HELPS CLEAR THE HEAD.
ANYWAY, SHOULDN'T YOU BE LOOKING AT THE SKY?
IDIOT.
GIVE HIM THE BENEFIT OF THE DOUBT. HE MIGHT BE PLAYING DUMB.
ZETCA, THE COMM IS YOURS. TRY NOT TO CRASH ANYTHING.
I'M GONNA GO GET MY STUPID LITTLE BROTHER...
"...AND STOP HIM BEFORE HE MAKES ANOTHER MISTAKE."
"NOTHING STOPS EVERYTHING..."

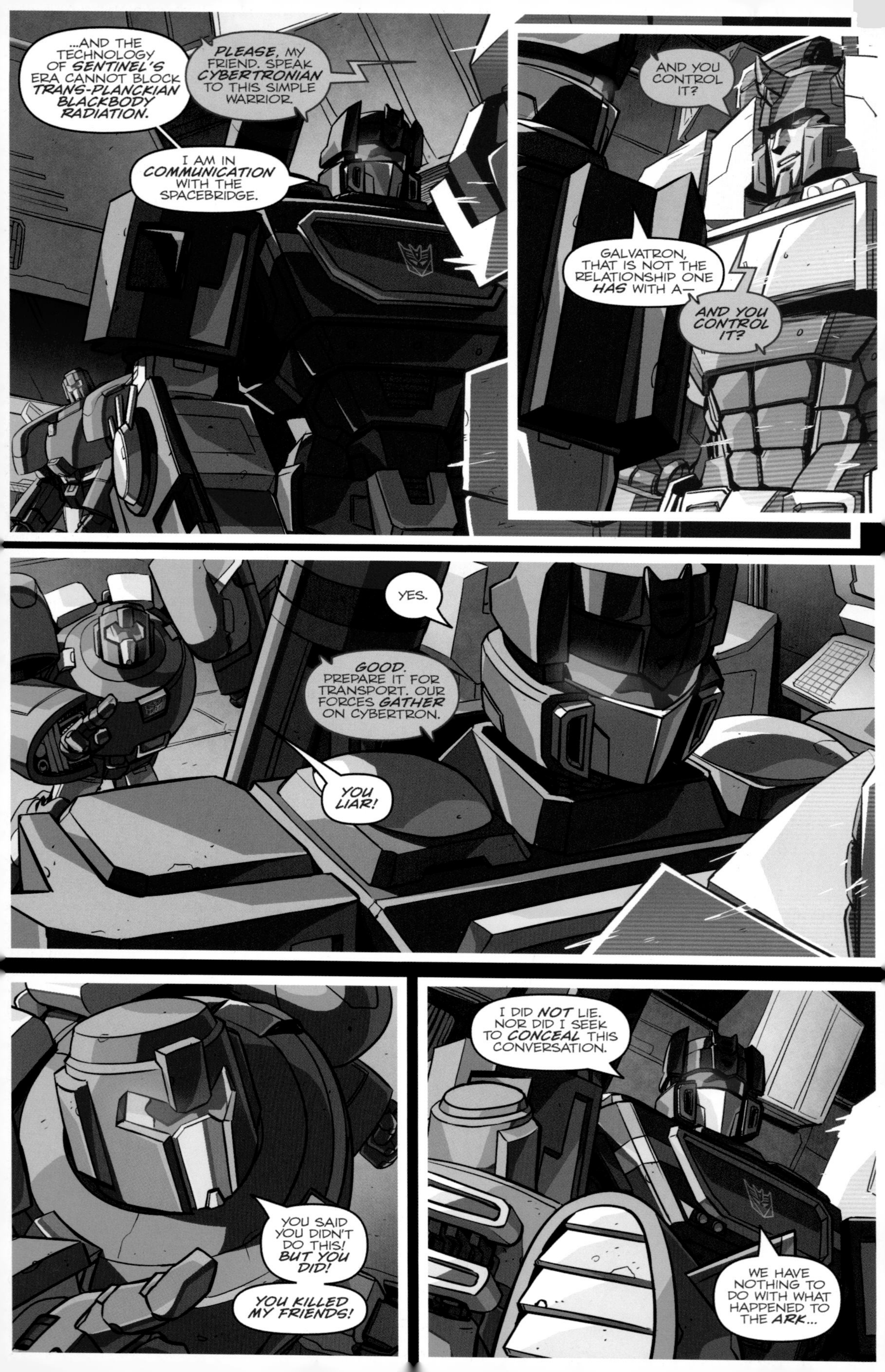

...AND THE TECHNOLOGY OF SENTINEL'S ERA CANNOT BLOCK TRANS-PLANCKIAN BLACKBODY RADIATION.
PLEASE, MY FRIEND. SPEAK CYBERTRONIAN TO THIS SIMPLE WARRIOR.
I AM IN COMMUNICATION WITH THE SPACEBRIDGE.
AND YOU CONTROL IT?
GALVATRON, THAT IS NOT THE RELATIONSHIP ONE HAS WITH A—
AND YOU CONTROL IT?
YES.
GOOD. PREPARE IT FOR TRANSPORT. OUR FORCES GATHER ON CYBERTRON.
YOU LIAR!
YOU SAID YOU DIDN'T DO THIS! BUT YOU DID!
YOU KILLED MY FRIENDS!
I DID NOT LIE. NOR DID I SEEK TO CONCEAL THIS CONVERSATION.
WE HAVE NOTHING TO DO WITH WHAT HAPPENED TO THE ARK...

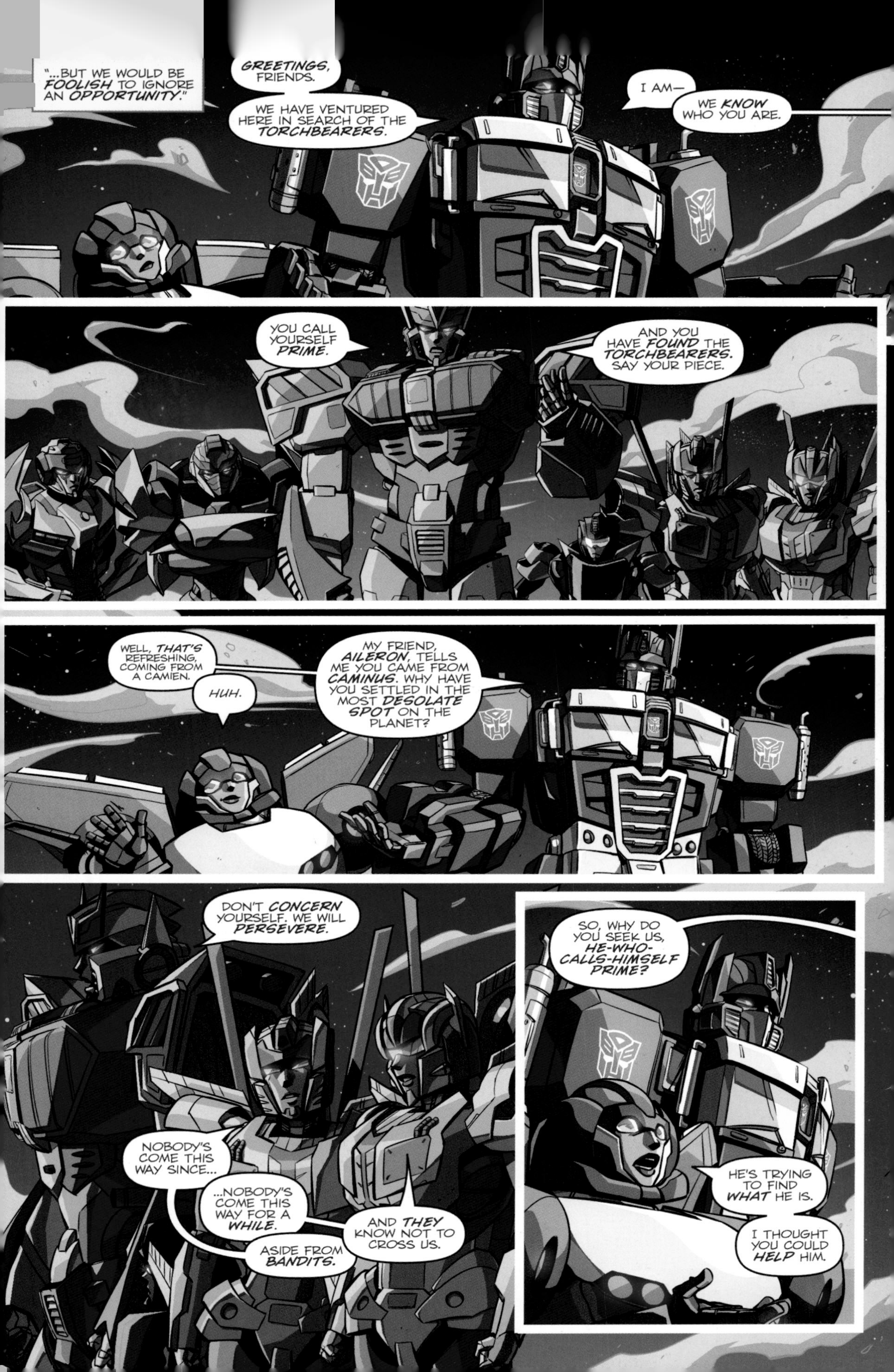
"...BUT WE WOULD BE FOOLISH TO IGNORE AN OPPORTUNITY."
GREETINGS, FRIENDS.
WE HAVE VENTURED HERE IN SEARCH OF THE TORCHBEARERS.
I AM—
WE KNOW WHO YOU ARE.
YOU CALL YOURSELF PRIME.
AND YOU HAVE FOUND THE TORCHBEARERS. SAY YOUR PIECE.
WELL, THAT'S REFRESHING, COMING FROM A CAMIEN.
HUH.
MY FRIEND, AILERON, TELLS ME YOU CAME FROM CAMINUS. WHY HAVE YOU SETTLED IN THE MOST DESOLATE SPOT ON THE PLANET?
DON'T CONCERN YOURSELF. WE WILL PERSEVERE.
NOBODY'S COME THIS WAY SINCE...
...NOBODY'S COME THIS WAY FOR A WHILE.
AND THEY KNOW NOT TO CROSS US.
ASIDE FROM BANDITS.
SO, WHY DO YOU SEEK US, HE-WHO-CALLS-HIMSELF PRIME?
HE'S TRYING TO FIND WHAT HE IS.
I THOUGHT YOU COULD HELP HIM.

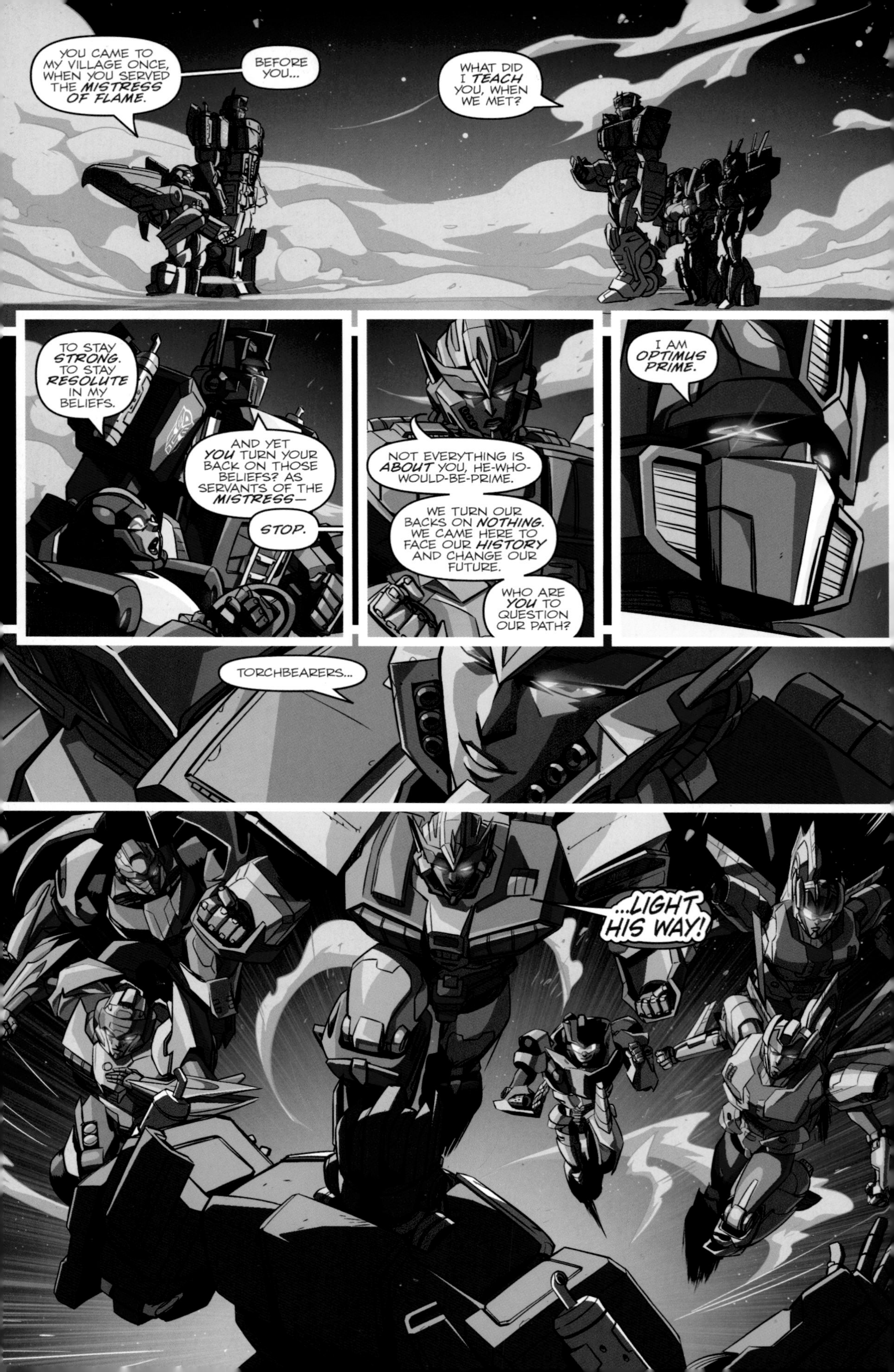
YOU CAME TO MY VILLAGE ONCE, WHEN YOU SERVED THE MISTRESS OF FLAME.
BEFORE YOU...
WHAT DID I TEACH YOU, WHEN WE MET?
TO STAY STRONG. TO STAY RESOLUTE IN MY BELIEFS.
AND YET YOU TURN YOUR BACK ON THOSE BELIEFS? AS SERVANTS OF THE MISTRESS—
STOP.
NOT EVERYTHING IS ABOUT YOU, HE-WHO-WOULD-BE-PRIME.
WE TURN OUR BACKS ON NOTHING. WE CAME HERE TO FACE OUR HISTORY AND CHANGE OUR FUTURE.
WHO ARE YOU TO QUESTION OUR PATH?
I AM OPTIMUS PRIME.
TORCHBEARERS...
...LIGHT HIS WAY!

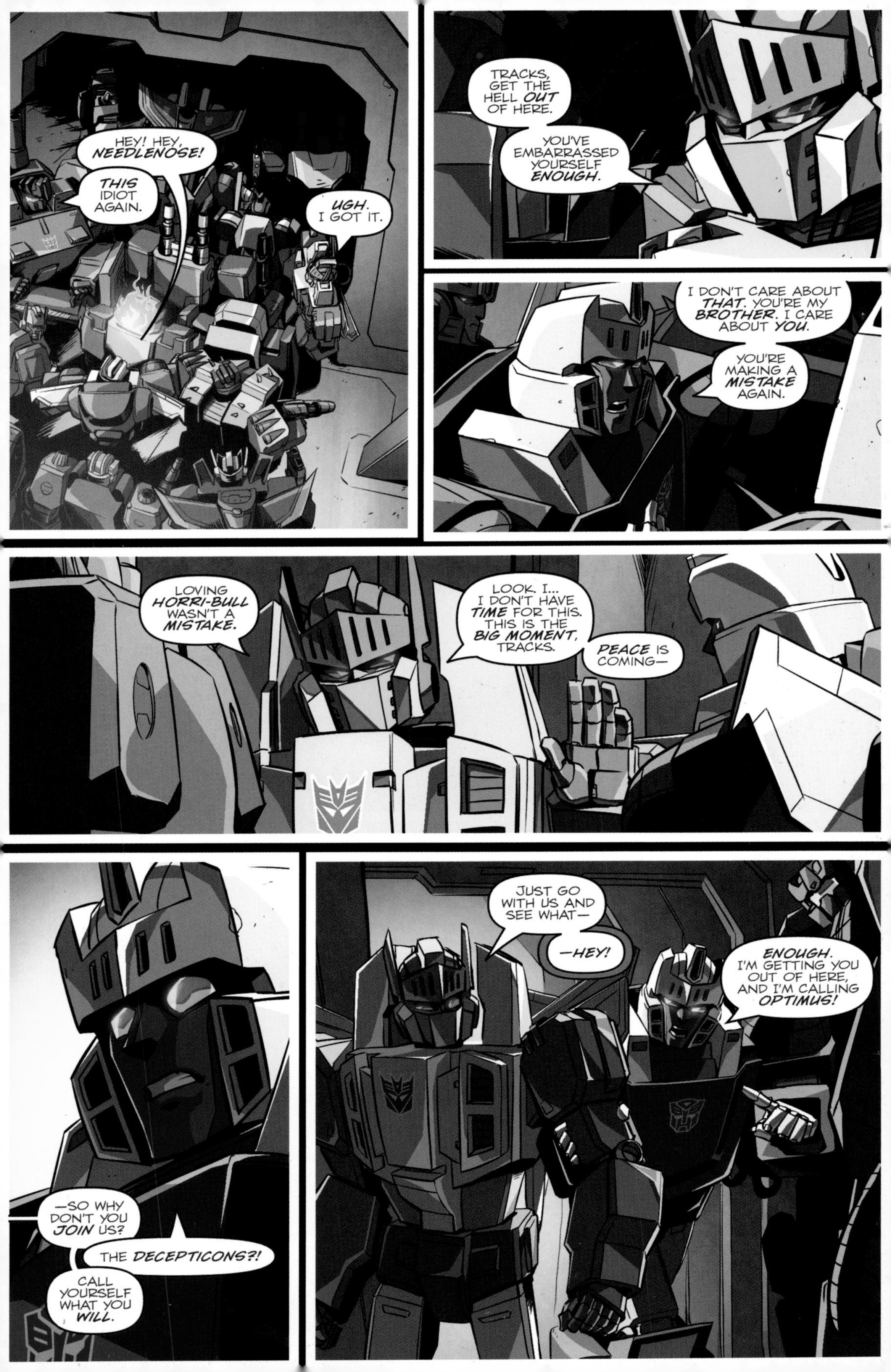
HEY! HEY, NEEDLENOSE!
THIS IDIOT AGAIN.
UGH. I GOT IT.
TRACKS, GET THE HELL OUT OF HERE.
YOU'VE EMBARRASSED YOURSELF ENOUGH.
I DON'T CARE ABOUT THAT. YOU'RE MY BROTHER. I CARE ABOUT YOU.
YOU'RE MAKING A MISTAKE AGAIN.
LOVING HORRI-BULL WASN'T A MISTAKE.
LOOK. I... I DON'T HAVE TIME FOR THIS. THIS IS THE BIG MOMENT, TRACKS.
PEACE IS COMING—
—SO WHY DON'T YOU JOIN US?
THE DECEPTICONS?!
CALL YOURSELF WHAT YOU WILL.
JUST GO WITH US AND SEE WHAT—
—HEY!
ENOUGH. I'M GETTING YOU OUT OF HERE, AND I'M CALLING OPTIMUS!

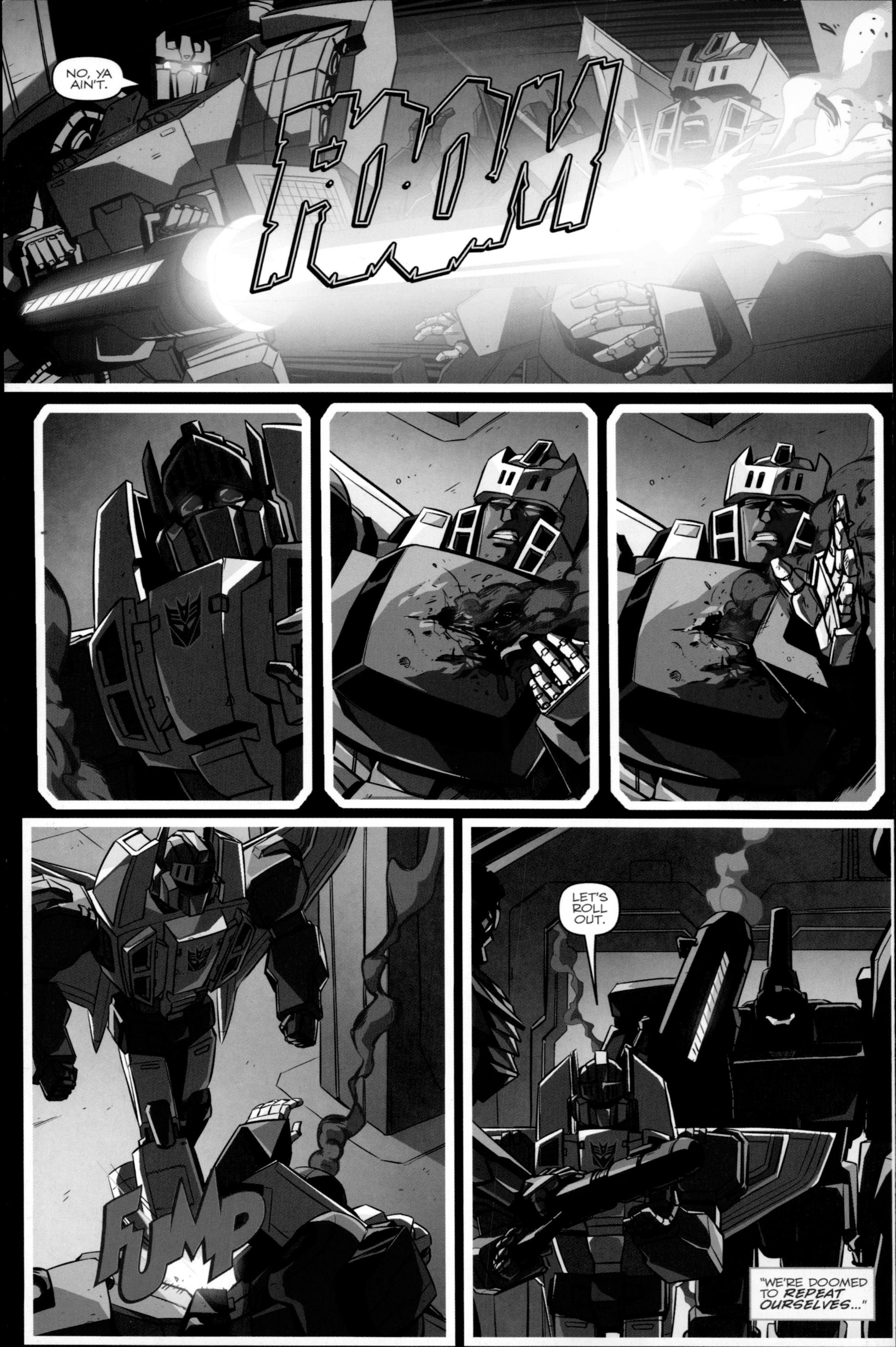
NO, YA AIN'T.
FROOM
FUMP
LET'S ROLL OUT.
"WE'RE DOOMED TO REPEAT OURSELVES..."

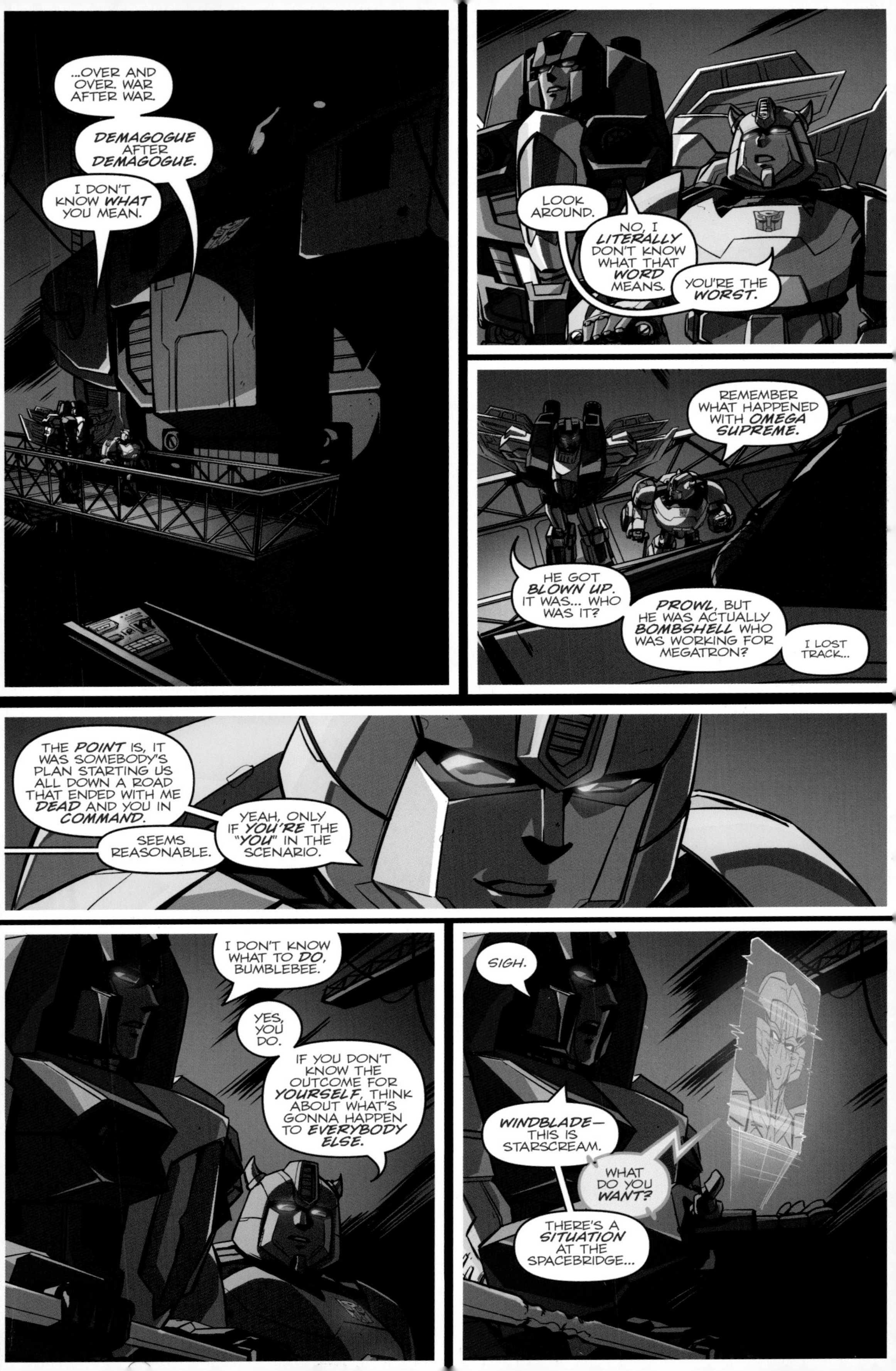
...OVER AND OVER. WAR AFTER WAR.
DEMAGOGUE AFTER DEMAGOGUE.
I DON'T KNOW WHAT YOU MEAN.
LOOK AROUND.
NO, I LITERALLY DON'T KNOW WHAT THAT WORD MEANS.
YOU'RE THE WORST.
REMEMBER WHAT HAPPENED WITH OMEGA SUPREME.
HE GOT BLOWN UP. IT WAS... WHO WAS IT?
PROWL, BUT HE WAS ACTUALLY BOMBSHELL WHO WAS WORKING FOR MEGATRON?
I LOST TRACK...
THE POINT IS, IT WAS SOMEBODY'S PLAN STARTING US ALL DOWN A ROAD THAT ENDED WITH ME DEAD AND YOU IN COMMAND.
SEEMS REASONABLE.
YEAH, ONLY IF YOU'RE THE "YOU" IN THE SCENARIO.
I DON'T KNOW WHAT TO DO, BUMBLEBEE.
YES, YOU DO.
IF YOU DON'T KNOW THE OUTCOME FOR YOURSELF, THINK ABOUT WHAT'S GONNA HAPPEN TO EVERYBODY ELSE.
SIGH.
WINDBLADE— THIS IS STARSCREAM.
WHAT DO YOU WANT?
THERE'S A SITUATION AT THE SPACEBRIDGE...

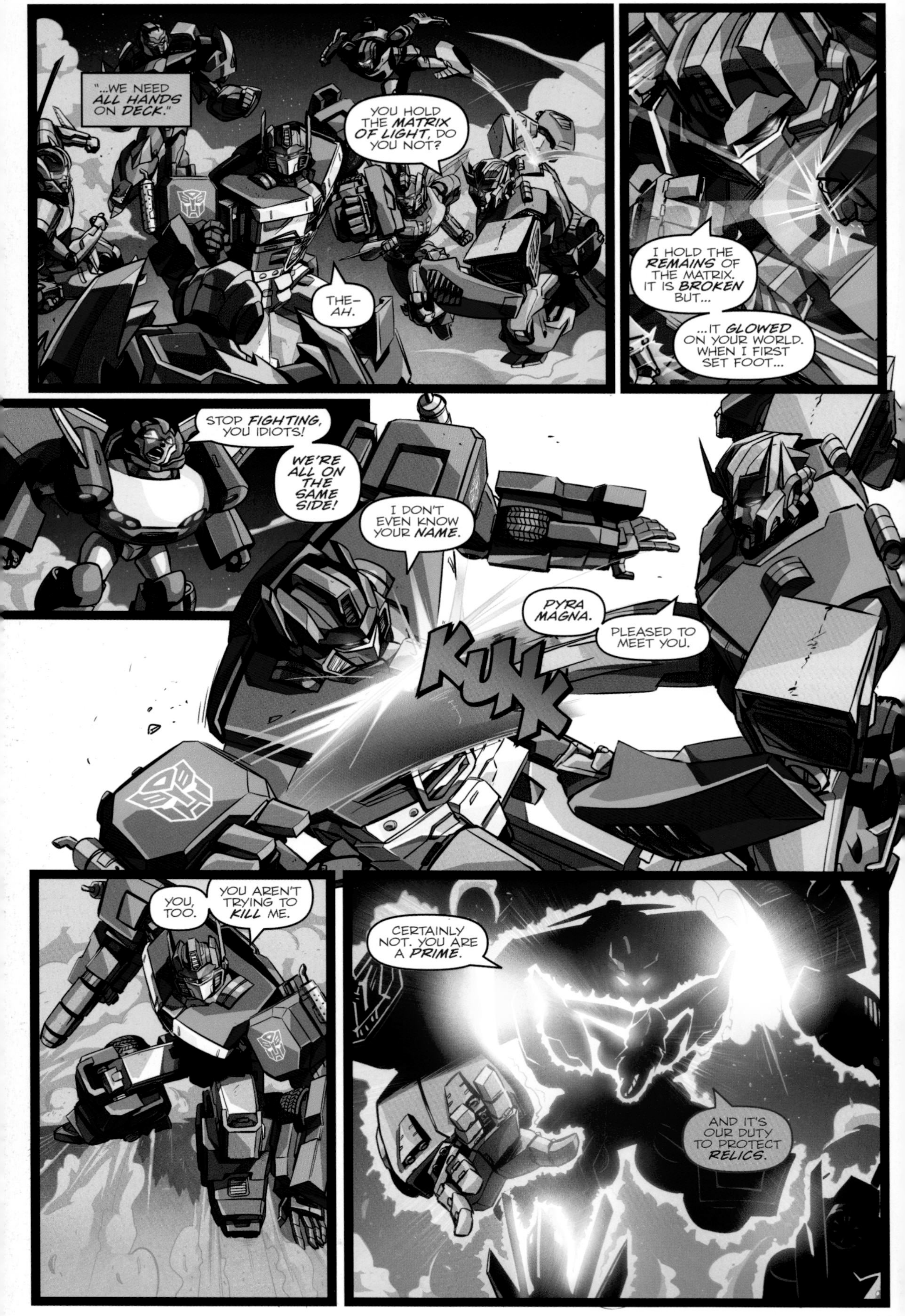
"...WE NEED ALL HANDS ON DECK."
YOU HOLD THE MATRIX OF LIGHT, DO YOU NOT?
THE-AH.
I HOLD THE REMAINS OF THE MATRIX. IT IS BROKEN BUT...
...IT GLOWED ON YOUR WORLD. WHEN I FIRST SET FOOT...
STOP FIGHTING, YOU IDIOTS!
WE'RE ALL ON THE SAME SIDE!
I DON'T EVEN KNOW YOUR NAME.
PYRA MAGNA.
PLEASED TO MEET YOU.
KLUNK
YOU, TOO.
YOU AREN'T TRYING TO KILL ME.
CERTAINLY NOT. YOU ARE A PRIME.
AND IT'S OUR DUTY TO PROTECT RELICS.

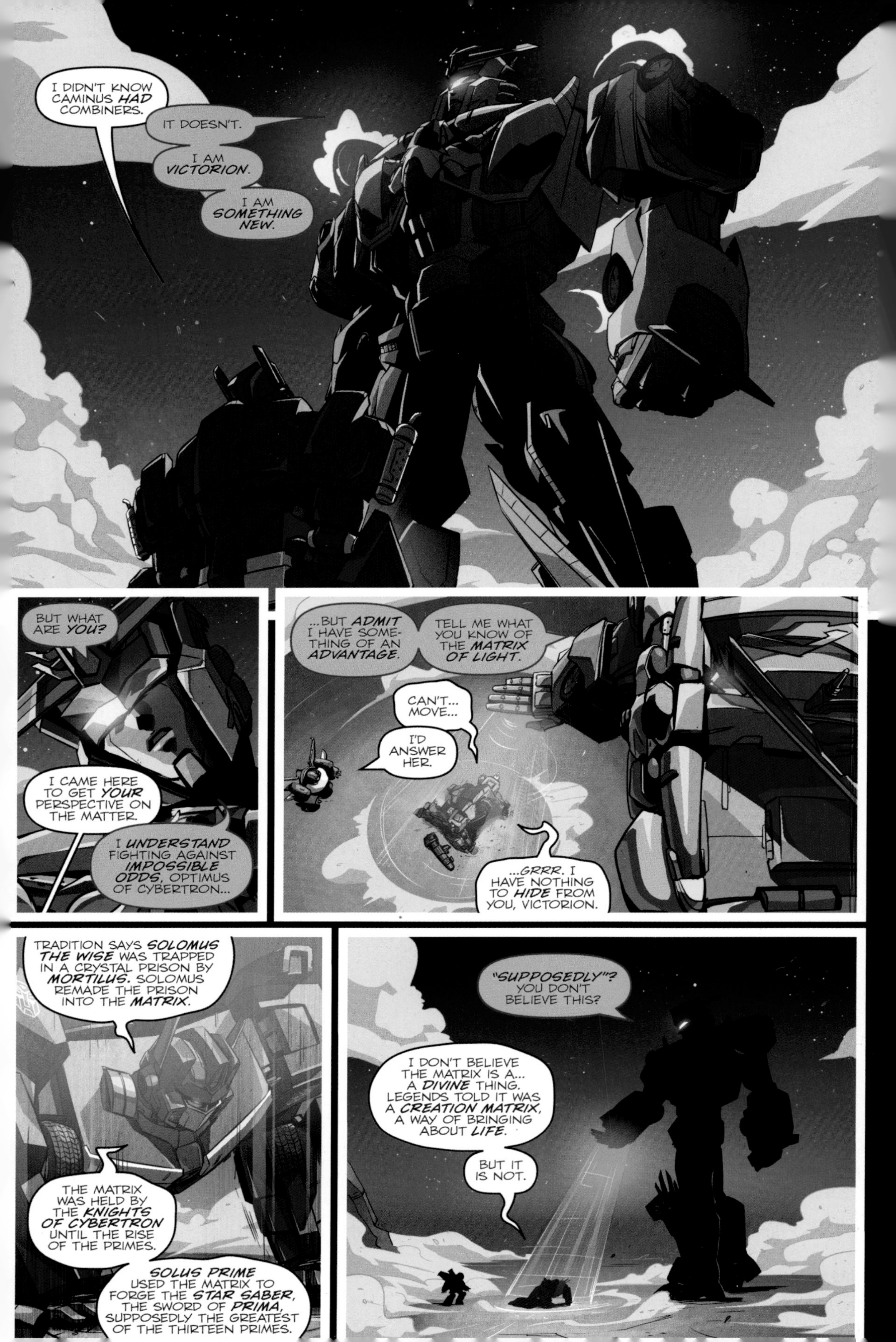

I DIDN'T KNOW CAMINUS *HAD* COMBINERS.
IT DOESN'T.
I AM *VICTORION*.
I AM *SOMETHING NEW*.
BUT WHAT ARE *YOU*?
I CAME HERE TO GET *YOUR* PERSPECTIVE ON THE MATTER.
I *UNDERSTAND* FIGHTING AGAINST *IMPOSSIBLE ODDS*, OPTIMUS OF CYBERTRON...
...BUT *ADMIT* I HAVE SOMETHING OF AN *ADVANTAGE*.
TELL ME WHAT YOU KNOW OF THE *MATRIX OF LIGHT*.
CAN'T... MOVE...
I'D ANSWER HER.
...GRRR. I HAVE NOTHING TO *HIDE* FROM YOU, VICTORION.
TRADITION SAYS *SOLOMUS THE WISE* WAS TRAPPED IN A CRYSTAL PRISON BY *MORTILUS*. SOLOMUS REMADE THE PRISON INTO THE *MATRIX*.
THE MATRIX WAS HELD BY THE *KNIGHTS OF CYBERTRON* UNTIL THE RISE OF THE PRIMES.
SOLUS PRIME USED THE MATRIX TO FORGE THE *STAR SABER*, THE SWORD OF *PRIMA*, SUPPOSEDLY THE GREATEST OF THE THIRTEEN PRIMES.
"SUPPOSEDLY"? YOU DON'T BELIEVE THIS?
I DON'T BELIEVE THE MATRIX IS A... A *DIVINE* THING. LEGENDS TOLD IT WAS A *CREATION MATRIX*, A WAY OF BRINGING ABOUT *LIFE*.
BUT IT IS NOT.

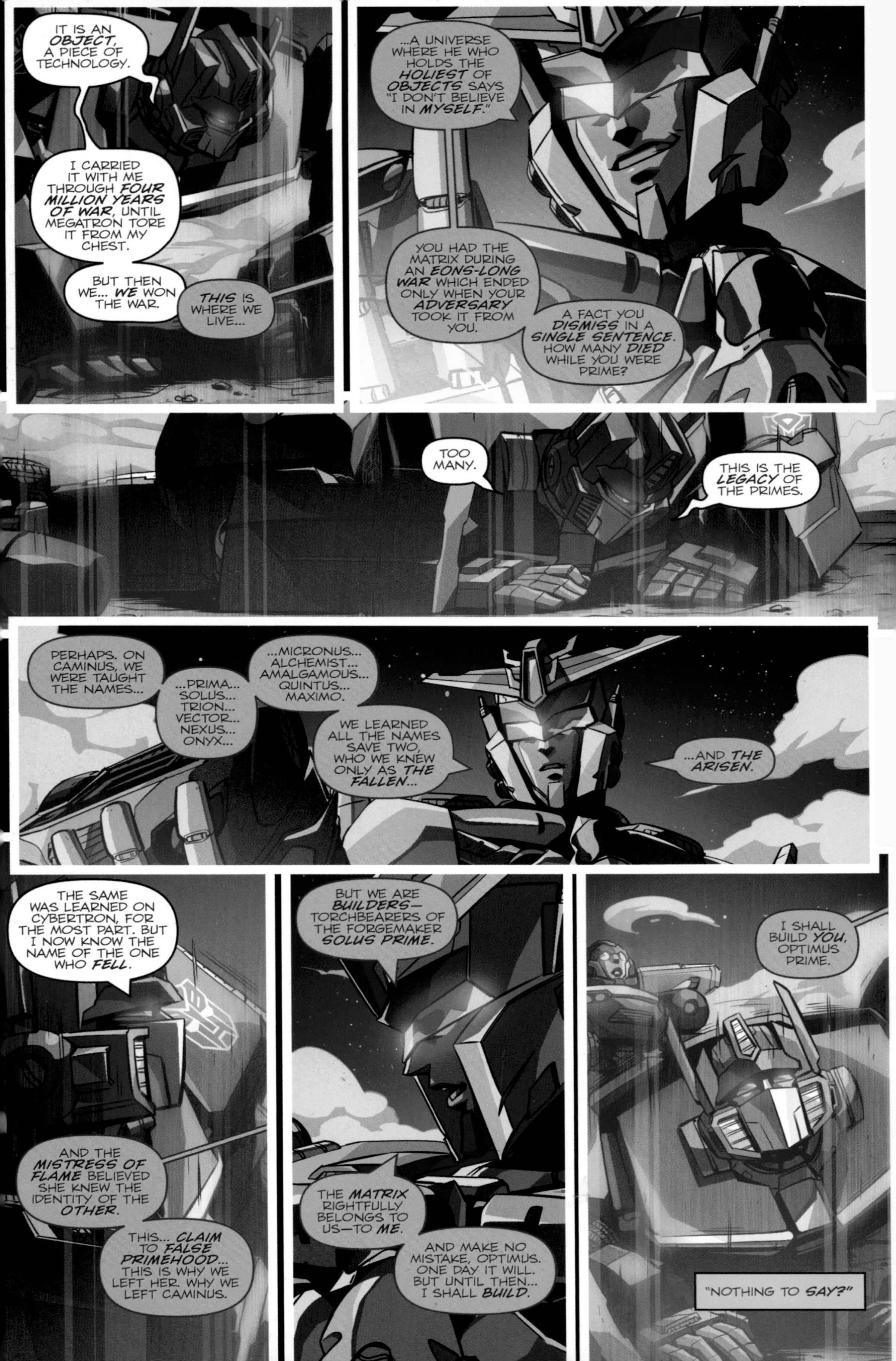
IT IS AN OBJECT, A PIECE OF TECHNOLOGY.
I CARRIED IT WITH ME THROUGH FOUR MILLION YEARS OF WAR, UNTIL MEGATRON TORE IT FROM MY CHEST.
BUT THEN WE... WE WON THE WAR.
THIS IS WHERE WE LIVE...
...A UNIVERSE WHERE HE WHO HOLDS THE HOLIEST OF OBJECTS SAYS "I DON'T BELIEVE IN MYSELF."
YOU HAD THE MATRIX DURING AN EONS-LONG WAR WHICH ENDED ONLY WHEN YOUR ADVERSARY TOOK IT FROM YOU.
A FACT YOU DISMISS IN A SINGLE SENTENCE. HOW MANY DIED WHILE YOU WERE PRIME?
TOO MANY.
THIS IS THE LEGACY OF THE PRIMES.
PERHAPS. ON CAMINUS, WE WERE TAUGHT THE NAMES...
...PRIMA... SOLUS... TRION... VECTOR... NEXUS... ONYX...
...MICRONUS... ALCHEMIST... AMALGAMOUS... QUINTUS... MAXIMO.
WE LEARNED ALL THE NAMES SAVE TWO, WHO WE KNEW ONLY AS THE FALLEN...
...AND THE ARISEN.
THE SAME WAS LEARNED ON CYBERTRON, FOR THE MOST PART. BUT I NOW KNOW THE NAME OF THE ONE WHO FELL.
AND THE MISTRESS OF FLAME BELIEVED SHE KNEW THE IDENTITY OF THE OTHER.
THIS... CLAIM TO FALSE PRIMEHOOD... THIS IS WHY WE LEFT HER. WHY WE LEFT CAMINUS.
BUT WE ARE BUILDERS—TORCHBEARERS OF THE FORGEMAKER SOLUS PRIME.
THE MATRIX RIGHTFULLY BELONGS TO US—TO ME.
AND MAKE NO MISTAKE, OPTIMUS. ONE DAY IT WILL. BUT UNTIL THEN... I SHALL BUILD.
I SHALL BUILD YOU, OPTIMUS PRIME.
"NOTHING TO SAY?"

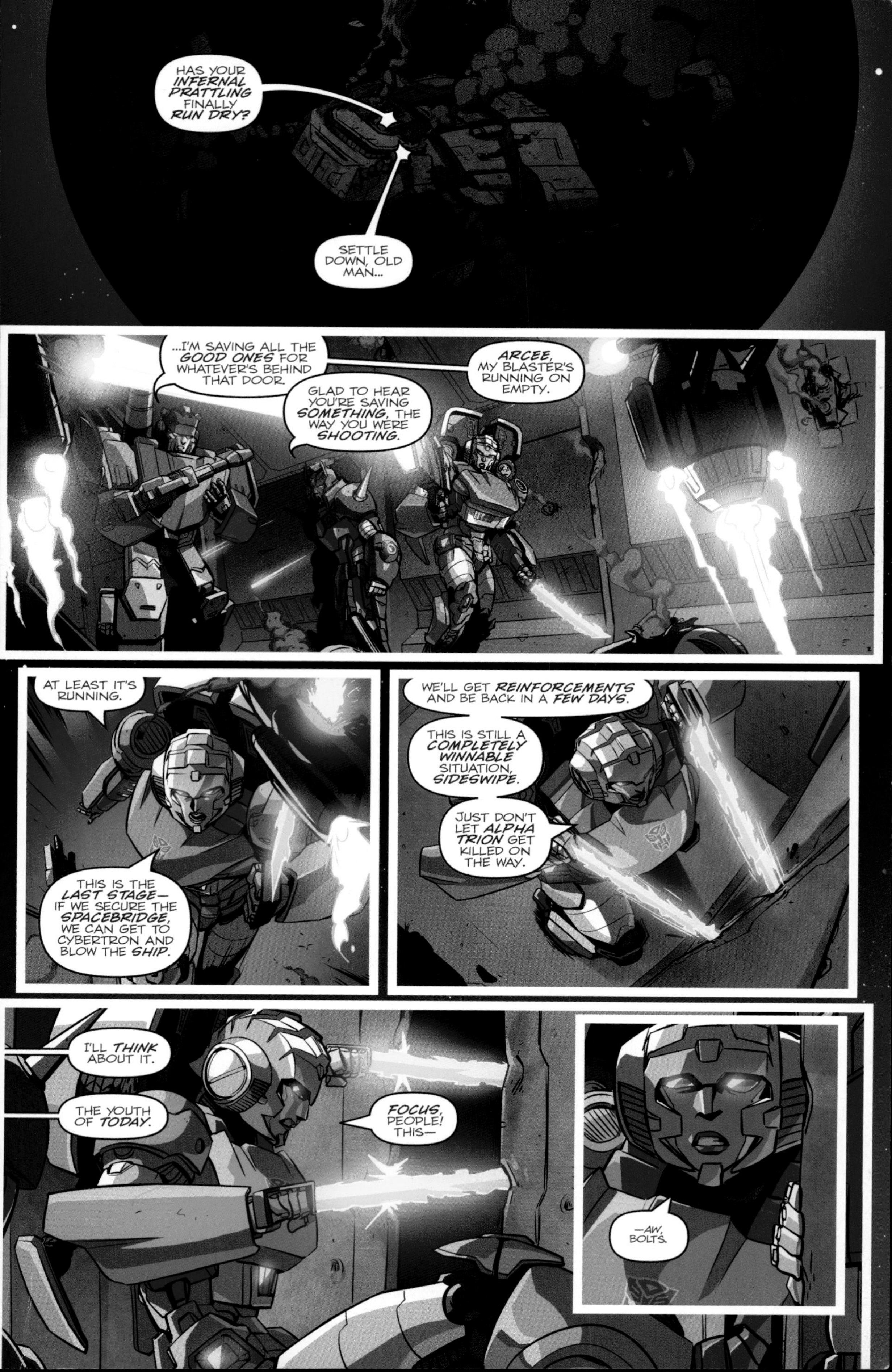
HAS YOUR INFERNAL PRATTLING FINALLY RUN DRY?
SETTLE DOWN, OLD MAN...
...I'M SAVING ALL THE GOOD ONES FOR WHATEVER'S BEHIND THAT DOOR.
GLAD TO HEAR YOU'RE SAVING SOMETHING, THE WAY YOU WERE SHOOTING.
ARCEE, MY BLASTER'S RUNNING ON EMPTY.
AT LEAST IT'S RUNNING.
THIS IS THE LAST STAGE— IF WE SECURE THE SPACEBRIDGE, WE CAN GET TO CYBERTRON AND BLOW THE SHIP.
WE'LL GET REINFORCEMENTS AND BE BACK IN A FEW DAYS.
THIS IS STILL A COMPLETELY WINNABLE SITUATION, SIDESWIPE.
JUST DON'T LET ALPHA TRION GET KILLED ON THE WAY.
I'LL THINK ABOUT IT.
THE YOUTH OF TODAY.
FOCUS, PEOPLE! THIS—
—AW, BOLTS.

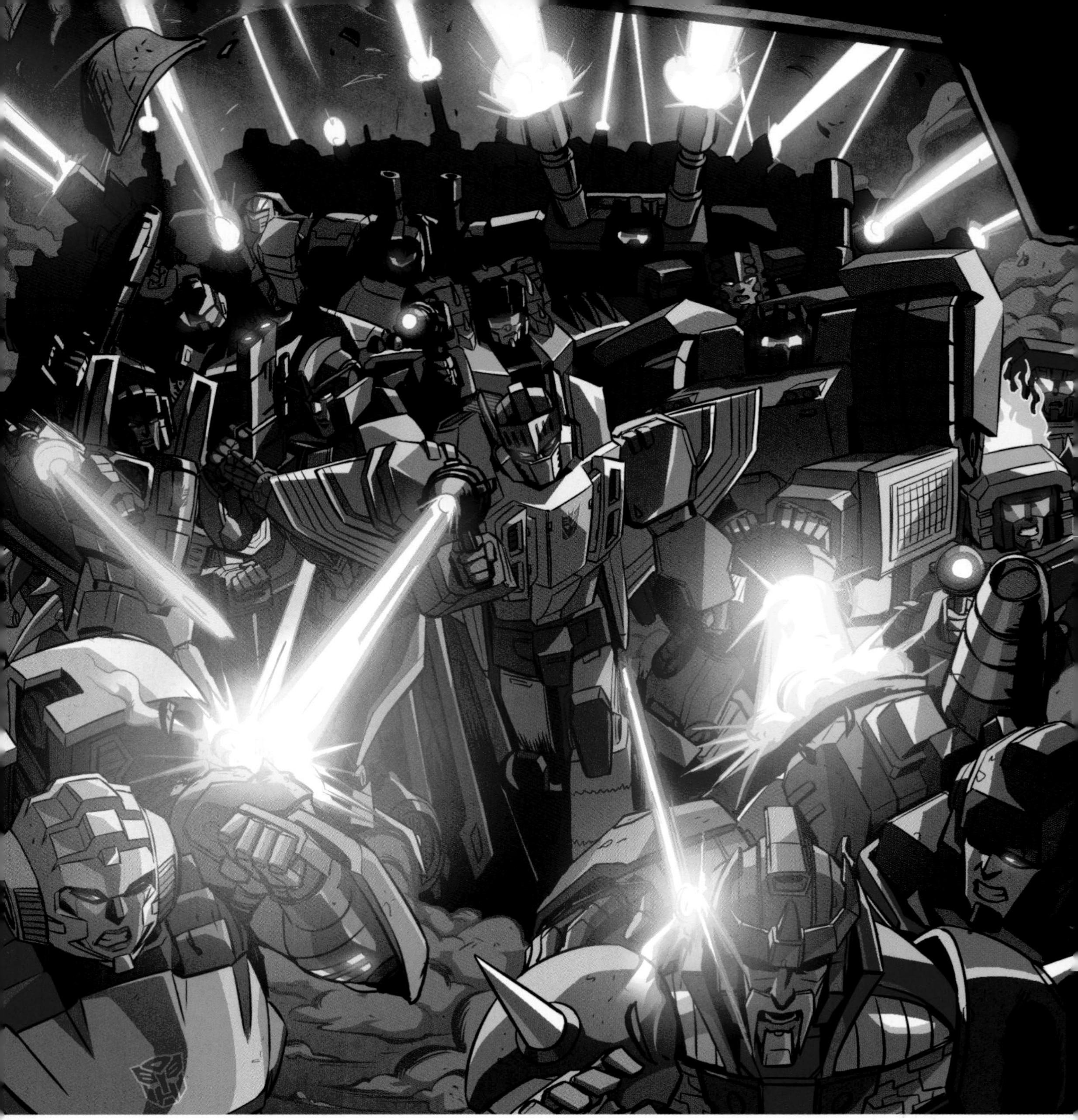

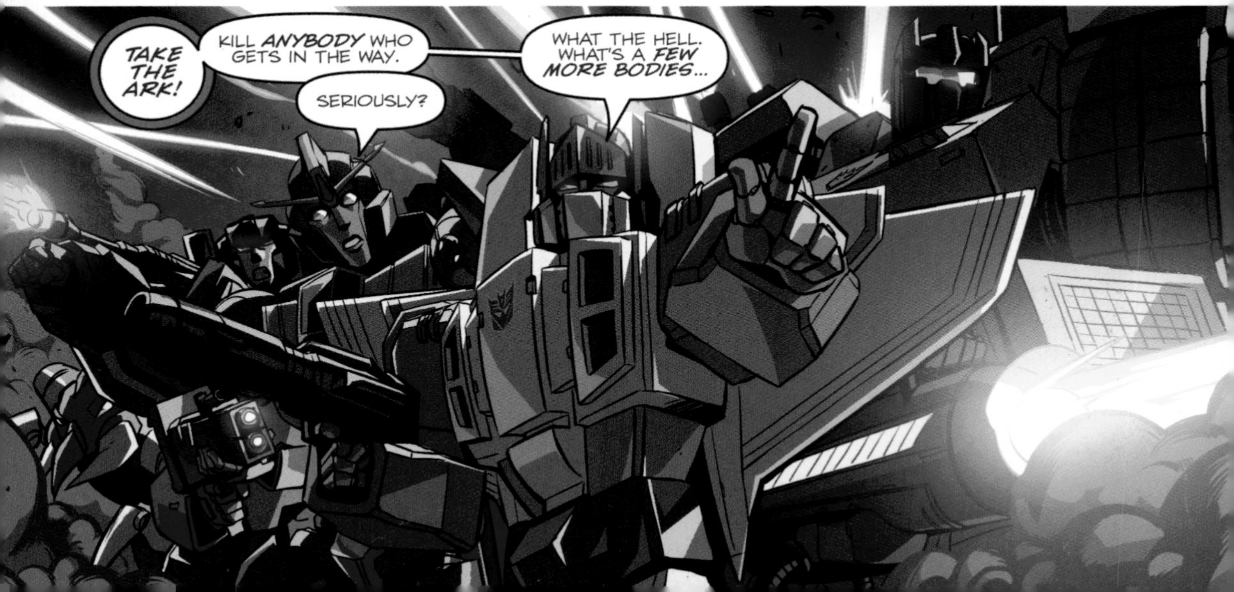
TAKE THE ARK!
KILL ANYBODY WHO GETS IN THE WAY.
SERIOUSLY?
WHAT THE HELL. WHAT'S A FEW MORE BODIES...

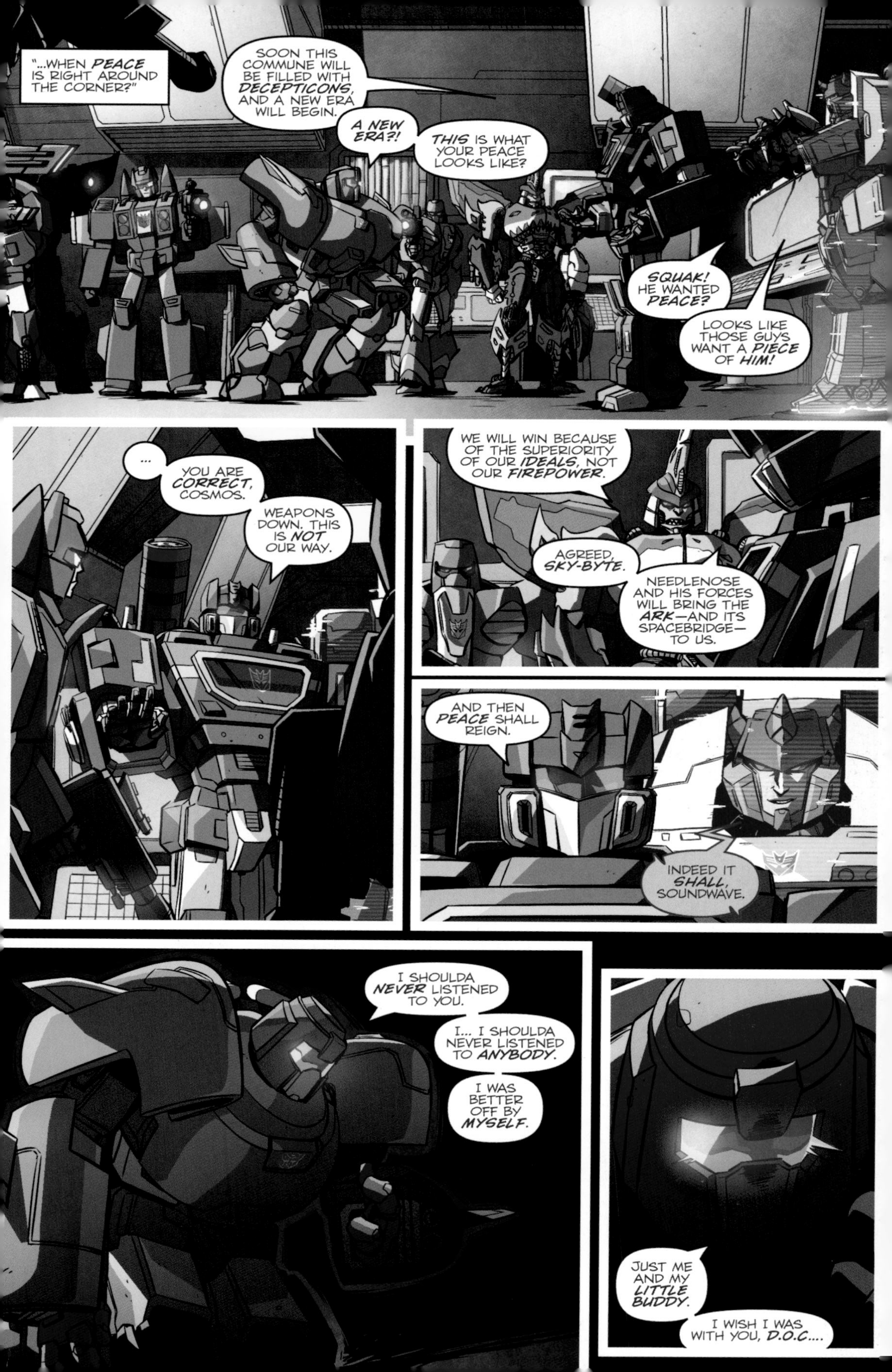

"...WHEN PEACE IS RIGHT AROUND THE CORNER?"
SOON THIS COMMUNE WILL BE FILLED WITH DECEPTICONS, AND A NEW ERA WILL BEGIN.
A NEW ERA?!
THIS IS WHAT YOUR PEACE LOOKS LIKE?
SQUAK! HE WANTED PEACE?
LOOKS LIKE THOSE GUYS WANT A PIECE OF HIM!
...
YOU ARE CORRECT, COSMOS.
WEAPONS DOWN. THIS IS NOT OUR WAY.
WE WILL WIN BECAUSE OF THE SUPERIORITY OF OUR IDEALS, NOT OUR FIREPOWER.
AGREED, SKY-BYTE.
NEEDLENOSE AND HIS FORCES WILL BRING THE ARK—AND ITS SPACEBRIDGE—TO US.
AND THEN PEACE SHALL REIGN.
INDEED IT SHALL, SOUNDWAVE.
I SHOULDA NEVER LISTENED TO YOU.
I... I SHOULDA NEVER LISTENED TO ANYBODY.
I WAS BETTER OFF BY MYSELF.
JUST ME AND MY LITTLE BUDDY.
I WISH I WAS WITH YOU, D.O.C....

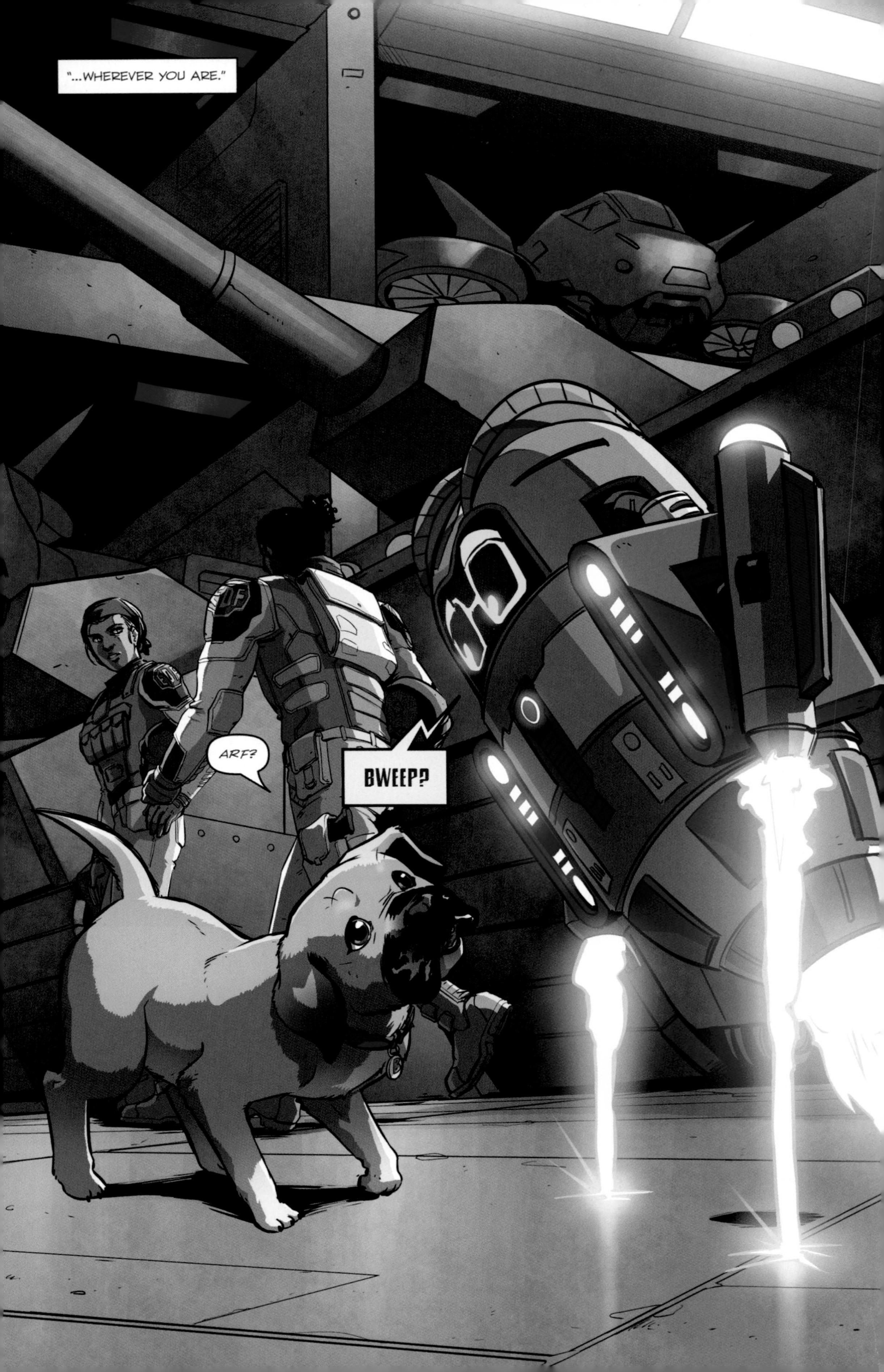
"...WHEREVER YOU ARE."
ARF?
BWEEP?

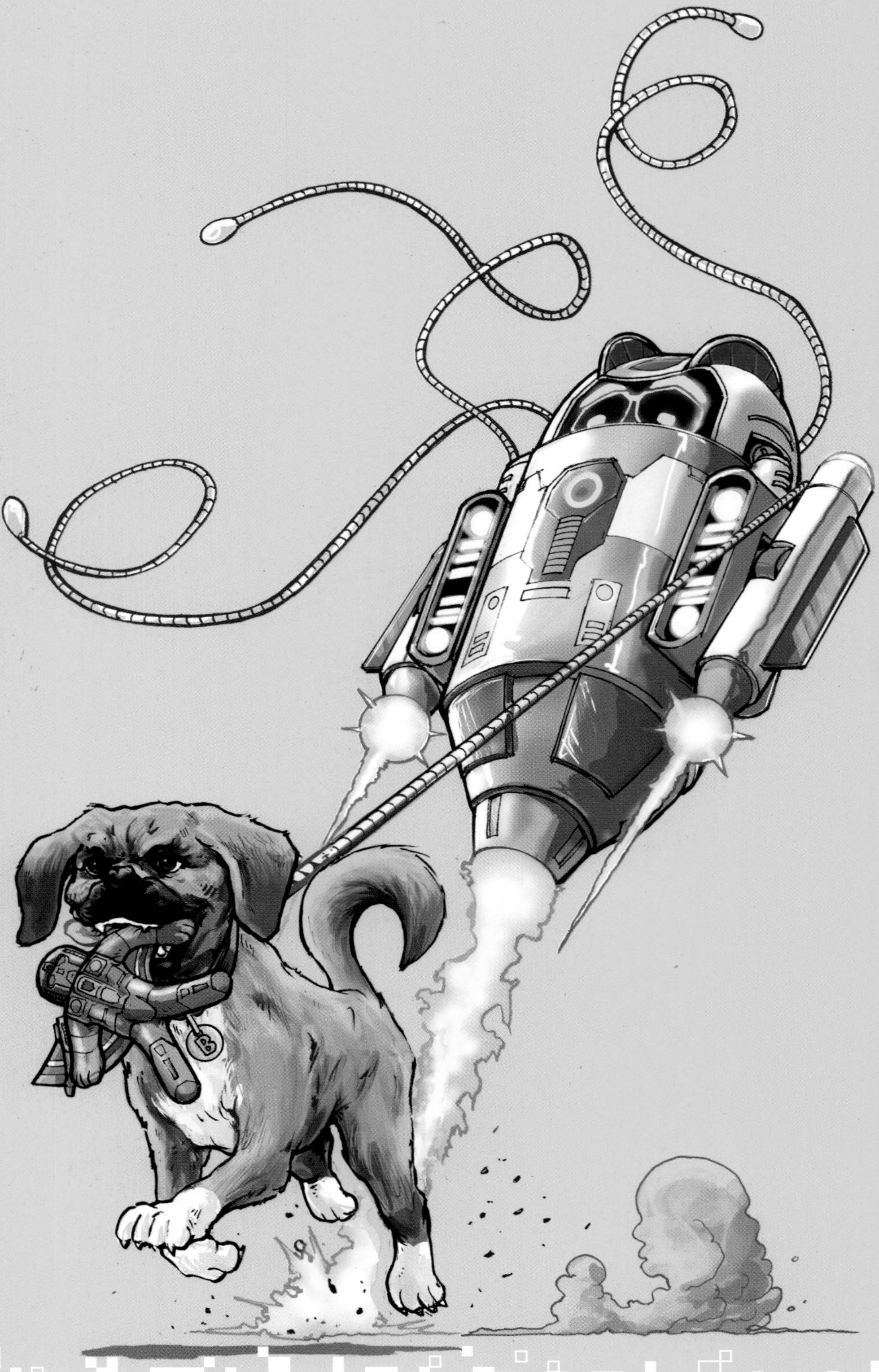

TRANSFORMERS #48 COVER A

by **ANDREW GRIFFITH**

CONQUERORS
Part 3 "HELDEN"

BREEP.

WOOF!

MISSION: RESCUE *MASTER JETFIRE AND AUTOBOT ALLIES.*

OBJECT: EARTH CREATURE. NON-CYBERTRONIAN. NON-HUMAN.

SYNTAX: INDECIPHERABLE.

USEFULNESS TOWARDS MISSION: NONE.

BUSTER! THERE YOU ARE.

WHY ARE YOU HANGING OUT WITH A *DRONE?* THOSE THINGS AREN'T VERY *BRIGHT.*

IT MIGHT TRY TO... I DON'T KNOW. UPDATE YOUR *SOFTWARE* OR SOMETHING.

FLEEP

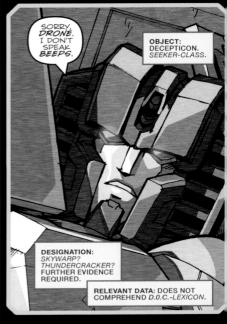

SORRY, *DRONE.* I DON'T SPEAK *BEEPS.*

OBJECT: DECEPTICON. *SEEKER-CLASS.*

DESIGNATION: *SKYWARP? THUNDERCRACKER?* FURTHER EVIDENCE REQUIRED.

RELEVANT DATA: DOES NOT COMPREHEND *D.O.C.-LEXICON.*

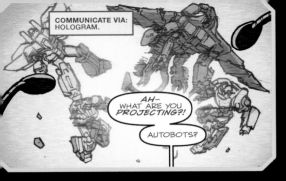

COMMUNICATE VIA: HOLOGRAM.

AH— WHAT ARE YOU *PROJECTING?!*

AUTOBOTS?

REPLAY MEMORY: VISUAL ONLY.

WHAT ARE *THOSE* THINGS?

REPLAY DATA: RECEIVED BROADCAST.

THAT'S AN *ARK!*

REPLAY DATA: BROADCAST *SOURCE.*

SOUNDWAVE— AND AN AUTOBOT... THAT'S THE *JUPITER COMMUNE.*

HOW ARE YOU *GETTING* THIS?

RESULT: COMPREHENSION?

LITTLE DRONE... YOU'VE SEEN SOME REALLY *SERIOUS* STUFF.

RESULT: *LIMITED* COMPREHENSION.

THUNDERCRACKER—

—WHAT'S GOING *ON?!*

THIS ROBOT SHOWED ME *CRAZY BUSINESS!*

THERE'S NOTHING *BUT* CRAZINESS WITH YOU, T.C.

OBJECT: HUMAN AUTHORITY FIGURE.

STATEMENT: JOKE? INSULT?

ACTION: COMPLETE MISSION.

I'M SURE THAT DRONE HAS A *JOB* TO *DO,* AND YOU'RE WASTING ITS TIME.

BUT—DID YOU SEE THE *HOLOGRAM?*

WHAT ARE YOU *TALKING* ABOUT?

WHO KNOWS WHAT SOUNDWAVE PROGRAMMED THOSE THINGS WITH.

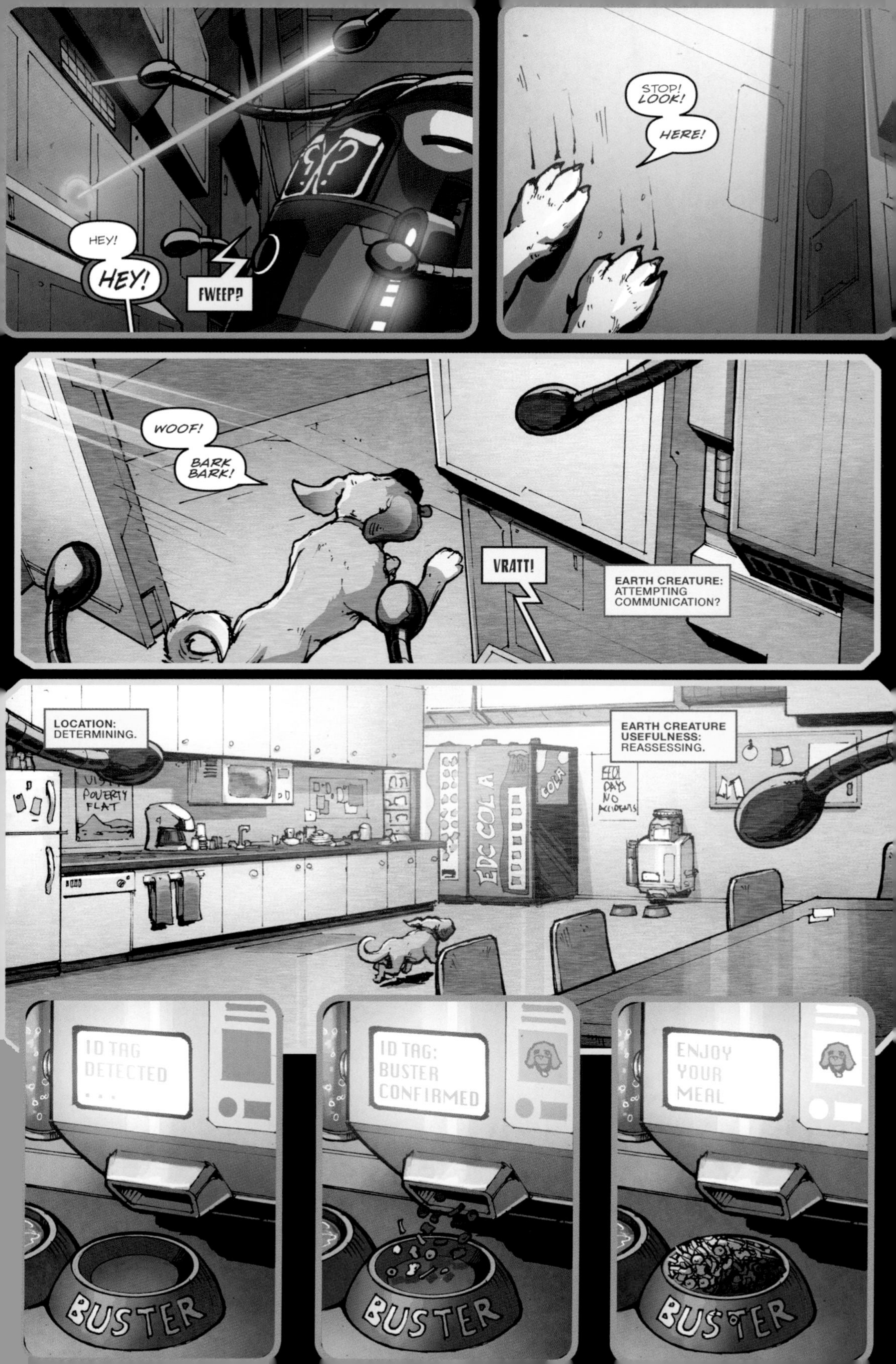
HEY!
HEY!
FWEEP?
STOP!
LOOK!
HERE!
WOOF!
BARK BARK!
VRATT!
EARTH CREATURE: ATTEMPTING COMMUNICATION?
LOCATION: DETERMINING.
POVERTY FLAT
EDC COLA
COLA
DAYS NO ACCIDENTS
EARTH CREATURE USEFULNESS: REASSESSING.
ID TAG DETECTED
...
BUSTER
ID TAG: BUSTER CONFIRMED
BUSTER
ENJOY YOUR MEAL
BUSTER

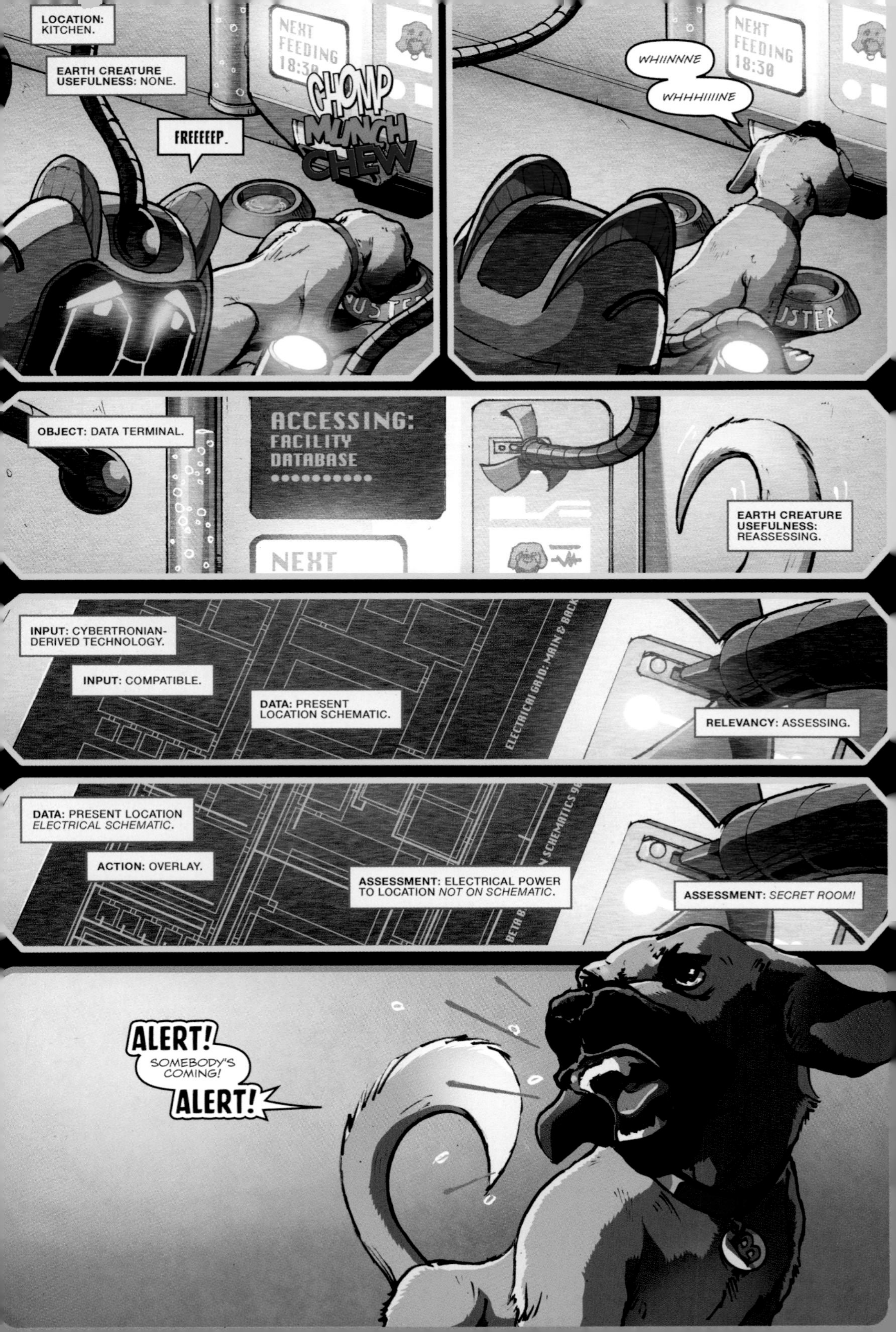
LOCATION: KITCHEN.
EARTH CREATURE USEFULNESS: NONE.
NEXT FEEDING 18:30
CHOMP
MUNCH
CHEW
FREEEEEP.
WHIINNNE
WHHHIIIINE
NEXT FEEDING 18:30
OBJECT: DATA TERMINAL.
ACCESSING: FACILITY DATABASE
NEXT
EARTH CREATURE USEFULNESS: REASSESSING.
INPUT: CYBERTRONIAN-DERIVED TECHNOLOGY.
INPUT: COMPATIBLE.
DATA: PRESENT LOCATION SCHEMATIC.
ELECTRICAL GRID: MAIN & BACK
RELEVANCY: ASSESSING.
DATA: PRESENT LOCATION *ELECTRICAL SCHEMATIC*.
ACTION: OVERLAY.
ASSESSMENT: ELECTRICAL POWER TO LOCATION *NOT ON SCHEMATIC*.
ASSESSMENT: *SECRET ROOM!*
ALERT!
SOMEBODY'S COMING!
ALERT!

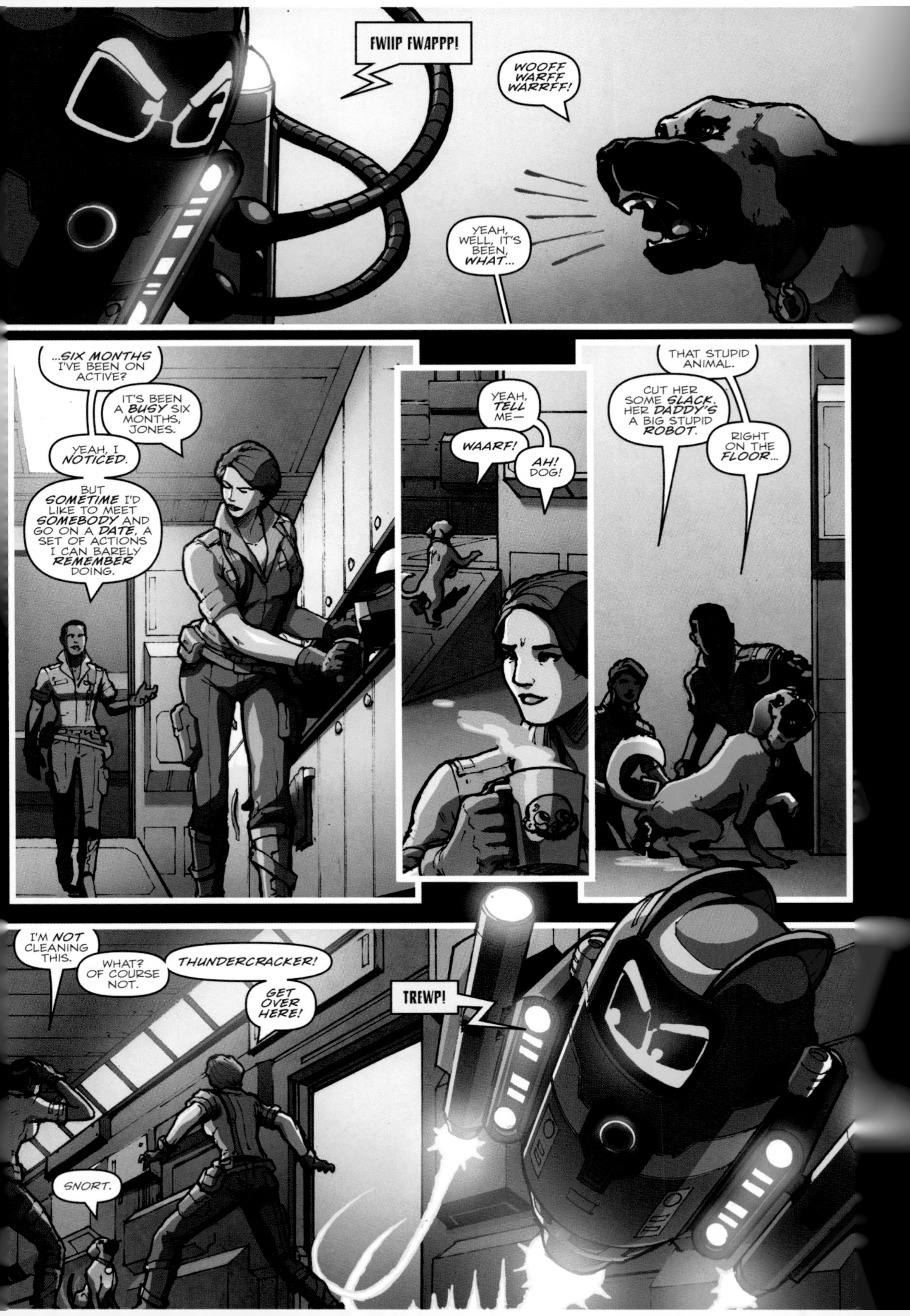

FWIIP FWAPPP!
WOOFF WARFF WARRFF!
YEAH, WELL, IT'S BEEN, WHAT...
...SIX MONTHS I'VE BEEN ON ACTIVE?
IT'S BEEN A BUSY SIX MONTHS, JONES.
YEAH, I NOTICED.
BUT SOMETIME I'D LIKE TO MEET SOMEBODY AND GO ON A DATE, A SET OF ACTIONS I CAN BARELY REMEMBER DOING.
YEAH, TELL ME—
WAARF!
AH! DOG!
THAT STUPID ANIMAL.
CUT HER SOME SLACK. HER DADDY'S A BIG STUPID ROBOT.
RIGHT ON THE FLOOR...
I'M NOT CLEANING THIS.
WHAT? OF COURSE NOT.
THUNDERCRACKER!
GET OVER HERE!
TREWP!
SNORT.

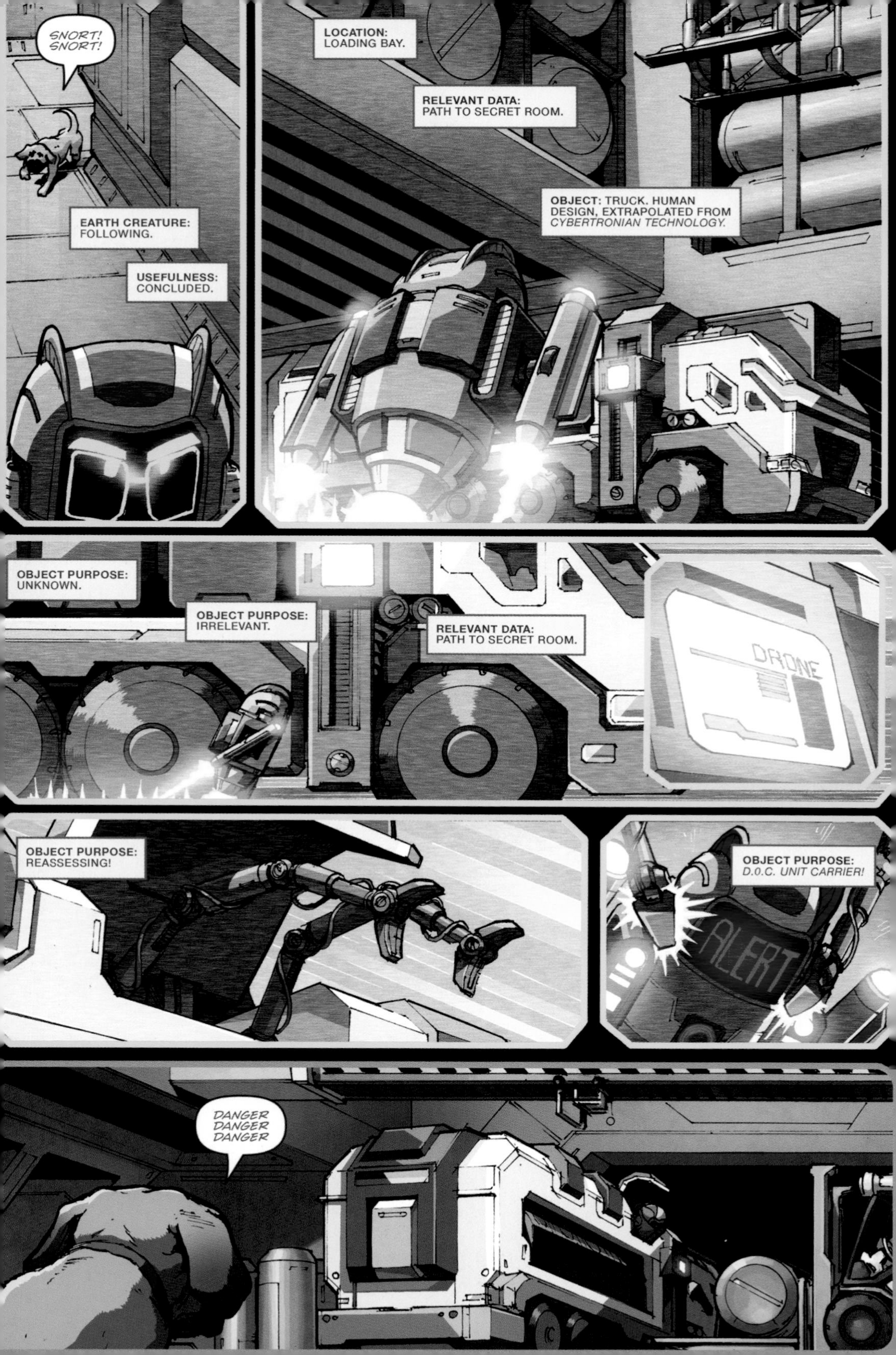
SNORT! SNORT!
EARTH CREATURE: FOLLOWING.
USEFULNESS: CONCLUDED.
LOCATION: LOADING BAY.
RELEVANT DATA: PATH TO SECRET ROOM.
OBJECT: TRUCK. HUMAN DESIGN, EXTRAPOLATED FROM CYBERTRONIAN TECHNOLOGY.
OBJECT PURPOSE: UNKNOWN.
OBJECT PURPOSE: IRRELEVANT.
RELEVANT DATA: PATH TO SECRET ROOM.
DRONE
OBJECT PURPOSE: REASSESSING!
OBJECT PURPOSE: D.0.C. UNIT CARRIER!
ALERT
DANGER DANGER DANGER

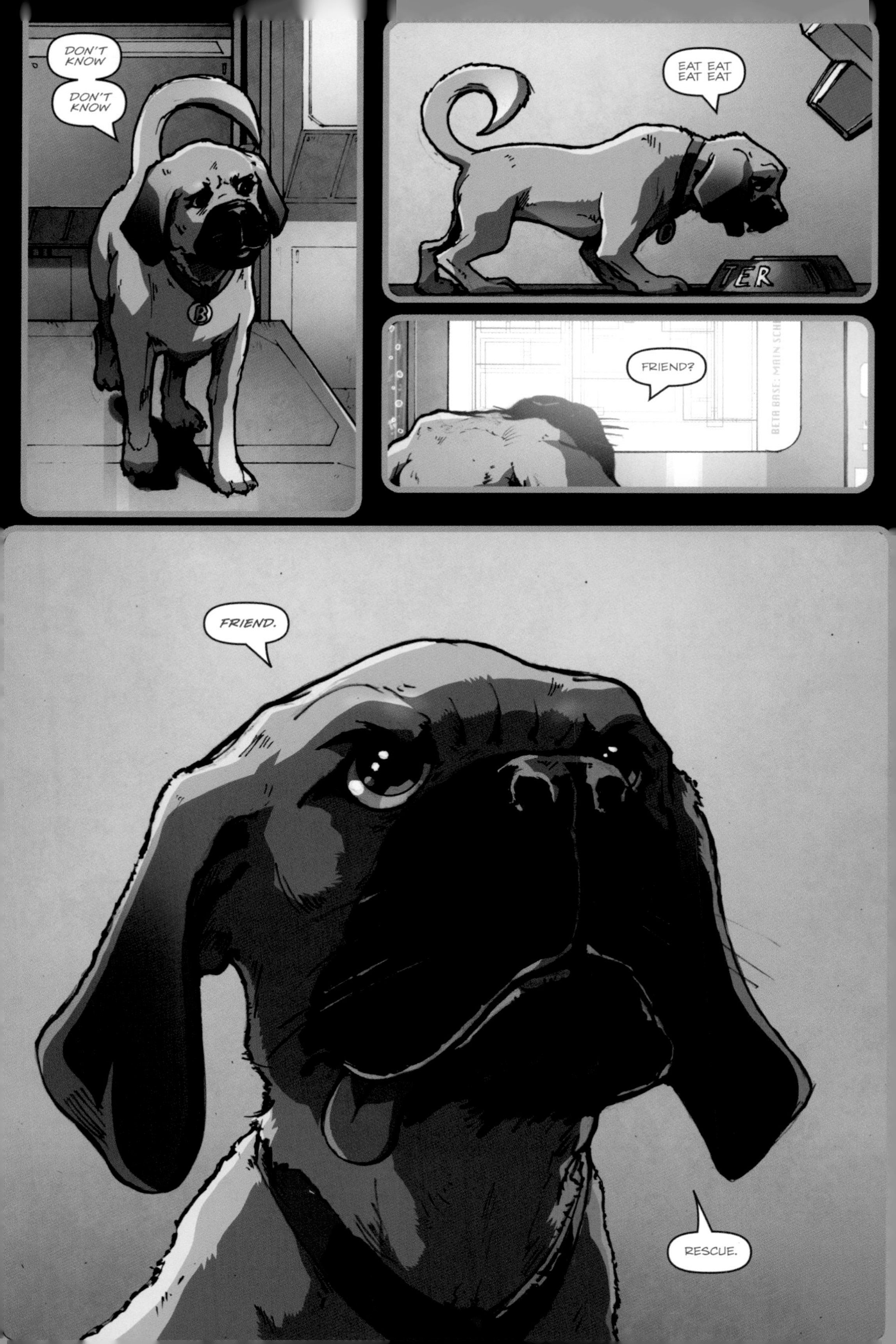
DON'T KNOW
DON'T KNOW
EAT EAT EAT EAT
TER
FRIEND?
BETA BASE: MAIN SCH
FRIEND.
RESCUE.

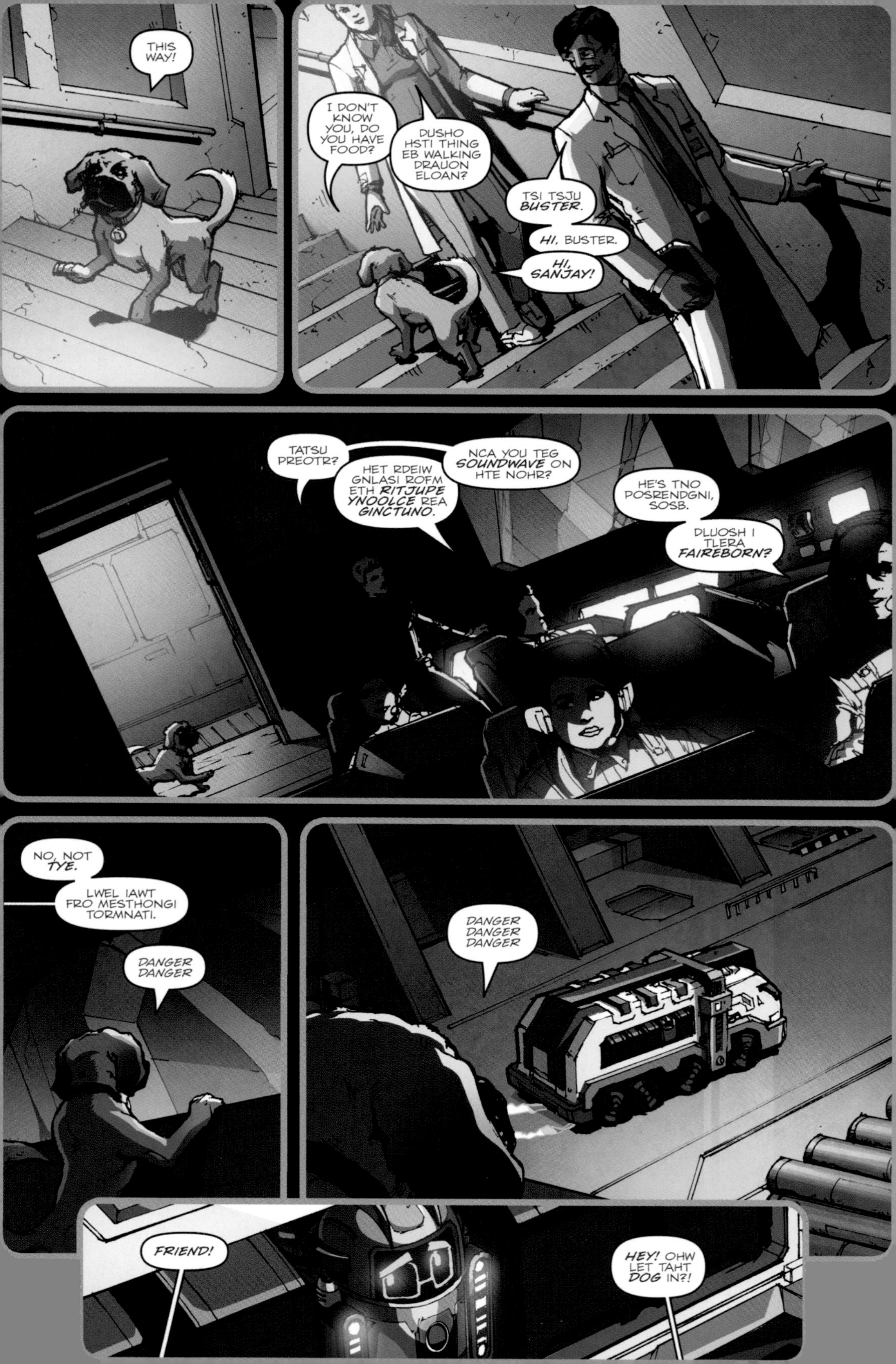
THIS WAY!
I DON'T KNOW YOU, DO YOU HAVE FOOD?
DUSHO HSTI THING EB WALKING DRAUON ELOAN?
TSI TSJU *BUSTER*.
HI, BUSTER.
HI, SANJAY!
TATSU PREOTR?
NCA YOU TEG *SOUNDWAVE* ON HTE NOHR?
HET RDEIW GNLASI ROFM ETH *RITJUPE YNOOLCE* REA *GINCTUNO*.
HE'S TNO POSRENDGNI, SOSB.
DLUOSH I TLERA *FAIREBORN?*
NO, NOT *TYE*.
LWEL IAWT FRO MESTHONGI TORMNATI.
DANGER DANGER
DANGER DANGER DANGER
FRIEND!
HEY! OHW LET TAHT *DOG* IN?!

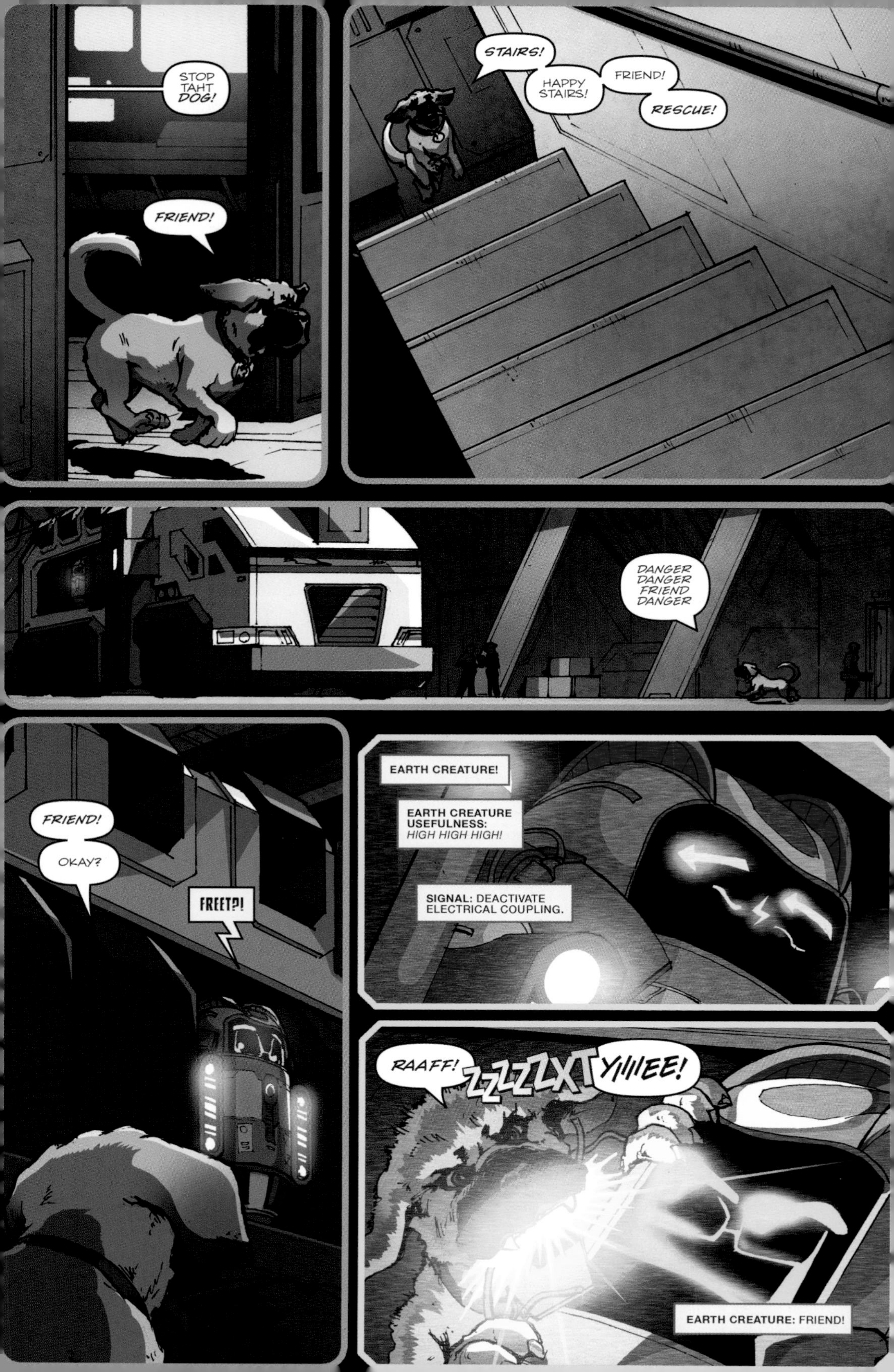
STOP TAHT DOG!
FRIEND!
STAIRS!
HAPPY STAIRS!
FRIEND!
RESCUE!
DANGER DANGER FRIEND DANGER
FRIEND!
OKAY?
FREET?!
EARTH CREATURE!
EARTH CREATURE USEFULNESS: HIGH HIGH HIGH!
SIGNAL: DEACTIVATE ELECTRICAL COUPLING.
RAAFF!
ZZZZZXT
YIIIIEE!
EARTH CREATURE: FRIEND!

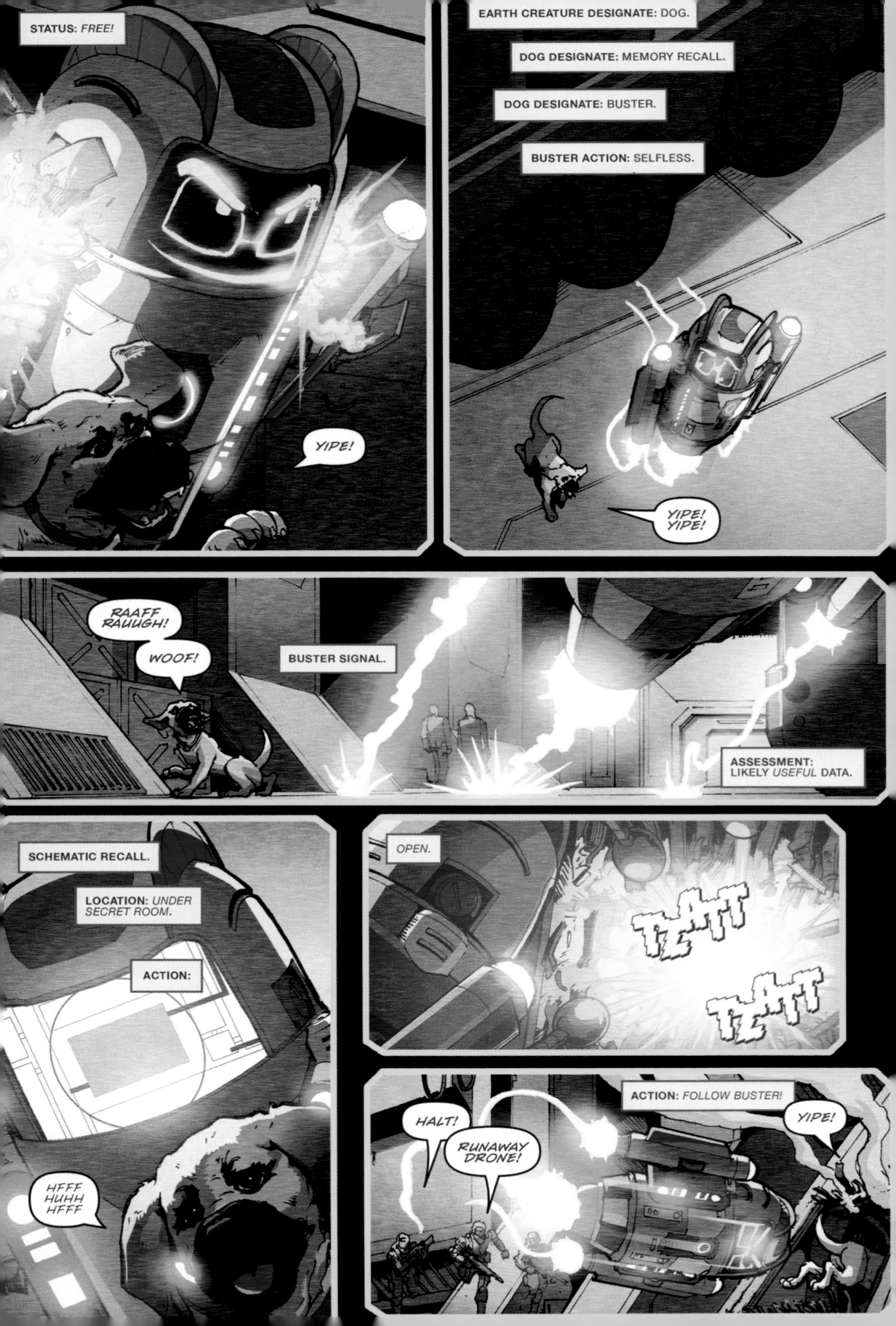
STATUS: FREE!
YIPE!
EARTH CREATURE DESIGNATE: DOG.
DOG DESIGNATE: MEMORY RECALL.
DOG DESIGNATE: BUSTER.
BUSTER ACTION: SELFLESS.
YIPE! YIPE!
RAAFF RAUUGH!
WOOF!
BUSTER SIGNAL.
ASSESSMENT: LIKELY USEFUL DATA.
SCHEMATIC RECALL.
LOCATION: UNDER SECRET ROOM.
ACTION:
HFFF HUHH HFFF
OPEN.
TZATT
TZATT
ACTION: FOLLOW BUSTER!
HALT!
RUNAWAY DRONE!
YIPE!

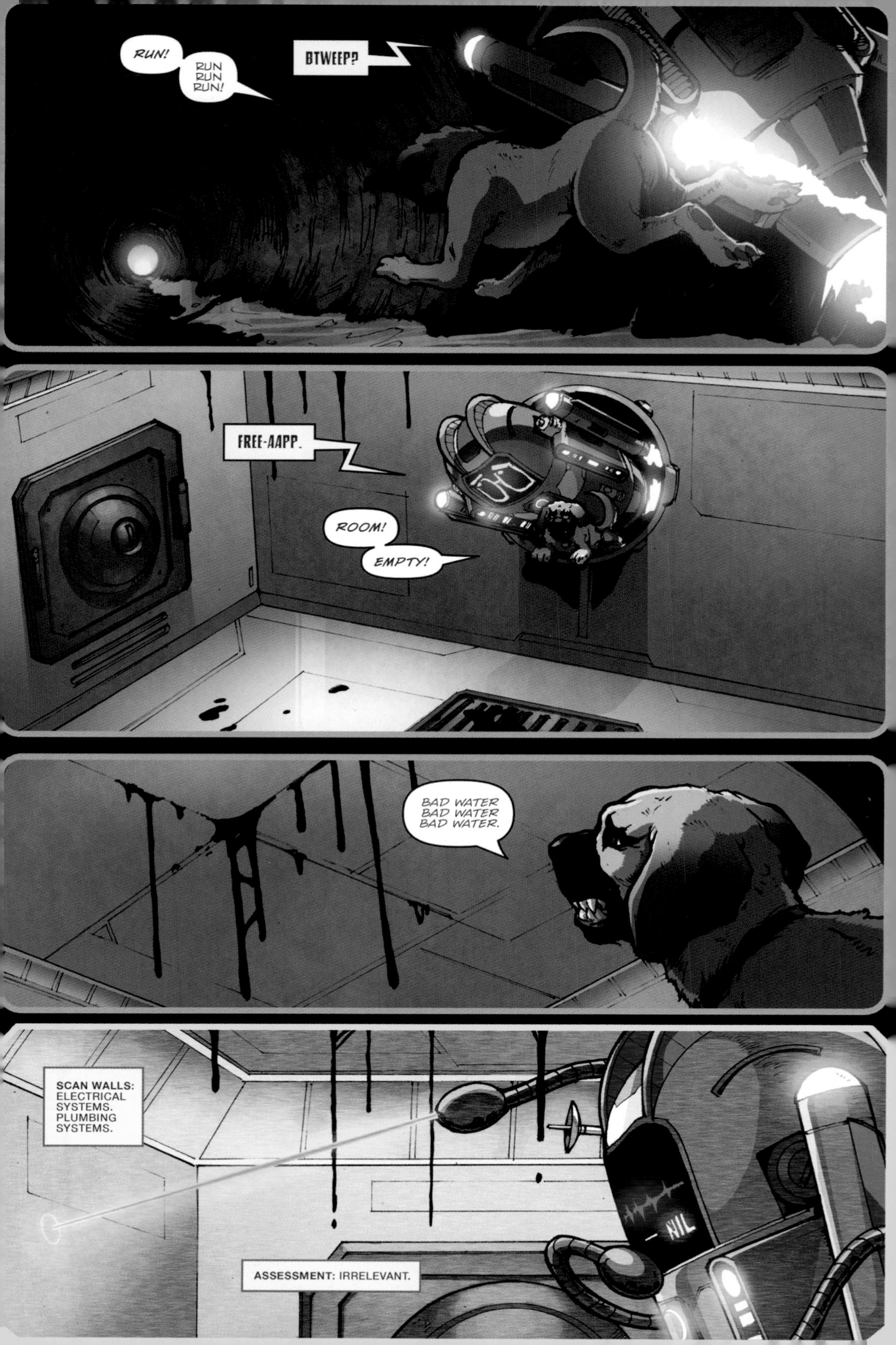
RUN!
RUN RUN RUN!
BTWEEP?
FREE-AAPP.
ROOM!
EMPTY!
BAD WATER BAD WATER BAD WATER.
SCAN WALLS: ELECTRICAL SYSTEMS. PLUMBING SYSTEMS.
NIL
ASSESSMENT: IRRELEVANT.

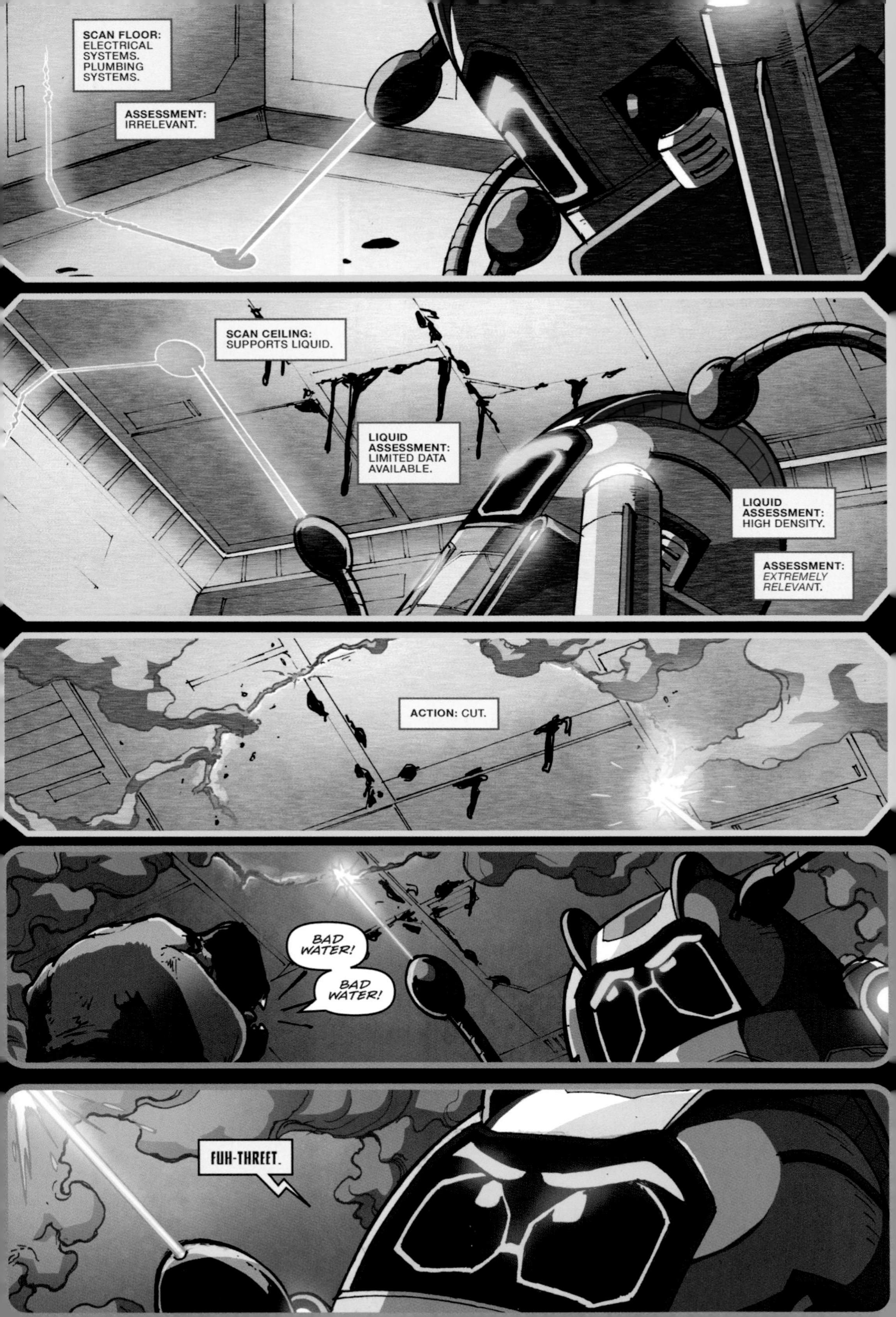
SCAN FLOOR: ELECTRICAL SYSTEMS. PLUMBING SYSTEMS.
ASSESSMENT: IRRELEVANT.
SCAN CEILING: SUPPORTS LIQUID.
LIQUID ASSESSMENT: LIMITED DATA AVAILABLE.
LIQUID ASSESSMENT: HIGH DENSITY.
ASSESSMENT: EXTREMELY RELEVANT.
ACTION: CUT.
BAD WATER!
BAD WATER!
FUH-THREET.

KRAKA-CRUKK

BAD BAD BAD!

FWEEP.

KRUH-THROOSH

REALLY BAD!

REALLY REALLY BAD!

BAD WATER!

NEED TO BREATHE!

ASSESSMENT: SECRET ROOM LOCATED.

ASSESSMENT: BUSTER NEEDS *OXYGEN* TO LIVE.

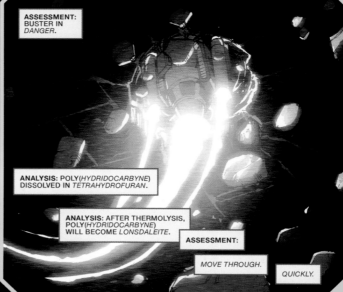

ASSESSMENT: BUSTER IN *DANGER*.

ANALYSIS: POLY(*HYDRIDOCARBYNE*) DISSOLVED IN *TETRAHYDROFURAN*.

ANALYSIS: AFTER THERMOLYSIS, POLY(*HYDRIDOCARBYNE*) WILL BECOME *LONSDALEITE*.

ASSESSMENT:

MOVE THROUGH.

QUICKLY.

AIR
LOCATED: AIR.
LOCATED: ALLIES. FRIENDS.
F-FANCY MEETING YOU HERE.
REMINDS M-ME OF A STORY...
...I'LL T-TELL YOU L-LATER...
DESIGNATE: SKY LYNX. FRIEND.
WOOOF!
HOW IN THE AFTERSPARK—
LAD, YOU'RE IN THE MIDDLE OF A WEIRD MIRACLE.
ROGER THAT.
D.O.C.! GET US OUT OF HERE!
DESIGNATE: KUP. FRIEND.
DESIGNATE: JETFIRE. COMMANDER.
ORDERS: FOLLOW!
FWAT.
EXIT: GENERATING.
I TAKE BACK EVERYTHING I EVER SAID 'BOUT YOU, D.O.C.!
DESIGNATE: JAZZ. FRIEND.

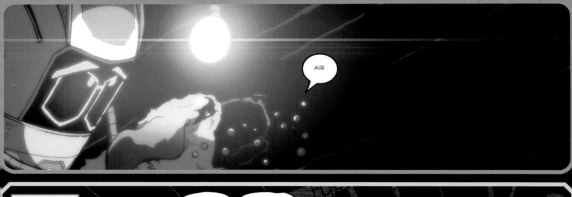

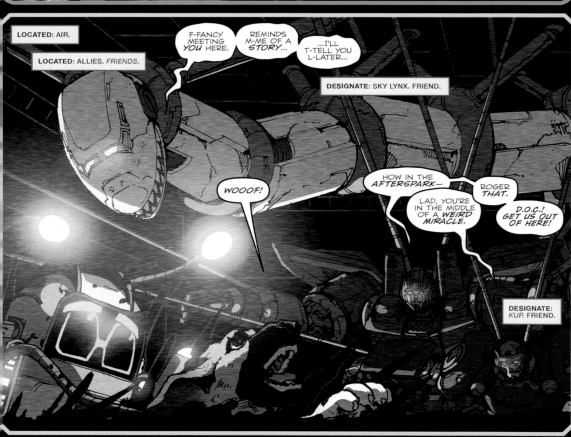

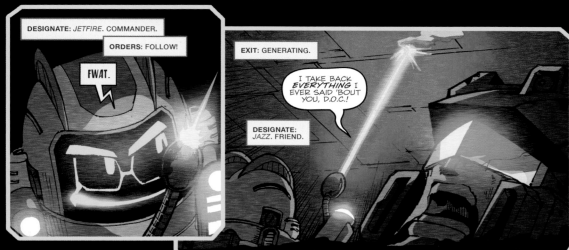

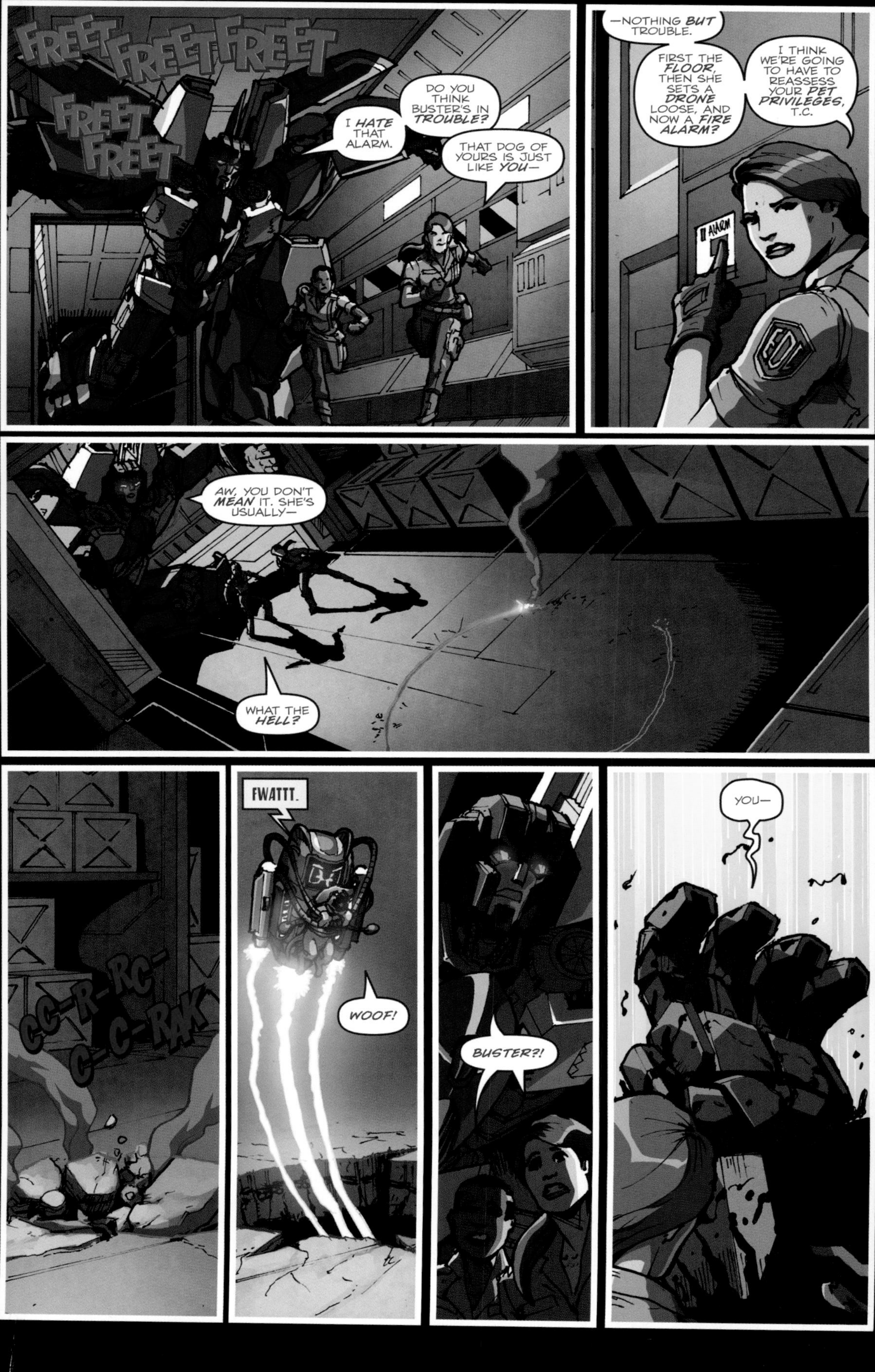
FREETFREETFREET
FREET FREET
I HATE THAT ALARM.
DO YOU THINK BUSTER'S IN TROUBLE?
THAT DOG OF YOURS IS JUST LIKE YOU—
—NOTHING BUT TROUBLE.
FIRST THE FLOOR, THEN SHE SETS A DRONE LOOSE, AND NOW A FIRE ALARM?
I THINK WE'RE GOING TO HAVE TO REASSESS YOUR PET PRIVILEGES, T.C.
ALARM
AW, YOU DON'T MEAN IT. SHE'S USUALLY—
WHAT THE HELL?
CC-R-RC-C-C-RAK
FWATTT.
WOOF!
BUSTER?!
YOU—

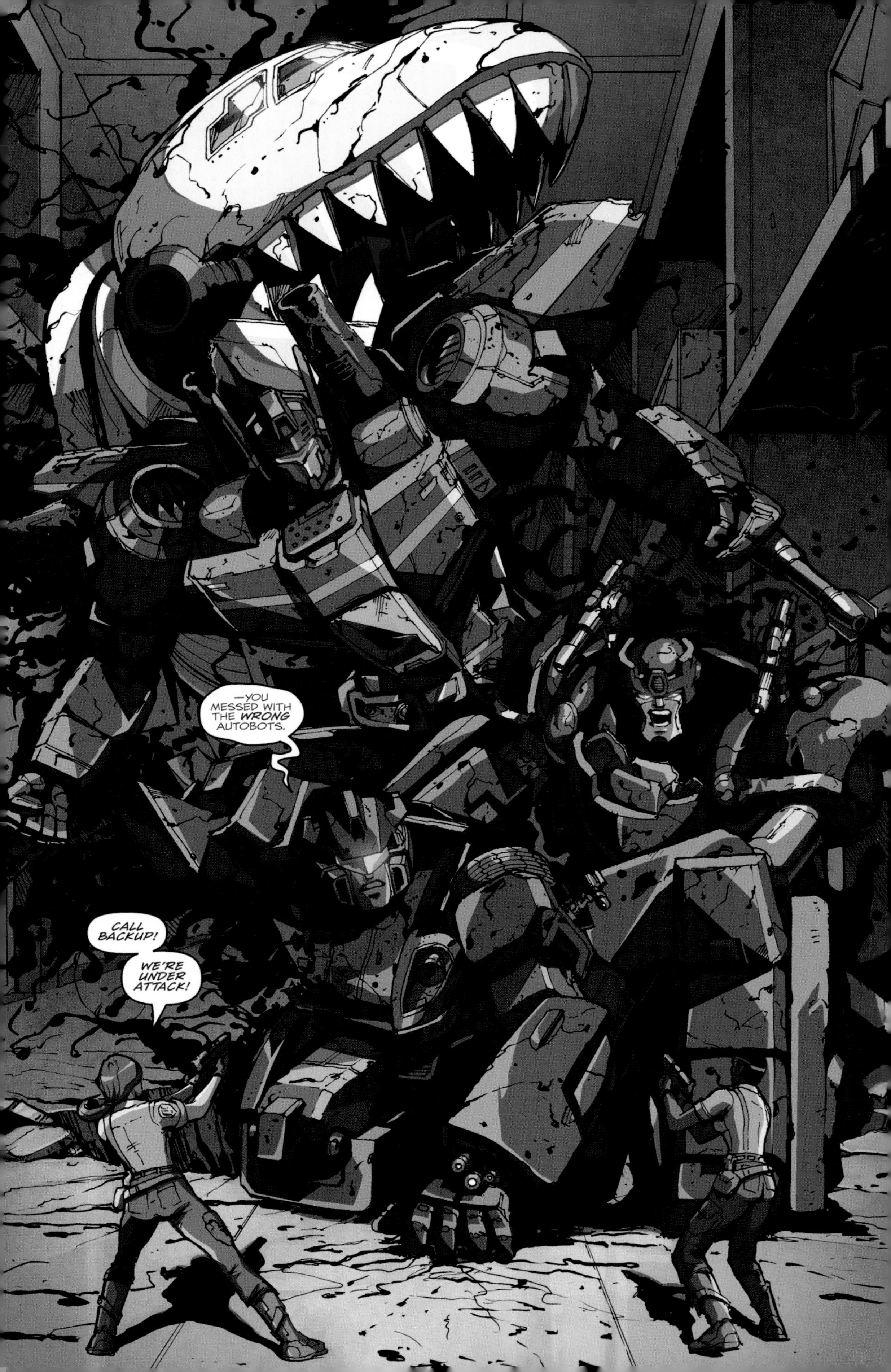
—YOU MESSED WITH THE WRONG AUTOBOTS.
CALL BACKUP!
WE'RE UNDER ATTACK!

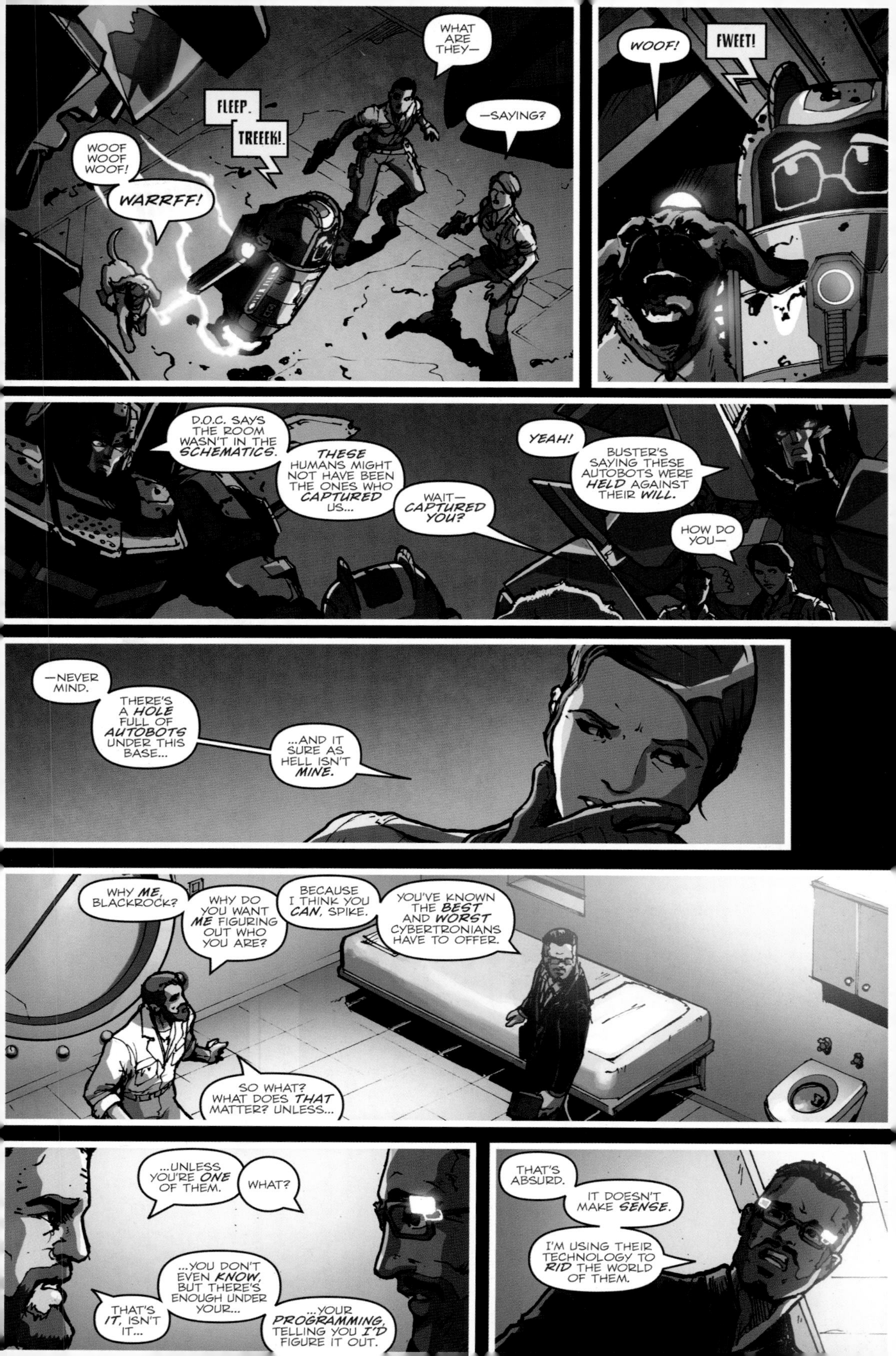
WHAT ARE THEY—
FLEEP.
TREEEK!.
—SAYING?
WOOF WOOF WOOF!
WARRFF!
WOOF!
FWEET!
D.O.C. SAYS THE ROOM WASN'T IN THE SCHEMATICS.
THESE HUMANS MIGHT NOT HAVE BEEN THE ONES WHO CAPTURED US...
WAIT— CAPTURED YOU?
YEAH!
BUSTER'S SAYING THESE AUTOBOTS WERE HELD AGAINST THEIR WILL.
HOW DO YOU—
—NEVER MIND.
THERE'S A HOLE FULL OF AUTOBOTS UNDER THIS BASE...
...AND IT SURE AS HELL ISN'T MINE.
WHY ME, BLACKROCK?
WHY DO YOU WANT ME FIGURING OUT WHO YOU ARE?
BECAUSE I THINK YOU CAN, SPIKE.
YOU'VE KNOWN THE BEST AND WORST CYBERTRONIANS HAVE TO OFFER.
SO WHAT? WHAT DOES THAT MATTER? UNLESS...
...UNLESS YOU'RE ONE OF THEM.
WHAT?
THAT'S IT, ISN'T IT...
...YOU DON'T EVEN KNOW, BUT THERE'S ENOUGH UNDER YOUR...
...YOUR PROGRAMMING, TELLING YOU I'D FIGURE IT OUT.
THAT'S ABSURD.
IT DOESN'T MAKE SENSE.
I'M USING THEIR TECHNOLOGY TO RID THE WORLD OF THEM.

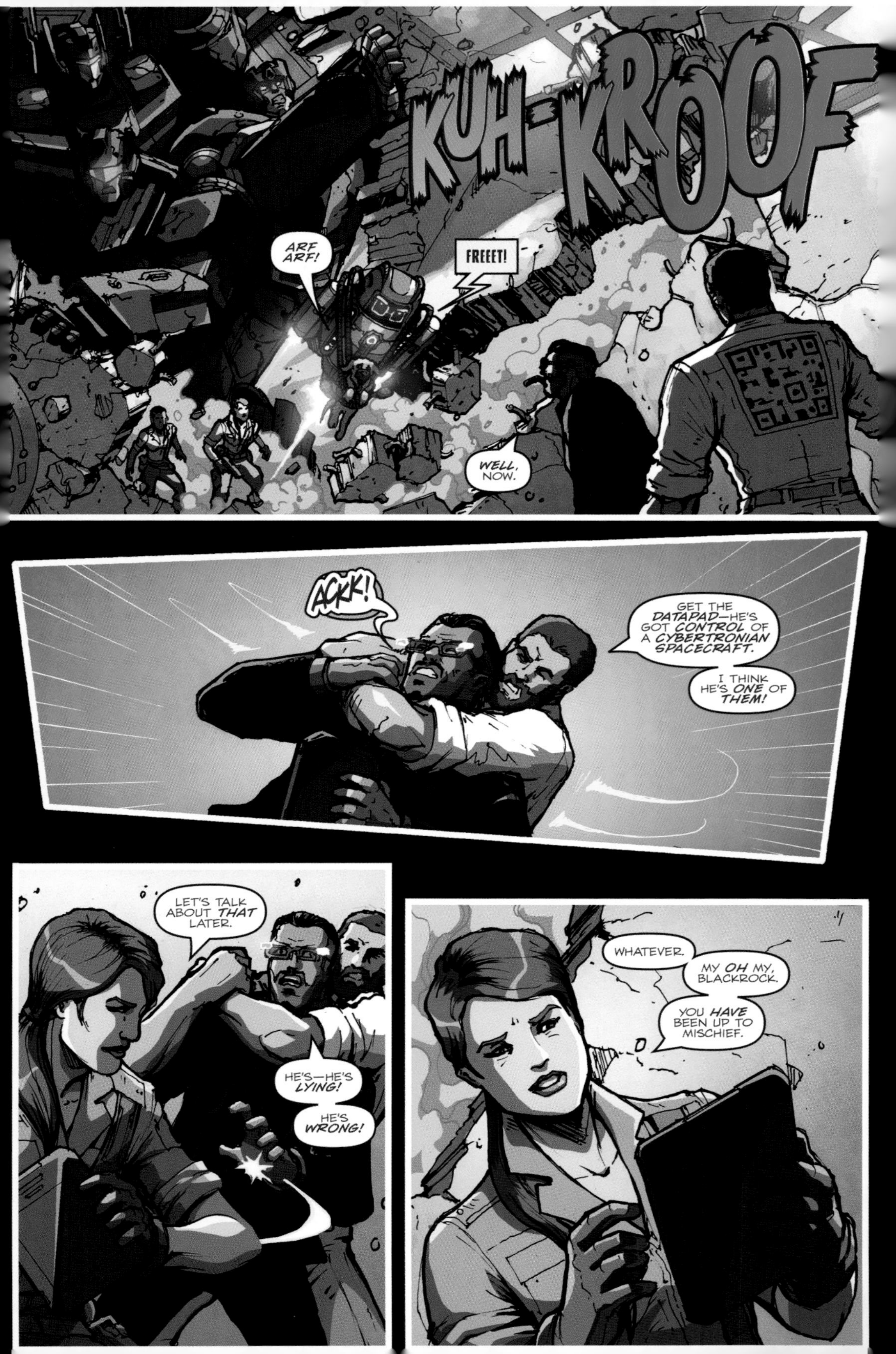
KUH-KROOF
ARF ARF!
FREEET!
WELL, NOW.
ACKK!
GET THE DATAPAD—HE'S GOT CONTROL OF A CYBERTRONIAN SPACECRAFT.
I THINK HE'S ONE OF THEM!
LET'S TALK ABOUT THAT LATER.
HE'S—HE'S LYING!
HE'S WRONG!
WHATEVER.
MY OH MY, BLACKROCK.
YOU HAVE BEEN UP TO MISCHIEF.

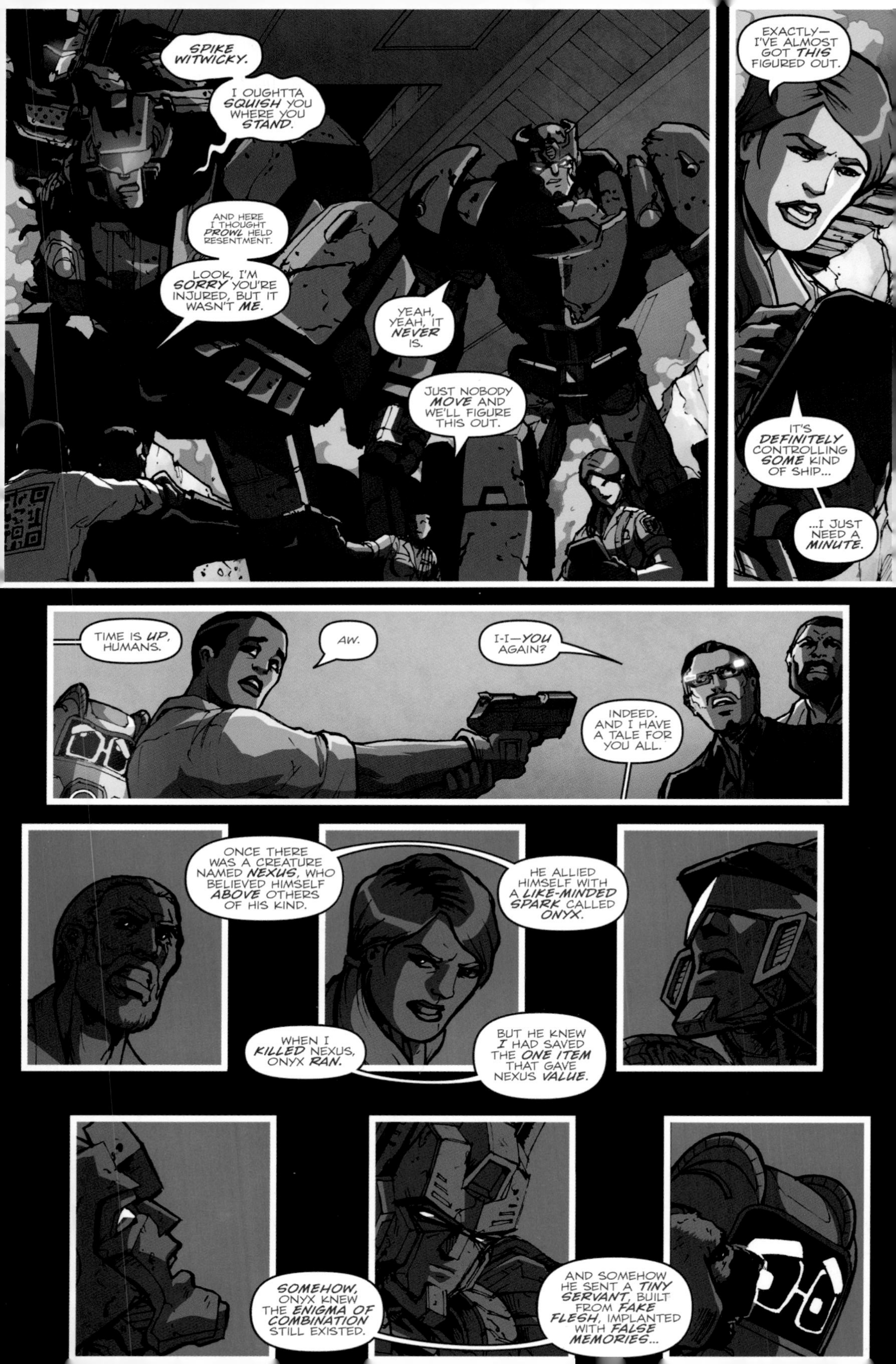
SPIKE WITWICKY.
I OUGHTTA SQUISH YOU WHERE YOU STAND.
AND HERE I THOUGHT PROWL HELD RESENTMENT.
LOOK, I'M SORRY YOU'RE INJURED, BUT IT WASN'T ME.
YEAH, YEAH, IT NEVER IS.
JUST NOBODY MOVE AND WE'LL FIGURE THIS OUT.
EXACTLY— I'VE ALMOST GOT THIS FIGURED OUT.
IT'S DEFINITELY CONTROLLING SOME KIND OF SHIP...
...I JUST NEED A MINUTE.
TIME IS UP, HUMANS.
AW.
I-I—YOU AGAIN?
INDEED. AND I HAVE A TALE FOR YOU ALL.
ONCE THERE WAS A CREATURE NAMED NEXUS, WHO BELIEVED HIMSELF ABOVE OTHERS OF HIS KIND.
HE ALLIED HIMSELF WITH A LIKE-MINDED SPARK CALLED ONYX.
WHEN I KILLED NEXUS, ONYX RAN.
BUT HE KNEW I HAD SAVED THE ONE ITEM THAT GAVE NEXUS VALUE.
SOMEHOW, ONYX KNEW THE ENIGMA OF COMBINATION STILL EXISTED.
AND SOMEHOW HE SENT A TINY SERVANT, BUILT FROM FAKE FLESH, IMPLANTED WITH FALSE MEMORIES...

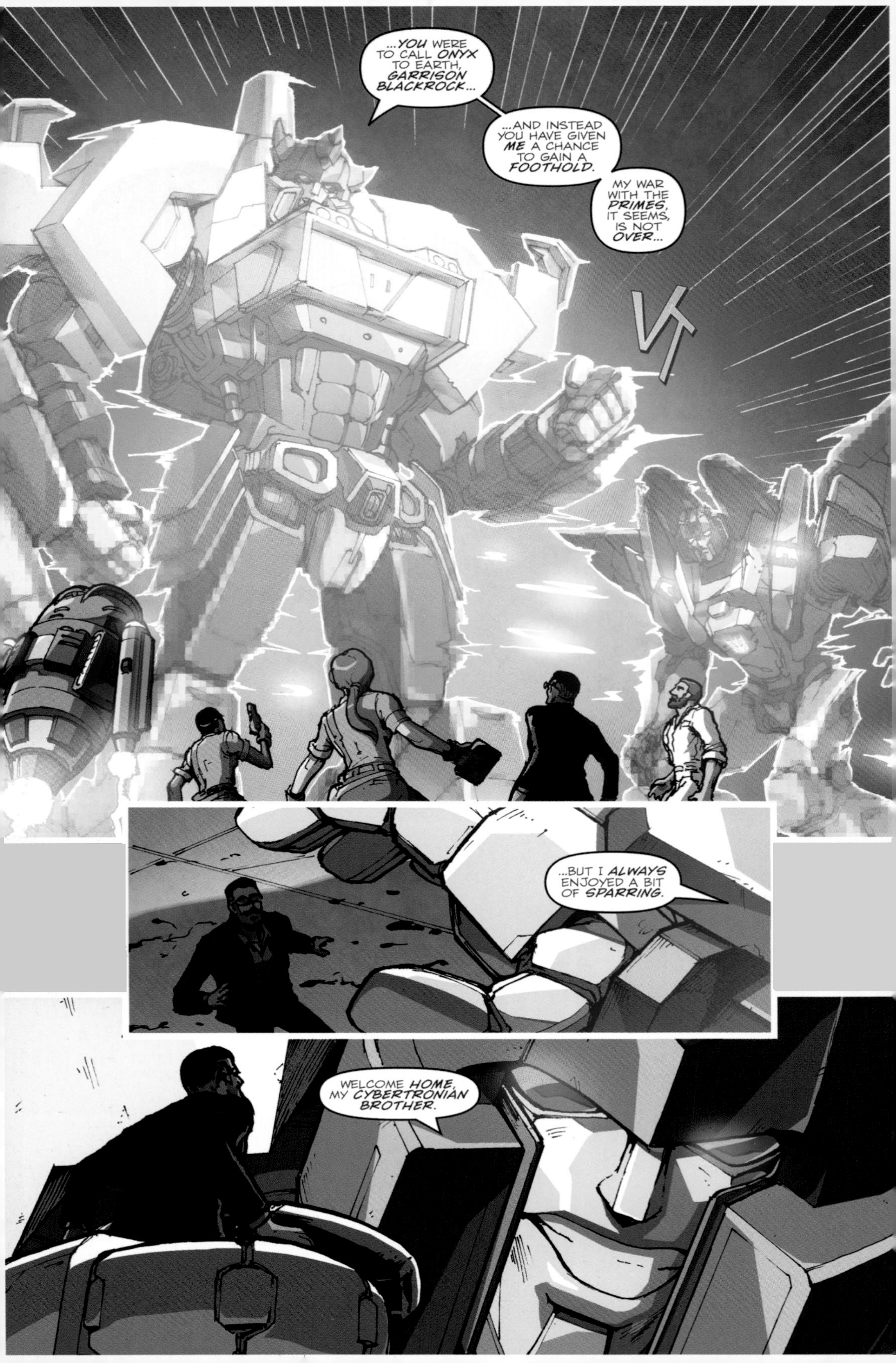
...YOU WERE TO CALL ONYX TO EARTH, GARRISON BLACKROCK...
...AND INSTEAD YOU HAVE GIVEN ME A CHANCE TO GAIN A FOOTHOLD.
MY WAR WITH THE PRIMES, IT SEEMS, IS NOT OVER...
VT
...BUT I ALWAYS ENJOYED A BIT OF SPARRING.
WELCOME HOME, MY CYBERTRONIAN BROTHER.

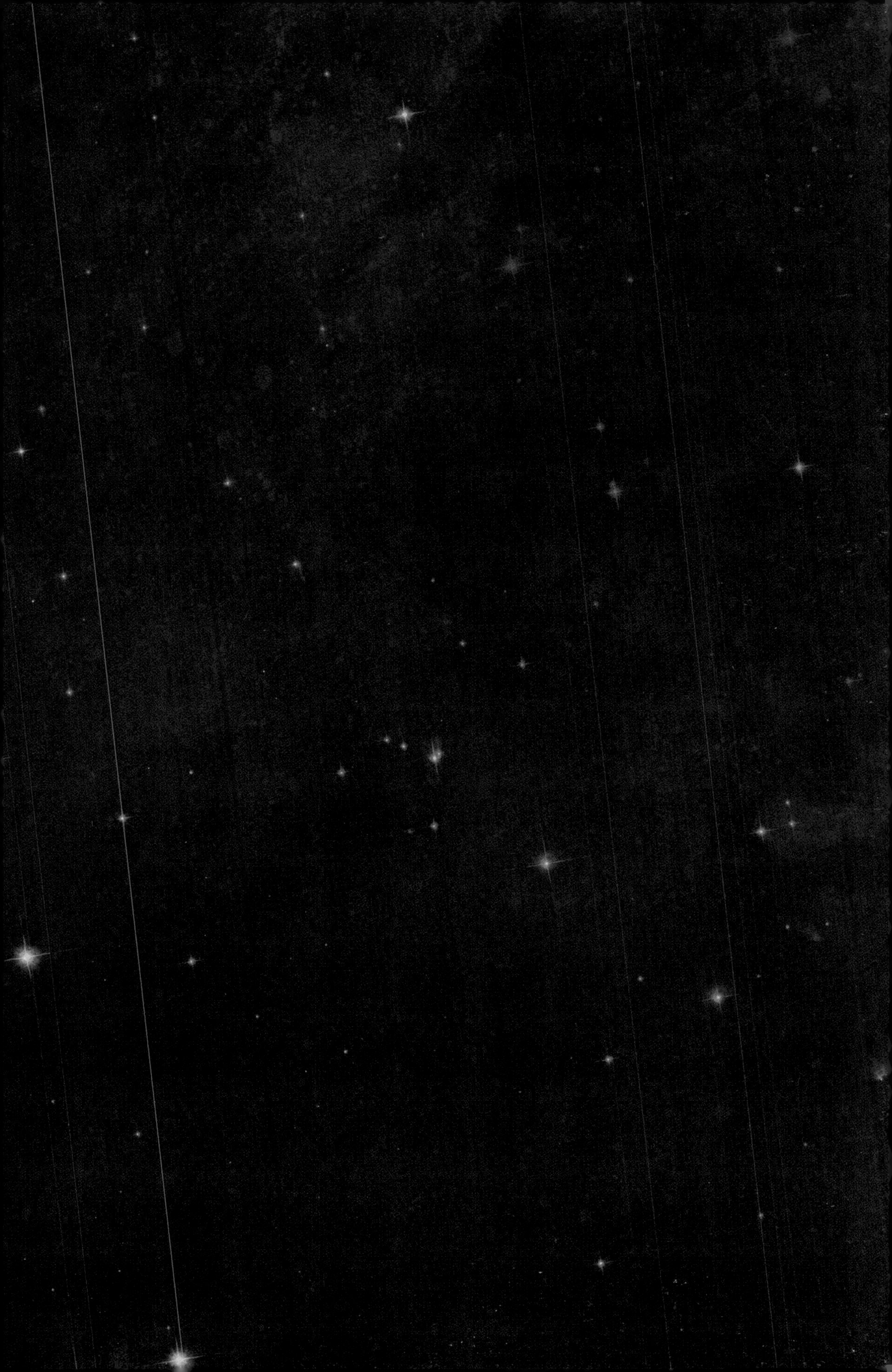

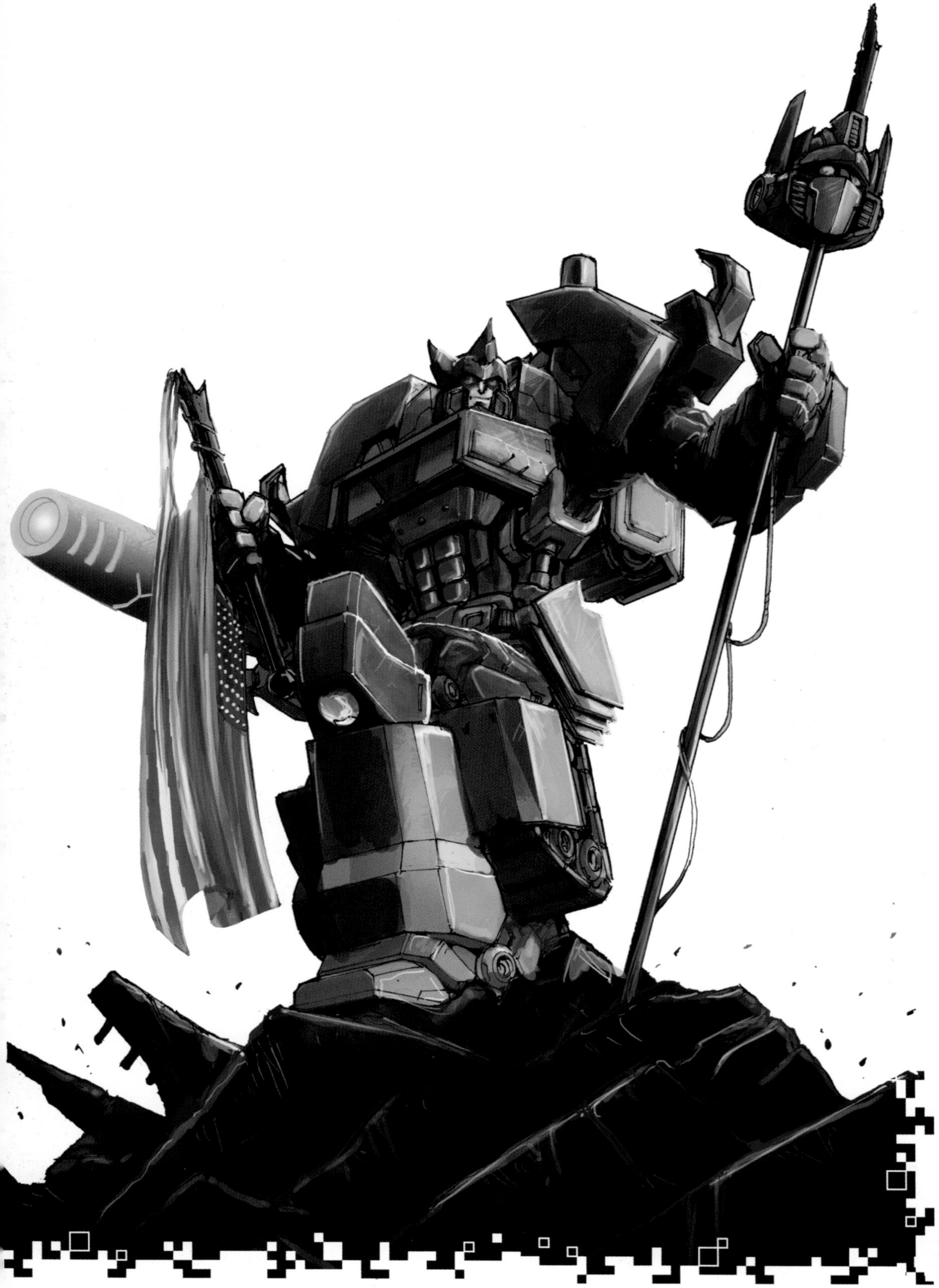

TRANSFORMERS #49 COVER A

by **ANDREW GRIFFITH** After **KLAUS SCHERWINSKI**

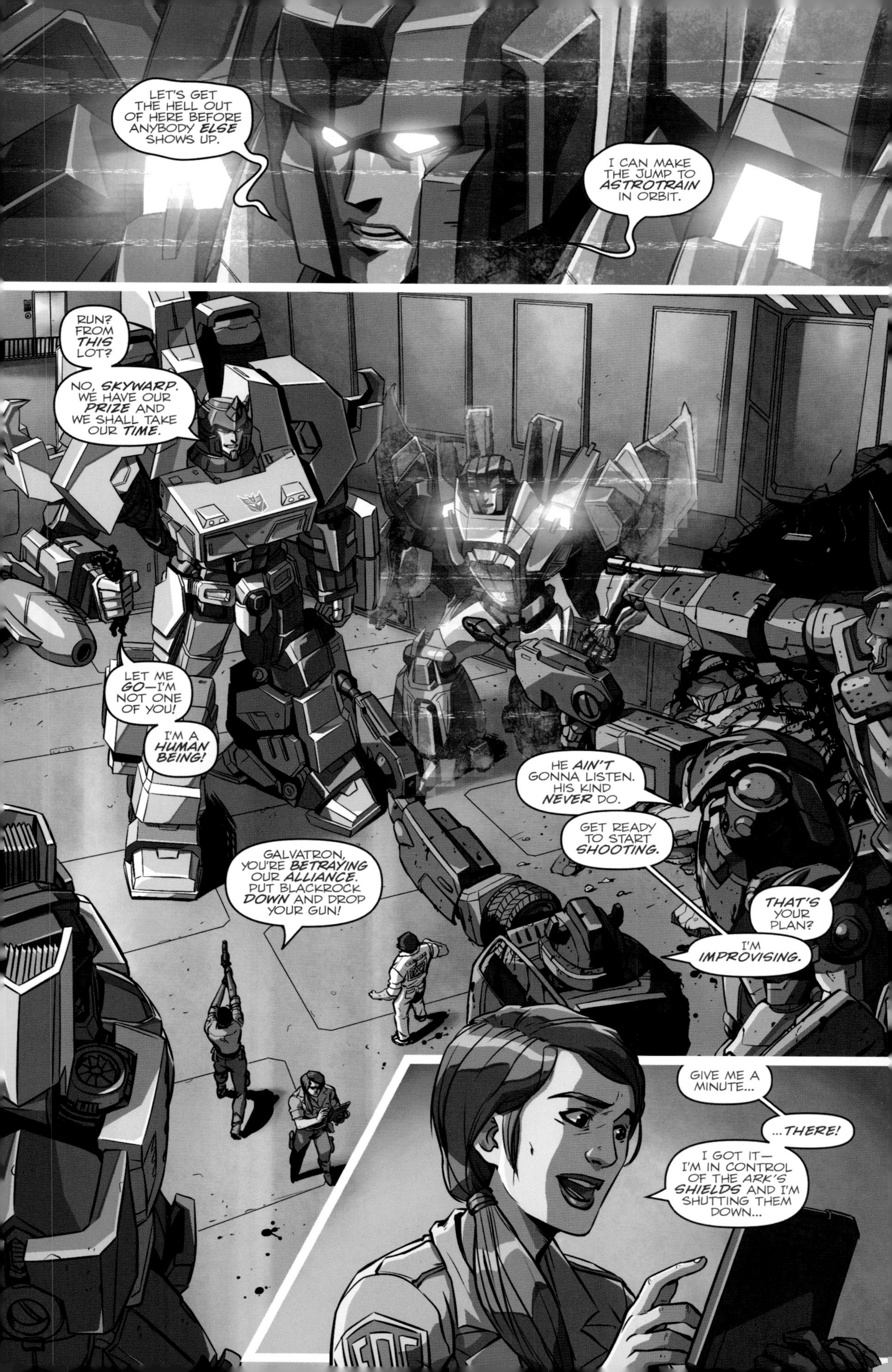
LET'S GET THE HELL OUT OF HERE BEFORE ANYBODY ELSE SHOWS UP.
I CAN MAKE THE JUMP TO ASTROTRAIN IN ORBIT.
RUN? FROM THIS LOT?
NO, SKYWARP. WE HAVE OUR PRIZE AND WE SHALL TAKE OUR TIME.
LET ME GO—I'M NOT ONE OF YOU!
I'M A HUMAN BEING!
HE AIN'T GONNA LISTEN. HIS KIND NEVER DO.
GET READY TO START SHOOTING.
GALVATRON, YOU'RE BETRAYING OUR ALLIANCE. PUT BLACKROCK DOWN AND DROP YOUR GUN!
THAT'S YOUR PLAN?
I'M IMPROVISING.
GIVE ME A MINUTE...
...THERE!
I GOT IT—I'M IN CONTROL OF THE ARK'S SHIELDS AND I'M SHUTTING THEM DOWN...

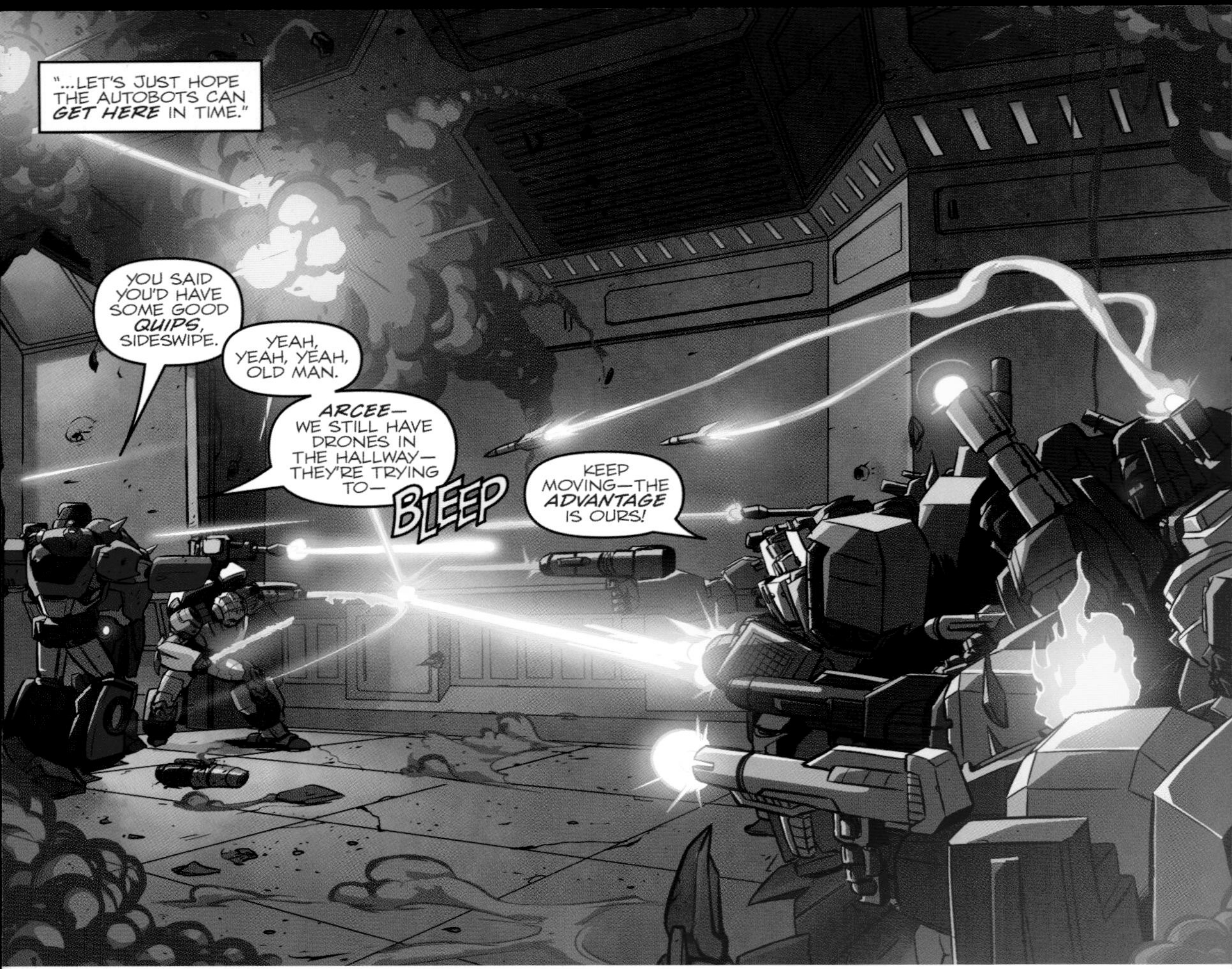
"...LET'S JUST HOPE THE AUTOBOTS CAN GET HERE IN TIME."
YOU SAID YOU'D HAVE SOME GOOD QUIPS, SIDESWIPE.
YEAH, YEAH, YEAH, OLD MAN.
ARCEE— WE STILL HAVE DRONES IN THE HALLWAY— THEY'RE TRYING TO—
BLEEP
KEEP MOVING—THE ADVANTAGE IS OURS!

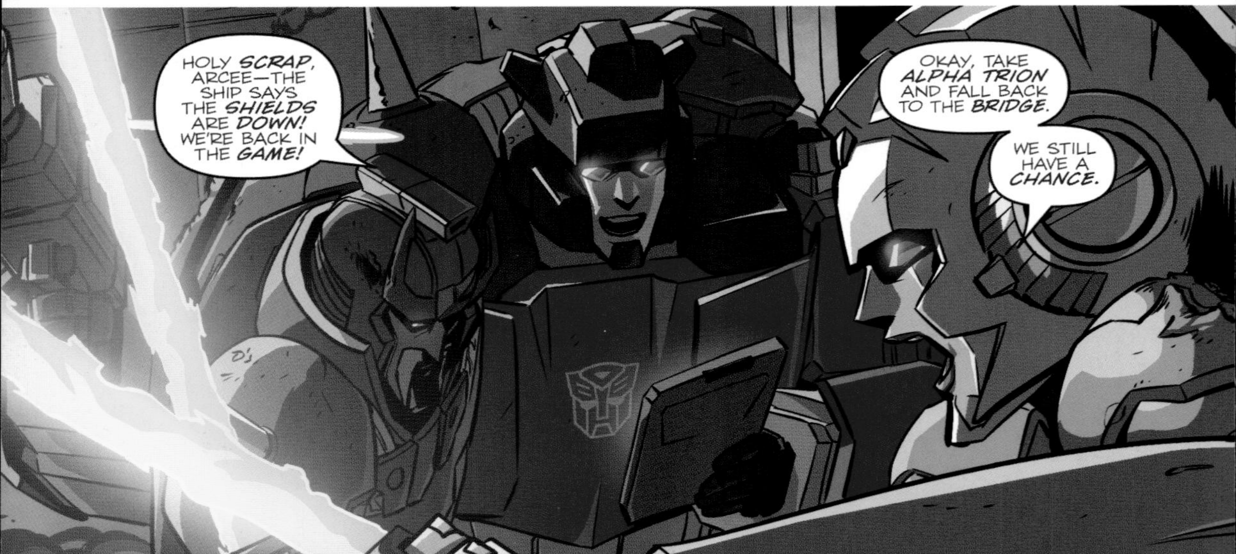
HOLY SCRAP, ARCEE—THE SHIP SAYS THE SHIELDS ARE DOWN! WE'RE BACK IN THE GAME!
OKAY, TAKE ALPHA TRION AND FALL BACK TO THE BRIDGE.
WE STILL HAVE A CHANCE.

CONQU

Part 4

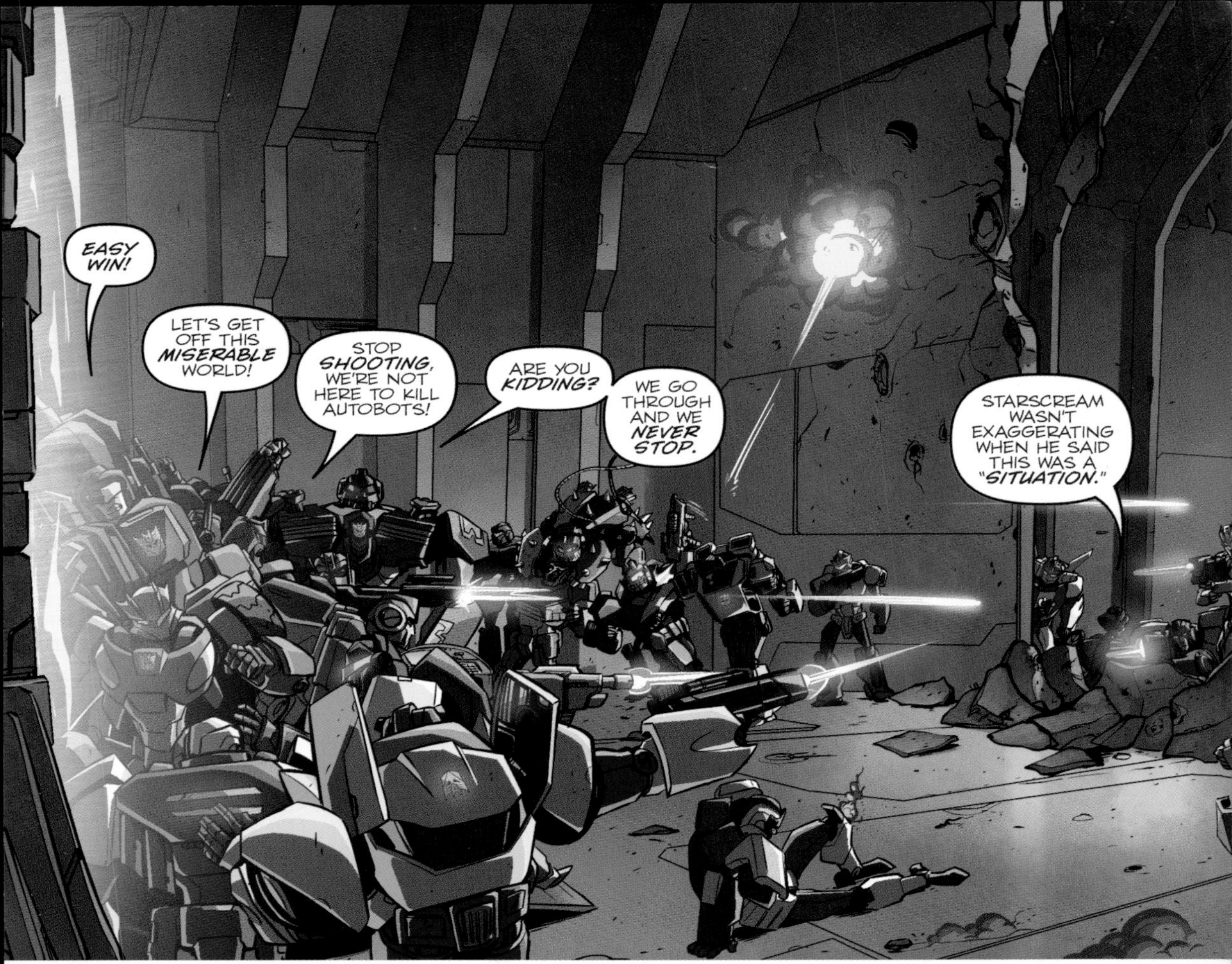
EASY WIN!
LET'S GET OFF THIS MISERABLE WORLD!
STOP SHOOTING, WE'RE NOT HERE TO KILL AUTOBOTS!
ARE YOU KIDDING?
WE GO THROUGH AND WE NEVER STOP.
STARSCREAM WASN'T EXAGGERATING WHEN HE SAID THIS WAS A "SITUATION."

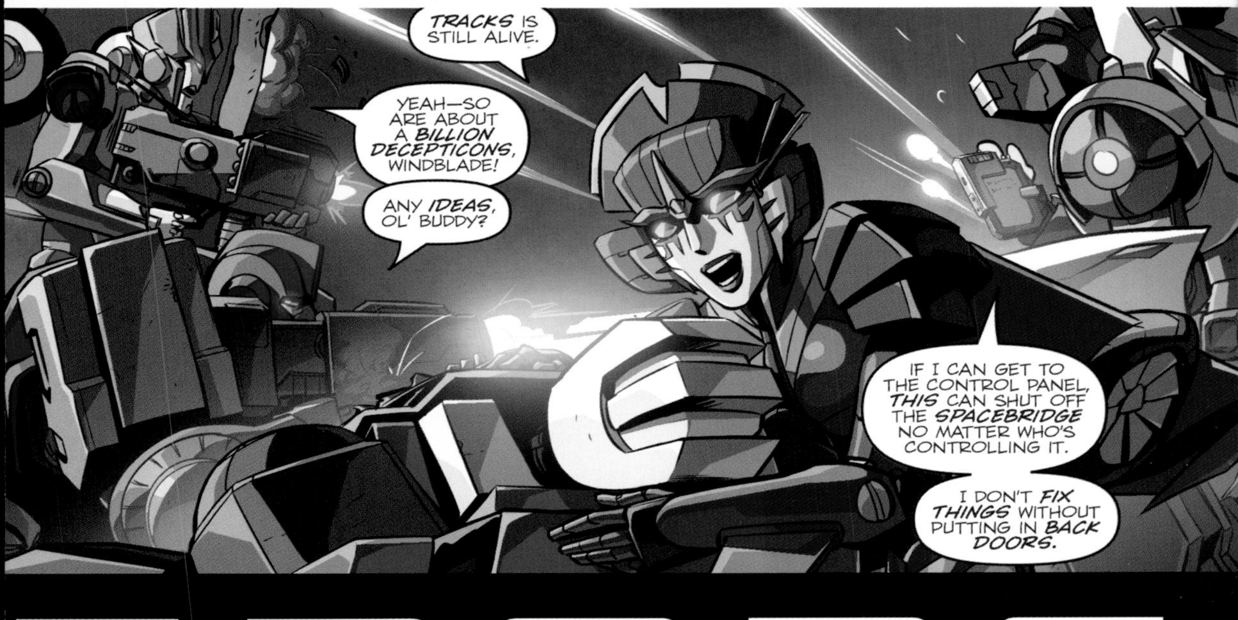
TRACKS IS STILL ALIVE.
YEAH—SO ARE ABOUT A BILLION DECEPTICONS, WINDBLADE!
ANY IDEAS, OL' BUDDY?
IF I CAN GET TO THE CONTROL PANEL, THIS CAN SHUT OFF THE SPACEBRIDGE NO MATTER WHO'S CONTROLLING IT.
I DON'T FIX THINGS WITHOUT PUTTING IN BACK DOORS.

ERORS

PERIHELION

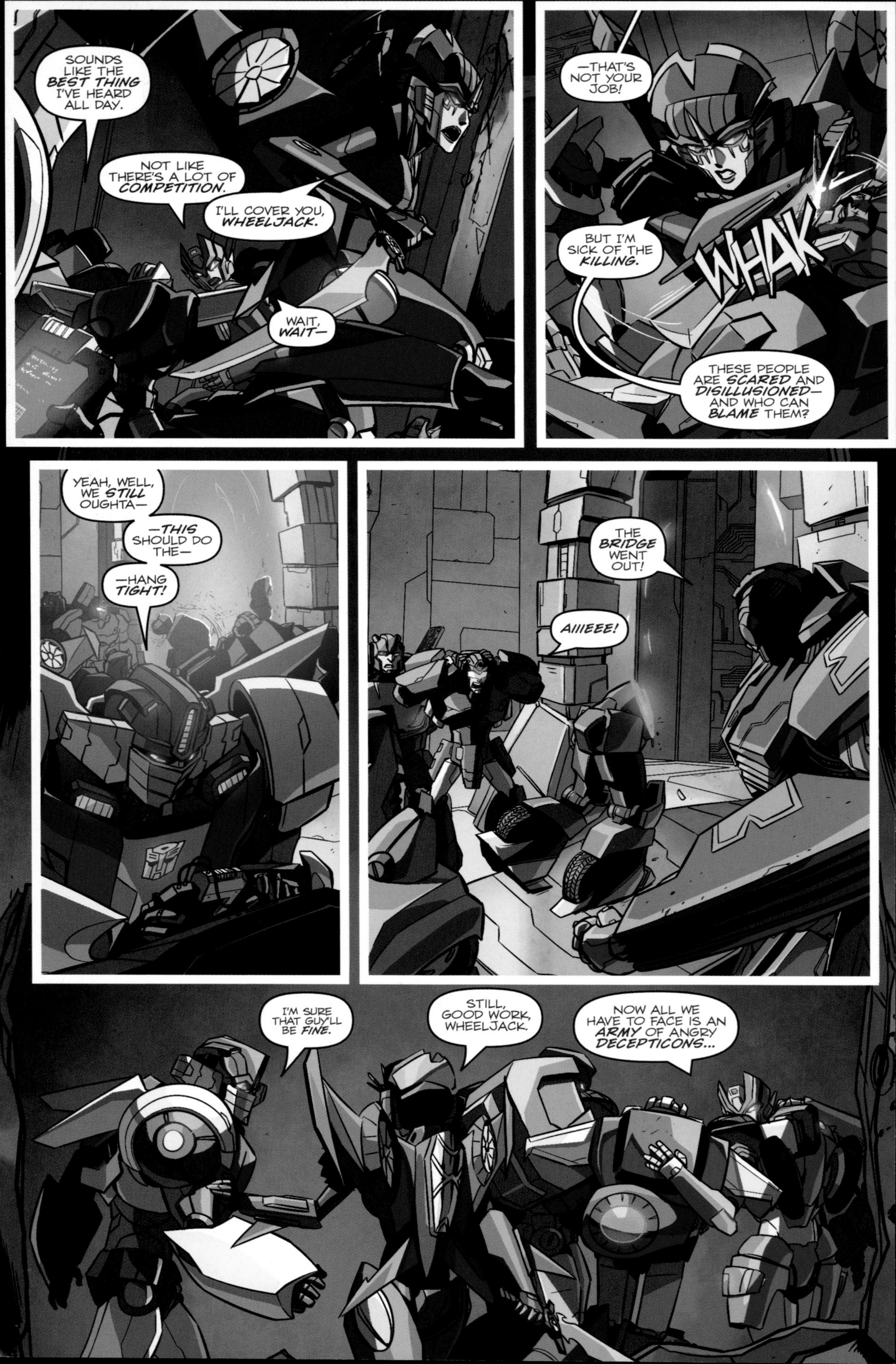
SOUNDS LIKE THE BEST THING I'VE HEARD ALL DAY.
NOT LIKE THERE'S A LOT OF COMPETITION.
I'LL COVER YOU, WHEELJACK.
WAIT, WAIT—
—THAT'S NOT YOUR JOB!
BUT I'M SICK OF THE KILLING.
WHAK
THESE PEOPLE ARE SCARED AND DISILLUSIONED—AND WHO CAN BLAME THEM?
YEAH, WELL, WE STILL OUGHTA—
—THIS SHOULD DO THE—
—HANG TIGHT!
THE BRIDGE WENT OUT!
AIIIEEE!
I'M SURE THAT GUY'LL BE FINE.
STILL, GOOD WORK, WHEELJACK.
NOW ALL WE HAVE TO FACE IS AN ARMY OF ANGRY DECEPTICONS...

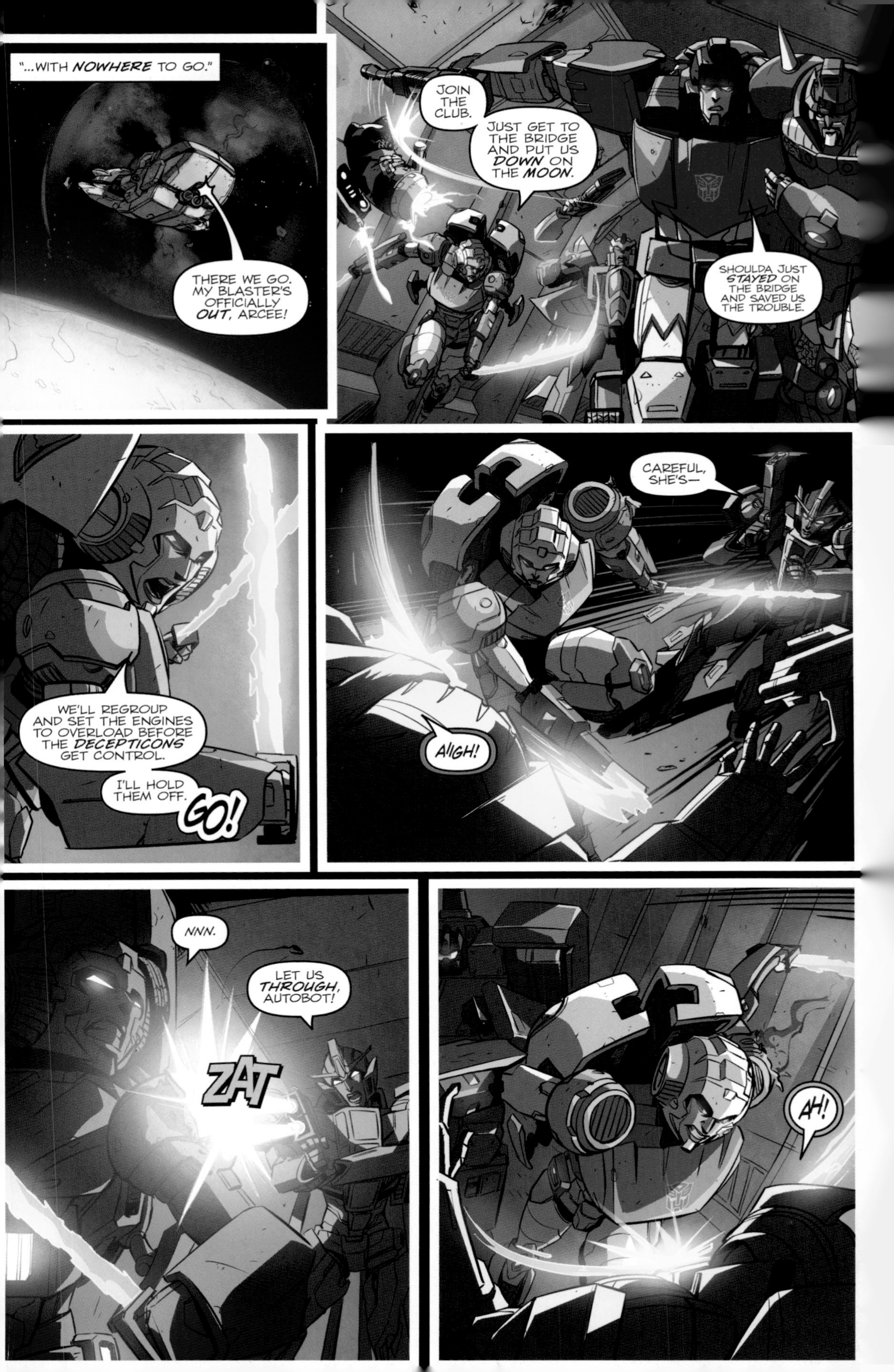
"...WITH NOWHERE TO GO."
THERE WE GO. MY BLASTER'S OFFICIALLY OUT, ARCEE!
JOIN THE CLUB.
JUST GET TO THE BRIDGE AND PUT US DOWN ON THE MOON.
SHOULDA JUST STAYED ON THE BRIDGE AND SAVED US THE TROUBLE.
WE'LL REGROUP AND SET THE ENGINES TO OVERLOAD BEFORE THE DECEPTICONS GET CONTROL.
I'LL HOLD THEM OFF.
GO!
CAREFUL, SHE'S—
AIIGH!
NNN.
LET US THROUGH, AUTOBOT!
ZAT
AH!

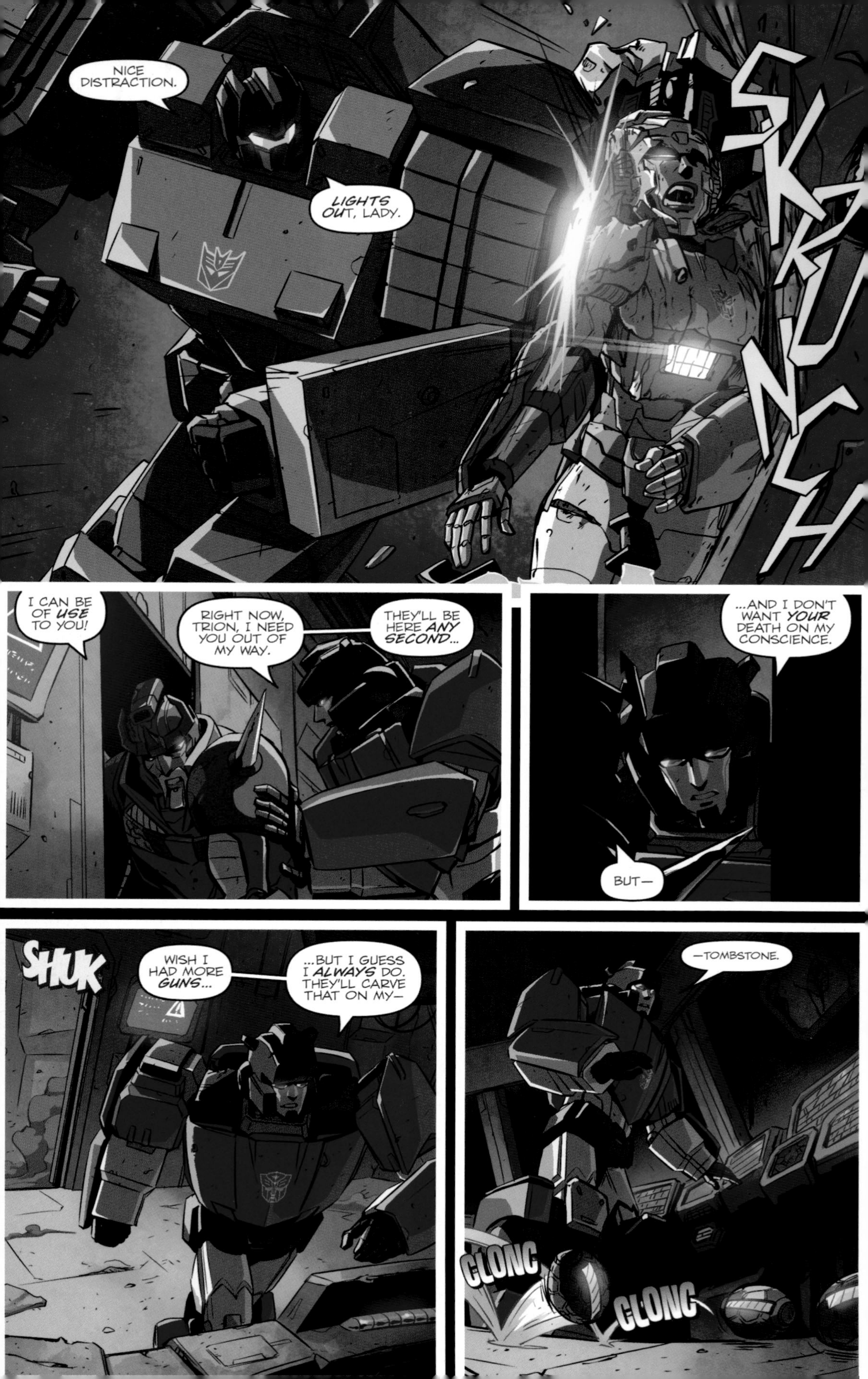
NICE DISTRACTION.
LIGHTS OUT, LADY.
SKKUNNCH
I CAN BE OF USE TO YOU!
RIGHT NOW, TRION, I NEED YOU OUT OF MY WAY.
THEY'LL BE HERE ANY SECOND...
...AND I DON'T WANT YOUR DEATH ON MY CONSCIENCE.
BUT—
SHUK
WISH I HAD MORE GUNS...
...BUT I GUESS I ALWAYS DO. THEY'LL CARVE THAT ON MY—
—TOMBSTONE.
CLONC
CLONC

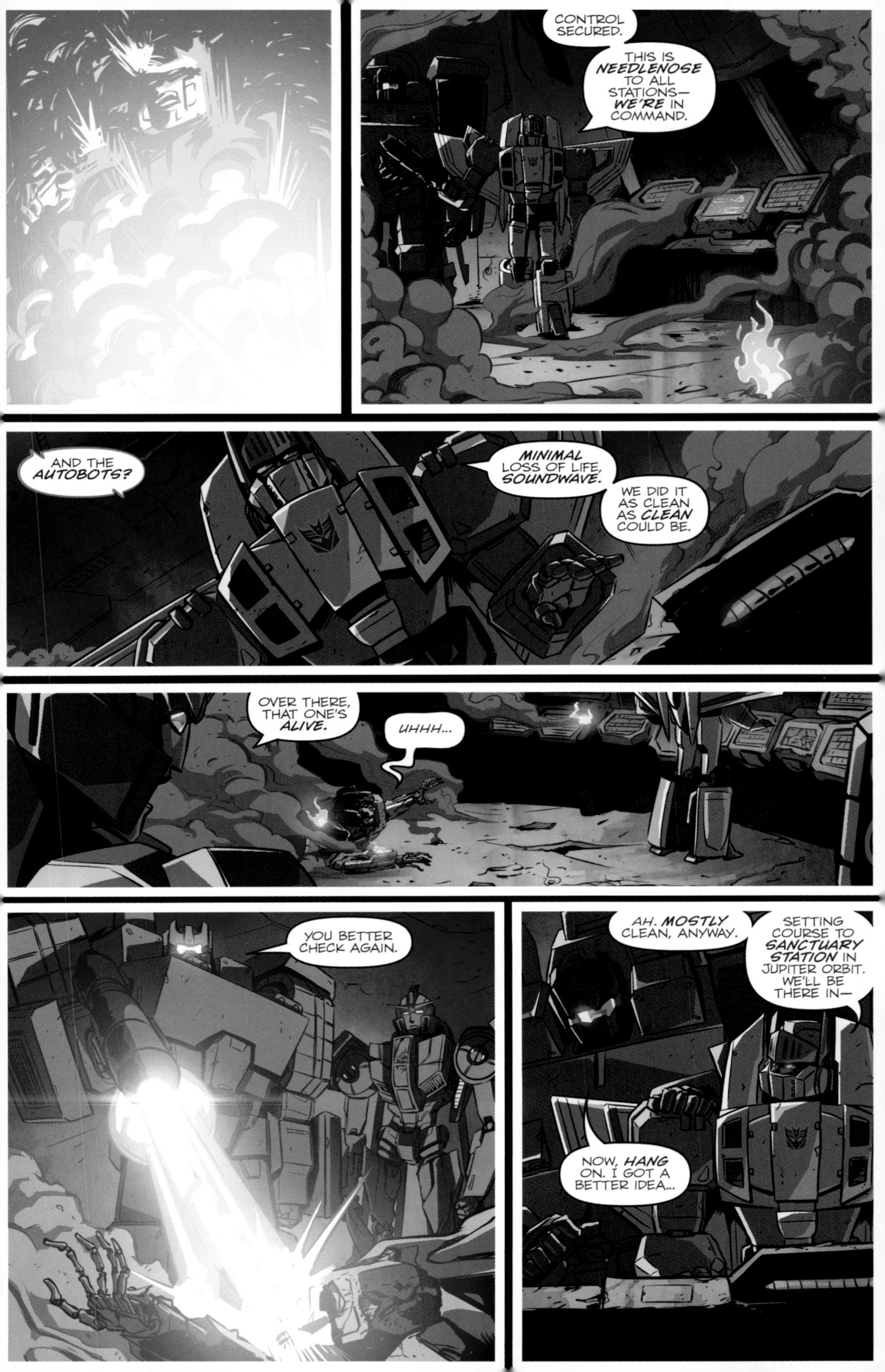
CONTROL SECURED.
THIS IS NEEDLENOSE TO ALL STATIONS— WE'RE IN COMMAND.
AND THE AUTOBOTS?
MINIMAL LOSS OF LIFE, SOUNDWAVE.
WE DID IT AS CLEAN AS CLEAN COULD BE.
OVER THERE, THAT ONE'S ALIVE.
UHHH...
YOU BETTER CHECK AGAIN.
AH. MOSTLY CLEAN, ANYWAY.
SETTING COURSE TO SANCTUARY STATION IN JUPITER ORBIT. WE'LL BE THERE IN—
NOW, HANG ON. I GOT A BETTER IDEA...

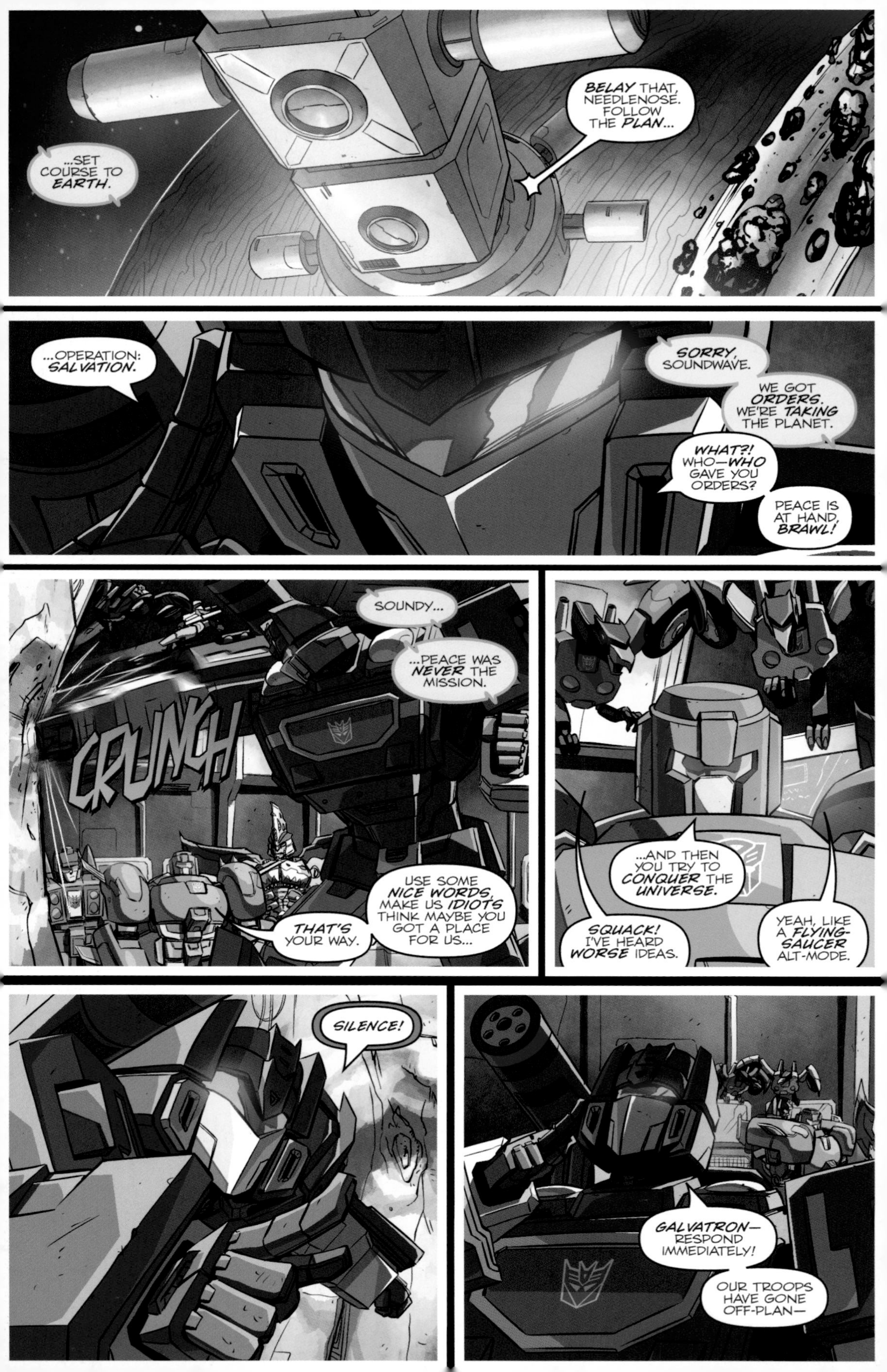
...SET COURSE TO EARTH.
BELAY THAT, NEEDLENOSE. FOLLOW THE PLAN...
...OPERATION: SALVATION.
SORRY, SOUNDWAVE.
WE GOT ORDERS. WE'RE TAKING THE PLANET.
WHAT?! WHO—WHO GAVE YOU ORDERS?
PEACE IS AT HAND, BRAWL!
SOUNDY...
...PEACE WAS NEVER THE MISSION.
CRUNCH
USE SOME NICE WORDS, MAKE US IDIOTS THINK MAYBE YOU GOT A PLACE FOR US...
THAT'S YOUR WAY.
...AND THEN YOU TRY TO CONQUER THE UNIVERSE.
SQUACK! I'VE HEARD WORSE IDEAS.
YEAH, LIKE A FLYING-SAUCER ALT-MODE.
SILENCE!
GALVATRON— RESPOND IMMEDIATELY!
OUR TROOPS HAVE GONE OFF-PLAN—

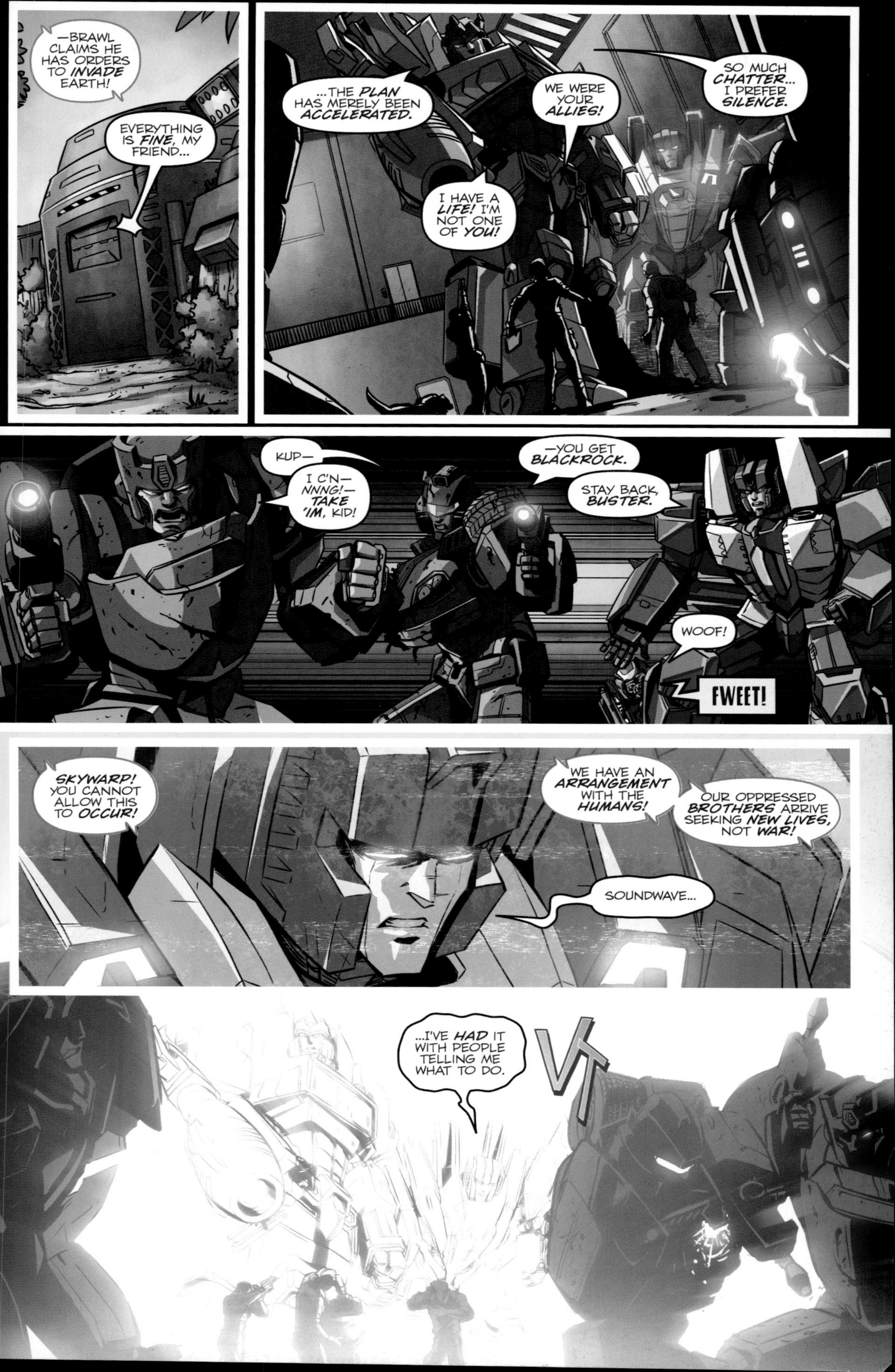
—BRAWL CLAIMS HE HAS ORDERS TO INVADE EARTH!
EVERYTHING IS FINE, MY FRIEND...
...THE PLAN HAS MERELY BEEN ACCELERATED.
WE WERE YOUR ALLIES!
I HAVE A LIFE! I'M NOT ONE OF YOU!
SO MUCH CHATTER... I PREFER SILENCE.
KUP—
I C'N—NNNG!—TAKE 'IM, KID!
—YOU GET BLACKROCK.
STAY BACK, BUSTER.
WOOF!
FWEET!
SKYWARP! YOU CANNOT ALLOW THIS TO OCCUR!
WE HAVE AN ARRANGEMENT WITH THE HUMANS!
OUR OPPRESSED BROTHERS ARRIVE SEEKING NEW LIVES, NOT WAR!
SOUNDWAVE...
...I'VE HAD IT WITH PEOPLE TELLING ME WHAT TO DO.
VT

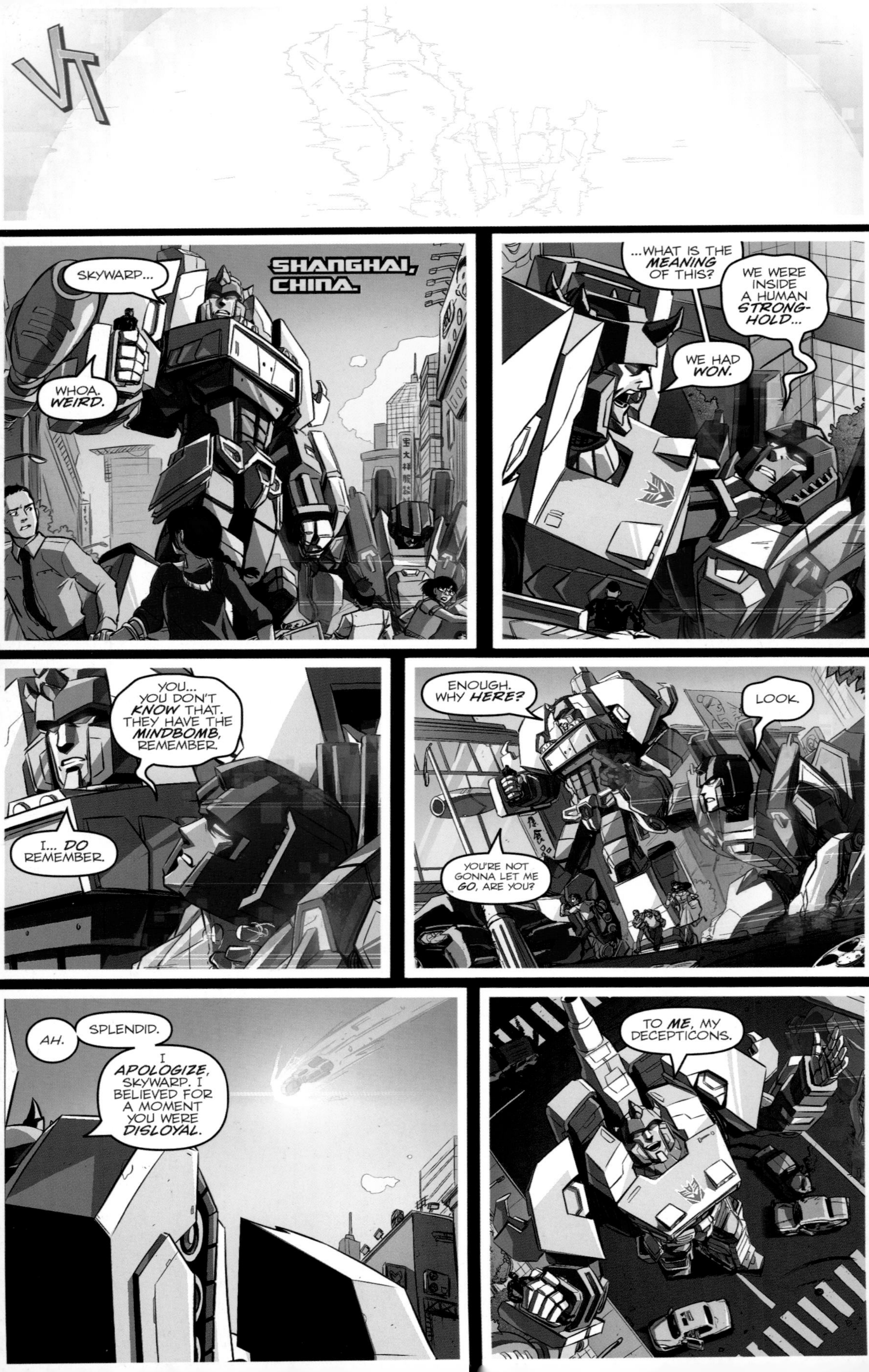

SHANGHAI, CHINA.
SKYWARP...
WHOA. WEIRD.
...WHAT IS THE MEANING OF THIS?
WE HAD WON.
WE WERE INSIDE A HUMAN STRONGHOLD...
YOU... YOU DON'T KNOW THAT. THEY HAVE THE MINDBOMB, REMEMBER.
I... DO REMEMBER.
ENOUGH. WHY HERE?
LOOK.
YOU'RE NOT GONNA LET ME GO, ARE YOU?
AH.
SPLENDID.
I APOLOGIZE, SKYWARP. I BELIEVED FOR A MOMENT YOU WERE DISLOYAL.
TO ME, MY DECEPTICONS.

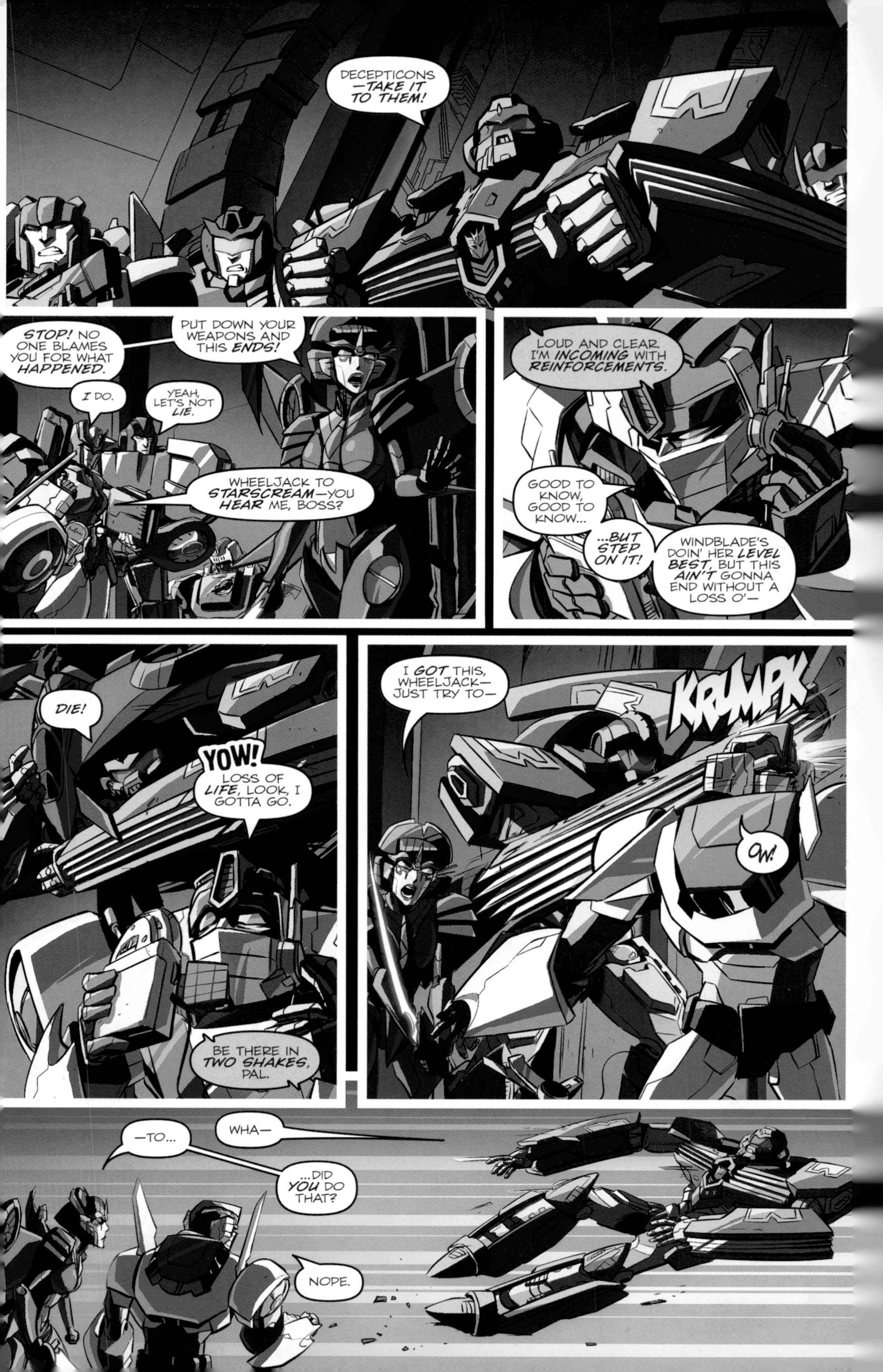
DECEPTICONS —TAKE IT TO THEM!
STOP! NO ONE BLAMES YOU FOR WHAT HAPPENED.
PUT DOWN YOUR WEAPONS AND THIS ENDS!
I DO.
YEAH, LET'S NOT LIE.
WHEELJACK TO STARSCREAM—YOU HEAR ME, BOSS?
LOUD AND CLEAR. I'M INCOMING WITH REINFORCEMENTS.
GOOD TO KNOW, GOOD TO KNOW...
...BUT STEP ON IT!
WINDBLADE'S DOIN' HER LEVEL BEST, BUT THIS AIN'T GONNA END WITHOUT A LOSS O'—
DIE!
YOW!
LOSS OF LIFE, LOOK, I GOTTA GO.
BE THERE IN TWO SHAKES, PAL.
I GOT THIS, WHEELJACK—JUST TRY TO—
KRUMPK
OW!
—TO...
WHA—
...DID YOU DO THAT?
NOPE.

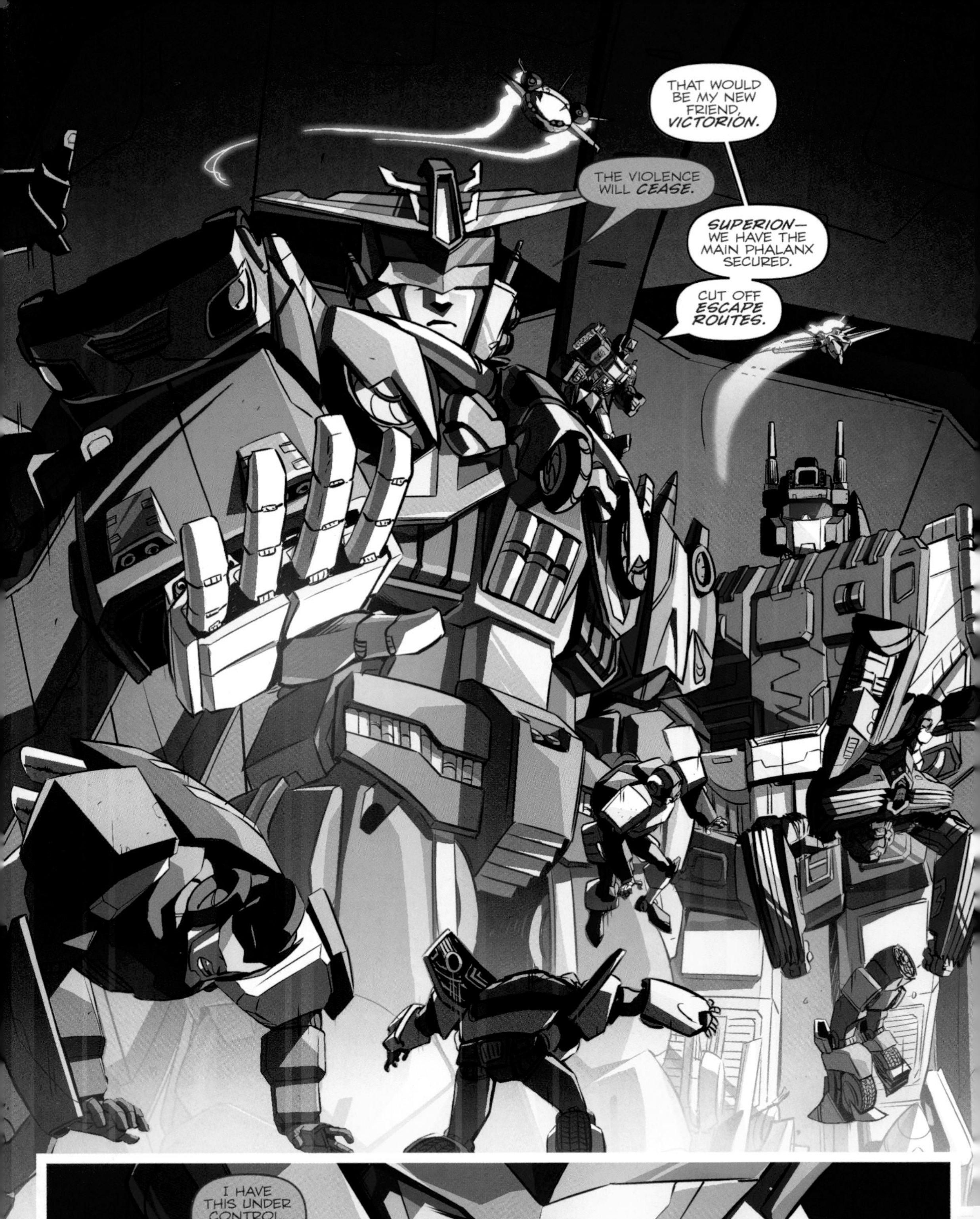

THE VIOLENCE WILL CEASE.
THAT WOULD BE MY NEW FRIEND, VICTORION.
SUPERION— WE HAVE THE MAIN PHALANX SECURED.
CUT OFF ESCAPE ROUTES.

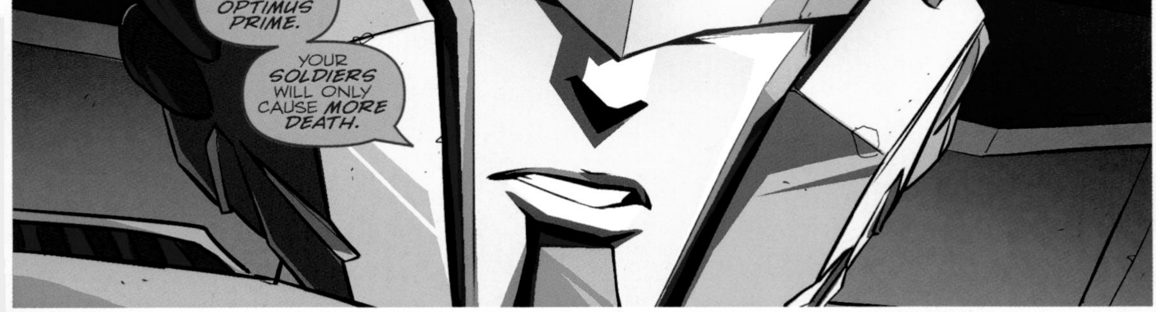

I HAVE THIS UNDER CONTROL, OPTIMUS PRIME.
YOUR SOLDIERS WILL ONLY CAUSE MORE DEATH.

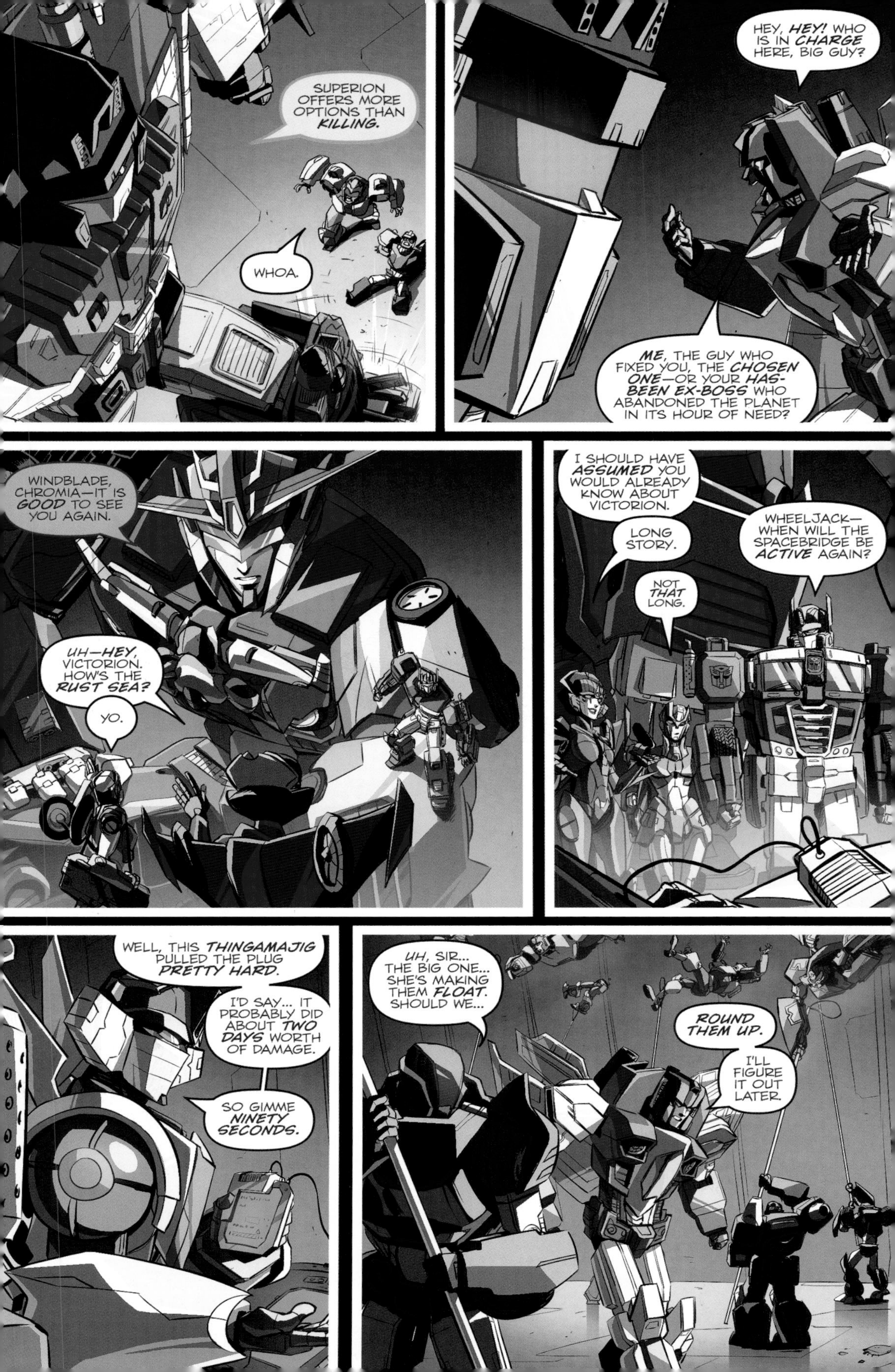
SUPERION OFFERS MORE OPTIONS THAN KILLING.
WHOA.
HEY, HEY! WHO IS IN CHARGE HERE, BIG GUY?
ME, THE GUY WHO FIXED YOU, THE CHOSEN ONE—OR YOUR HAS-BEEN EX-BOSS WHO ABANDONED THE PLANET IN ITS HOUR OF NEED?
WINDBLADE, CHROMIA—IT IS GOOD TO SEE YOU AGAIN.
UH—HEY, VICTORION. HOW'S THE RUST SEA?
YO.
I SHOULD HAVE ASSUMED YOU WOULD ALREADY KNOW ABOUT VICTORION.
LONG STORY.
NOT THAT LONG.
WHEELJACK—WHEN WILL THE SPACEBRIDGE BE ACTIVE AGAIN?
WELL, THIS THINGAMAJIG PULLED THE PLUG PRETTY HARD.
I'D SAY... IT PROBABLY DID ABOUT TWO DAYS WORTH OF DAMAGE.
SO GIMME NINETY SECONDS.
UH, SIR... THE BIG ONE... SHE'S MAKING THEM FLOAT. SHOULD WE...
ROUND THEM UP.
I'LL FIGURE IT OUT LATER.

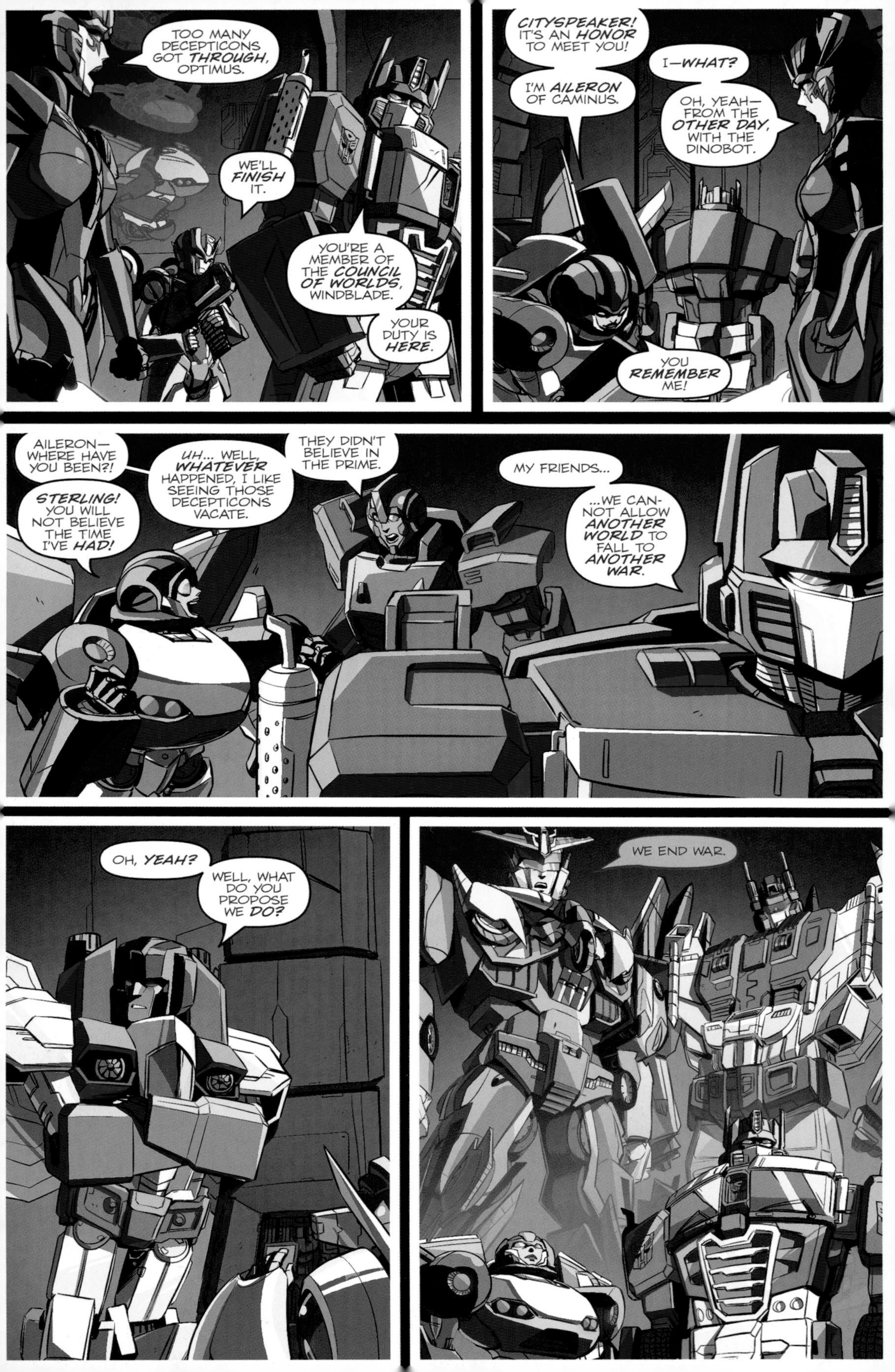
TOO MANY DECEPTICONS GOT THROUGH, OPTIMUS.
WE'LL FINISH IT.
YOU'RE A MEMBER OF THE COUNCIL OF WORLDS, WINDBLADE.
YOUR DUTY IS HERE.
CITYSPEAKER! IT'S AN HONOR TO MEET YOU!
I'M AILERON OF CAMINUS.
I—WHAT?
OH, YEAH— FROM THE OTHER DAY, WITH THE DINOBOT.
YOU REMEMBER ME!
AILERON— WHERE HAVE YOU BEEN?!
STERLING! YOU WILL NOT BELIEVE THE TIME I'VE HAD!
UH... WELL, WHATEVER HAPPENED, I LIKE SEEING THOSE DECEPTICONS VACATE.
THEY DIDN'T BELIEVE IN THE PRIME.
MY FRIENDS...
...WE CANNOT ALLOW ANOTHER WORLD TO FALL TO ANOTHER WAR.
OH, YEAH?
WELL, WHAT DO YOU PROPOSE WE DO?
WE END WAR.

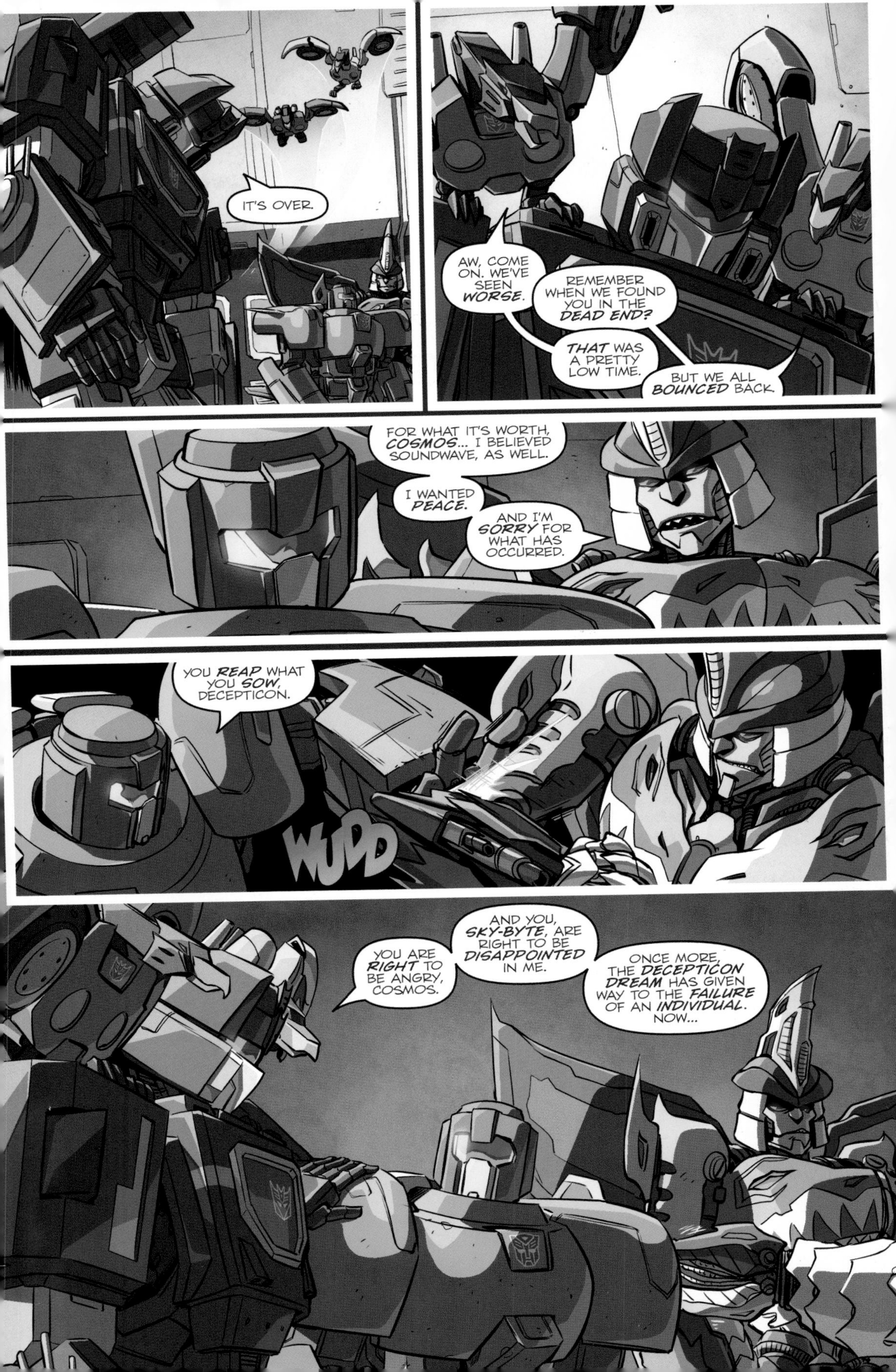
IT'S OVER.
AW, COME ON. WE'VE SEEN WORSE.
REMEMBER WHEN WE FOUND YOU IN THE DEAD END?
THAT WAS A PRETTY LOW TIME.
BUT WE ALL BOUNCED BACK.
FOR WHAT IT'S WORTH, COSMOS... I BELIEVED SOUNDWAVE, AS WELL.
I WANTED PEACE.
AND I'M SORRY FOR WHAT HAS OCCURRED.
YOU REAP WHAT YOU SOW, DECEPTICON.
WUDD
YOU ARE RIGHT TO BE ANGRY, COSMOS.
AND YOU, SKY-BYTE, ARE RIGHT TO BE DISAPPOINTED IN ME.
ONCE MORE, THE DECEPTICON DREAM HAS GIVEN WAY TO THE FAILURE OF AN INDIVIDUAL. NOW...

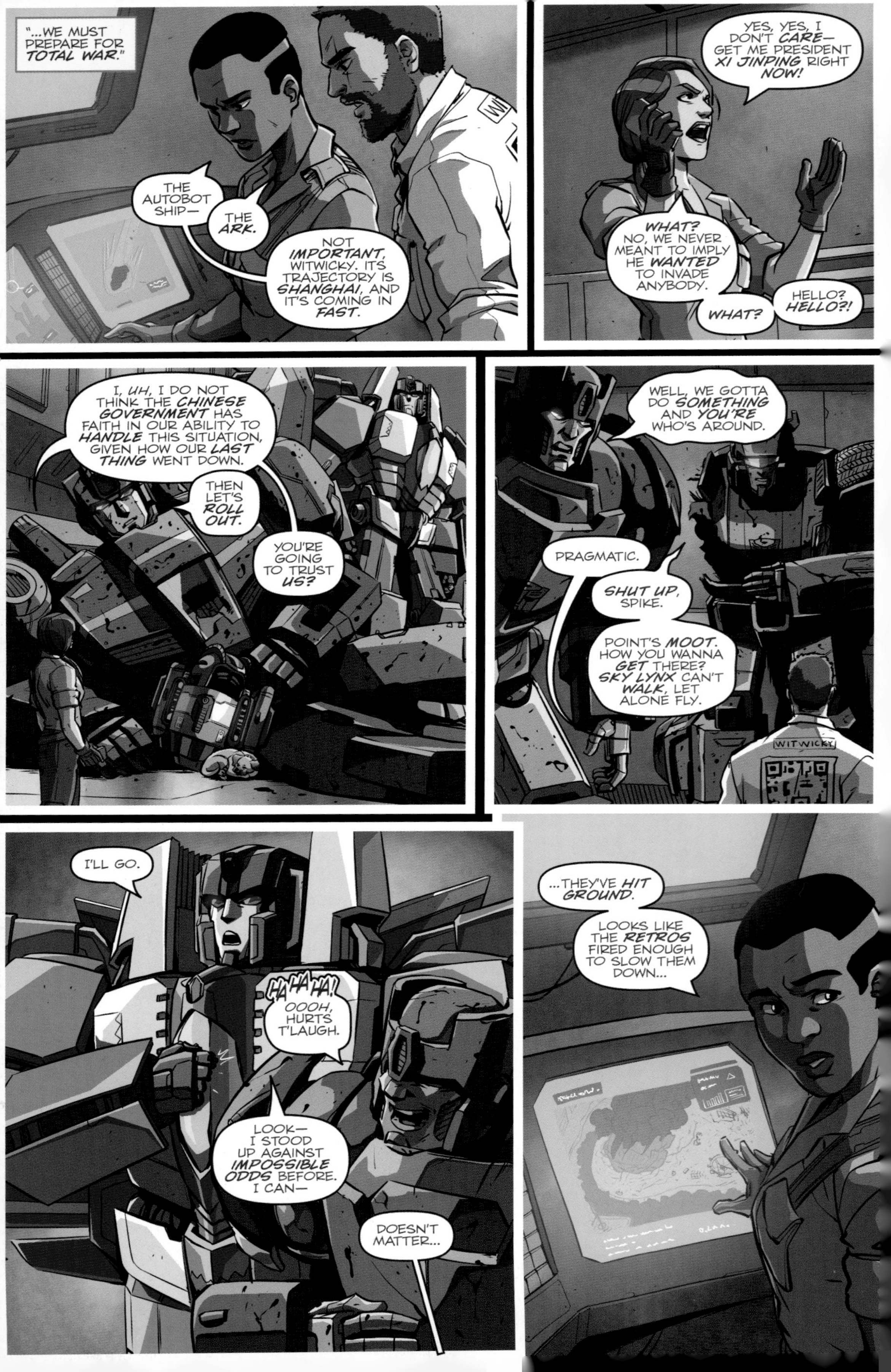
"...WE MUST PREPARE FOR TOTAL WAR."
THE AUTOBOT SHIP—
THE ARK.
NOT IMPORTANT, WITWICKY. ITS TRAJECTORY IS SHANGHAI, AND IT'S COMING IN FAST.
YES, YES, I DON'T CARE— GET ME PRESIDENT XI JINPING RIGHT NOW!
WHAT? NO, WE NEVER MEANT TO IMPLY HE WANTED TO INVADE ANYBODY.
WHAT?
HELLO? HELLO?!
I, UH, I DO NOT THINK THE CHINESE GOVERNMENT HAS FAITH IN OUR ABILITY TO HANDLE THIS SITUATION, GIVEN HOW OUR LAST THING WENT DOWN.
THEN LET'S ROLL OUT.
YOU'RE GOING TO TRUST US?
WELL, WE GOTTA DO SOMETHING AND YOU'RE WHO'S AROUND.
PRAGMATIC.
SHUT UP, SPIKE.
POINT'S MOOT. HOW YOU WANNA GET THERE? SKY LYNX CAN'T WALK, LET ALONE FLY.
WITWICKY
I'LL GO.
HA HA HA! OOOH, HURTS T'LAUGH.
LOOK— I STOOD UP AGAINST IMPOSSIBLE ODDS BEFORE. I CAN—
DOESN'T MATTER...
...THEY'VE HIT GROUND.
LOOKS LIKE THE RETROS FIRED ENOUGH TO SLOW THEM DOWN...

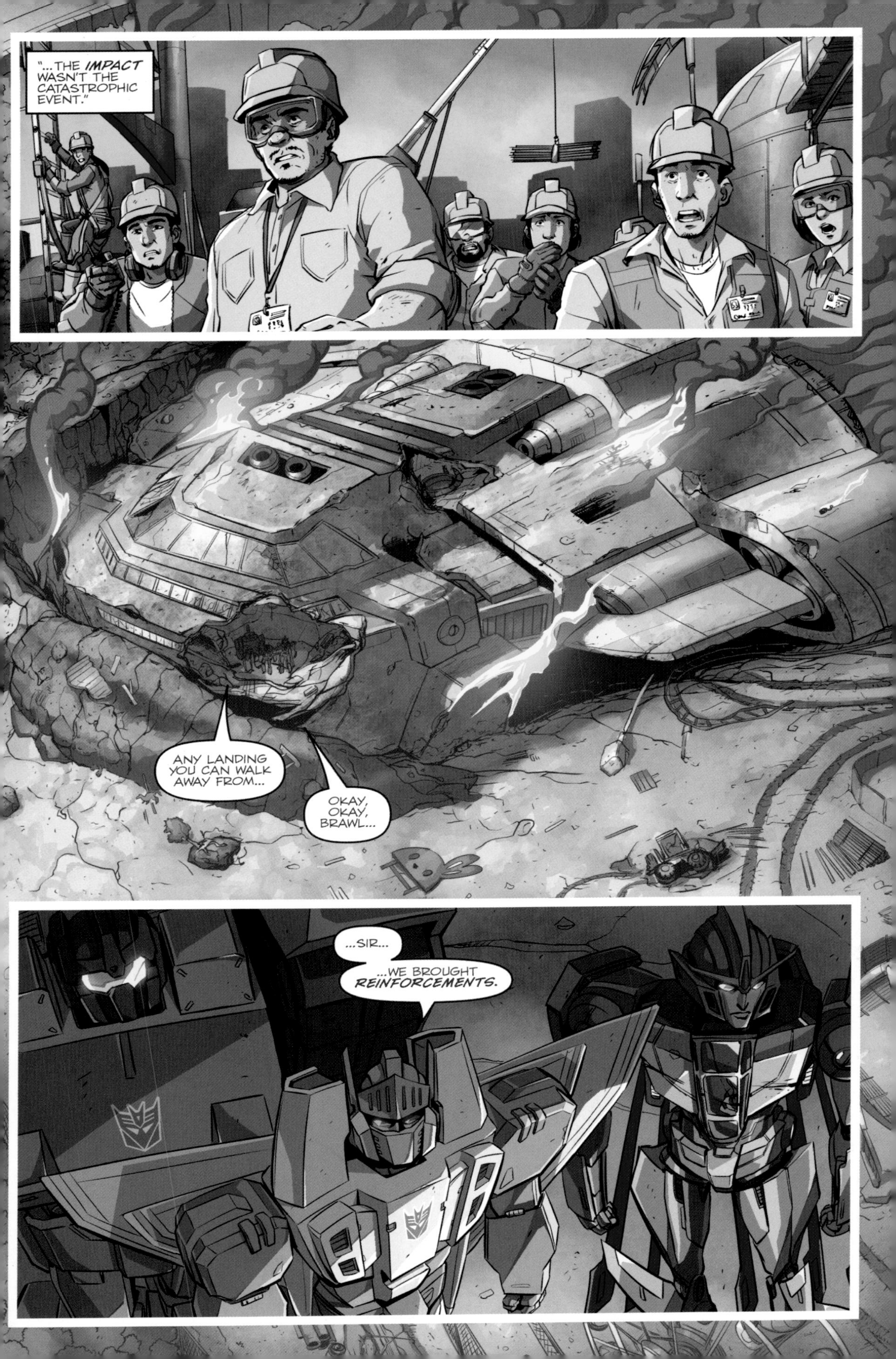
"...THE *IMPACT* WASN'T THE CATASTROPHIC EVENT."
ANY LANDING YOU CAN WALK AWAY FROM...
OKAY, OKAY, BRAWL...
...SIR...
...WE BROUGHT *REINFORCEMENTS*.

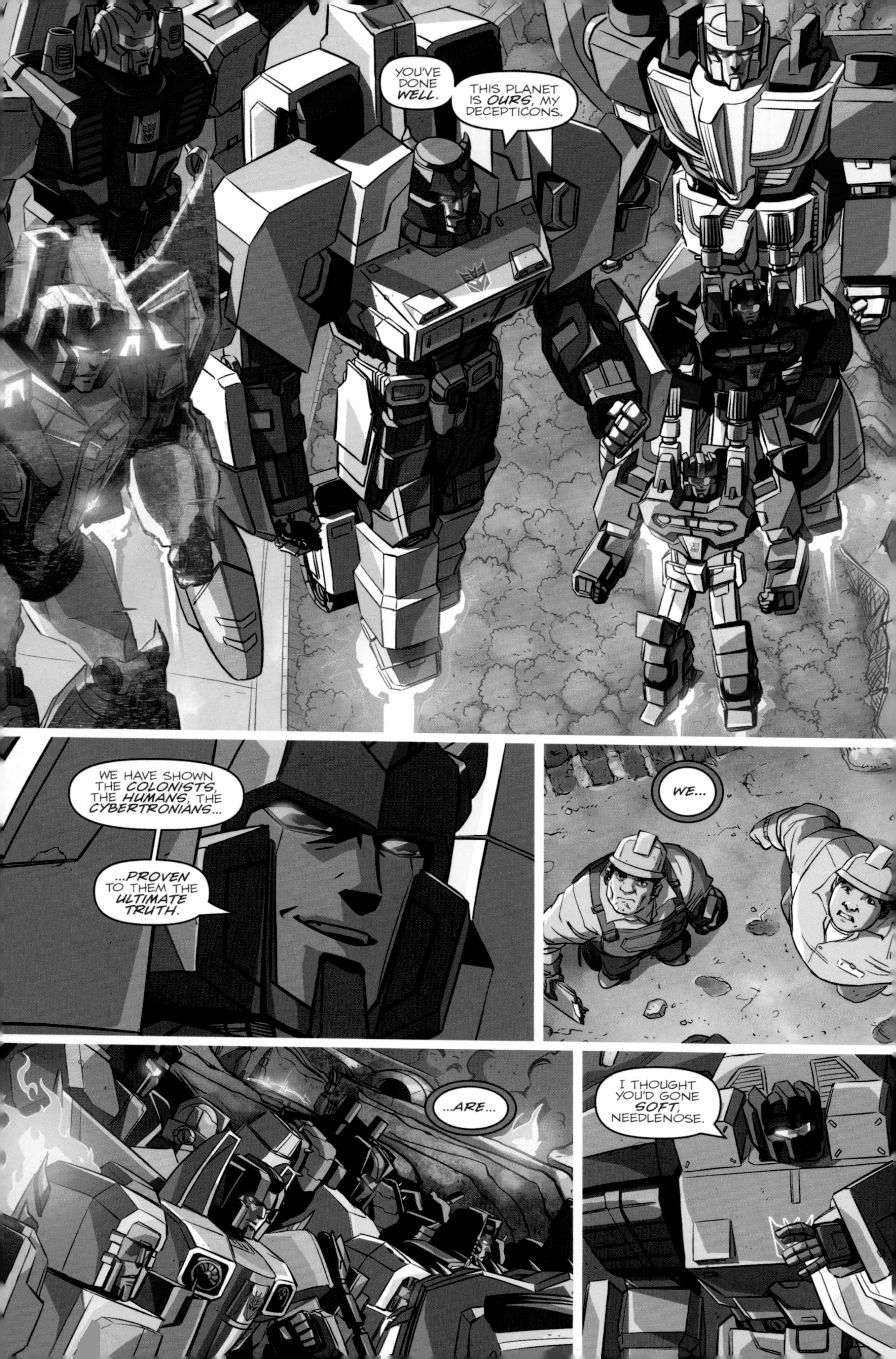
YOU'VE DONE **WELL**.
THIS PLANET IS **OURS**, MY DECEPTICONS.
WE HAVE SHOWN THE **COLONISTS**, THE **HUMANS**, THE **CYBERTRONIANS**...
...**PROVEN** TO THEM THE **ULTIMATE TRUTH**.
WE...
...ARE...
I THOUGHT YOU'D GONE **SOFT**, NEEDLENOSE.

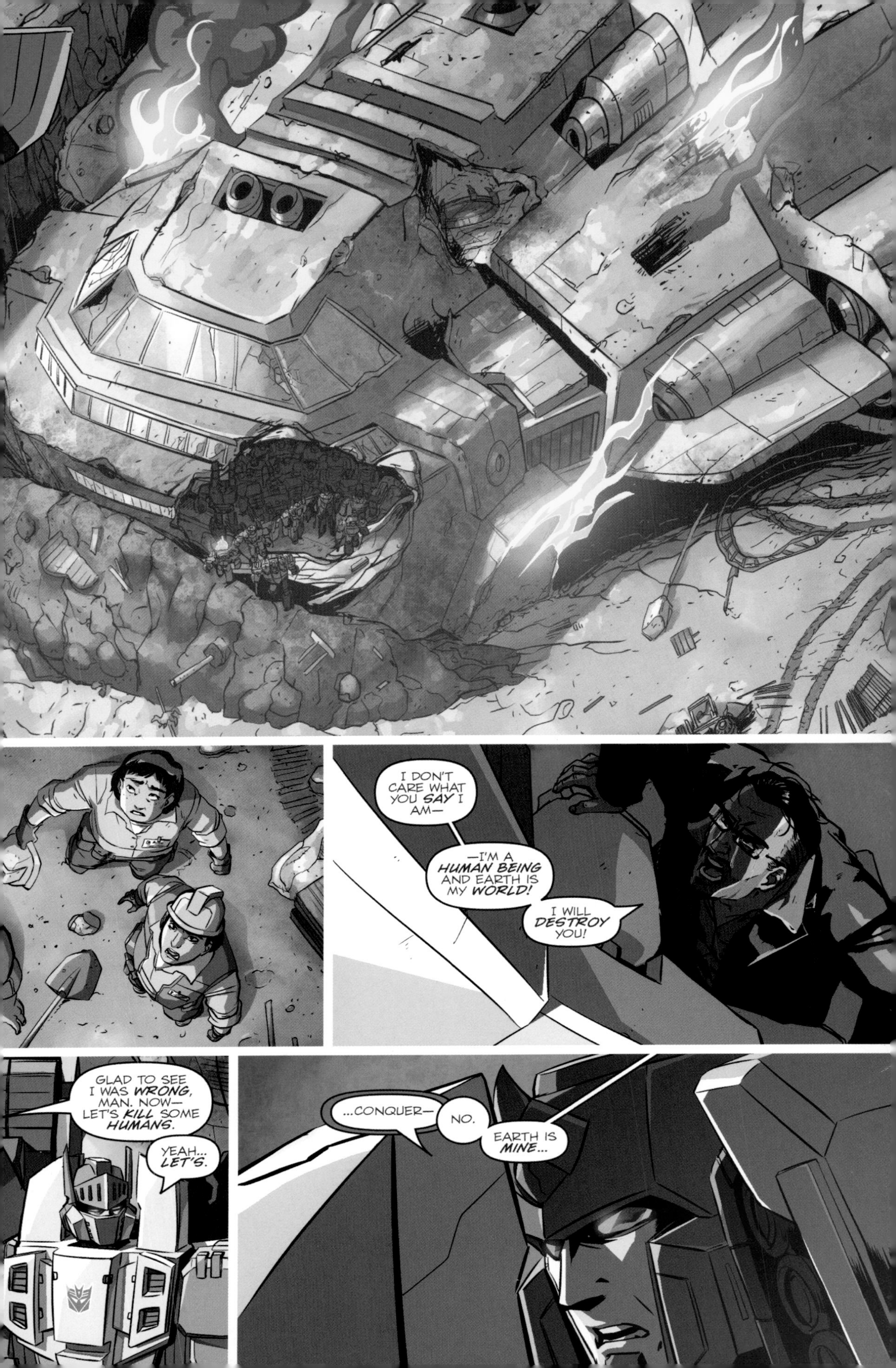
I DON'T CARE WHAT YOU SAY I AM—
—I'M A HUMAN BEING AND EARTH IS MY WORLD!
I WILL DESTROY YOU!
GLAD TO SEE I WAS WRONG, MAN. NOW— LET'S KILL SOME HUMANS.
YEAH... LET'S.
...CONQUER—
NO.
EARTH IS MINE...

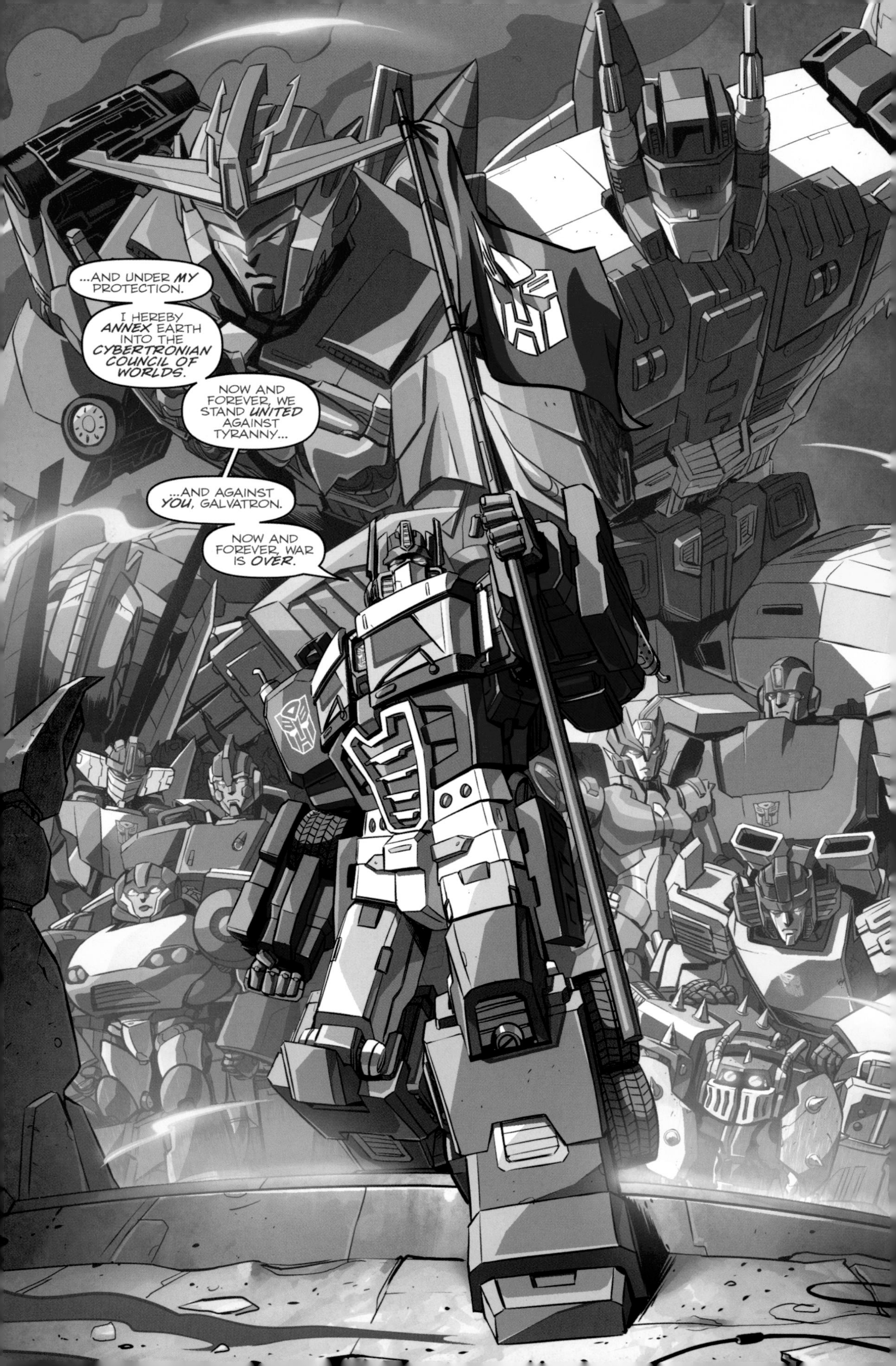
...AND UNDER MY PROTECTION.
I HEREBY ANNEX EARTH INTO THE CYBERTRONIAN COUNCIL OF WORLDS.
NOW AND FOREVER, WE STAND UNITED AGAINST TYRANNY...
...AND AGAINST YOU, GALVATRON.
NOW AND FOREVER, WAR IS OVER.

COVER GALLERY

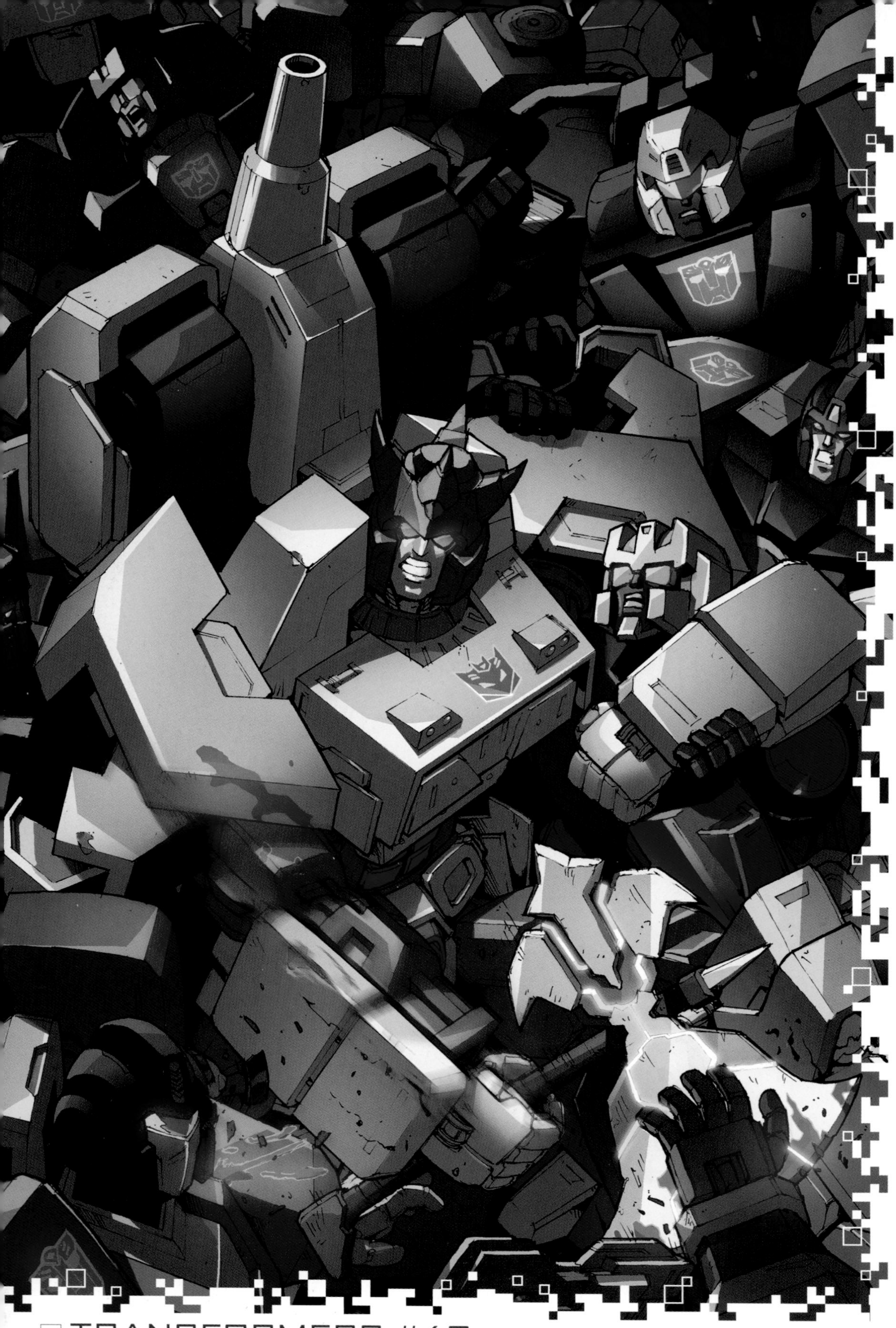

TRANSFORMERS #46 COVER A

by **ANDREW GRIFFITH** Colors by **JOSH PEREZ**

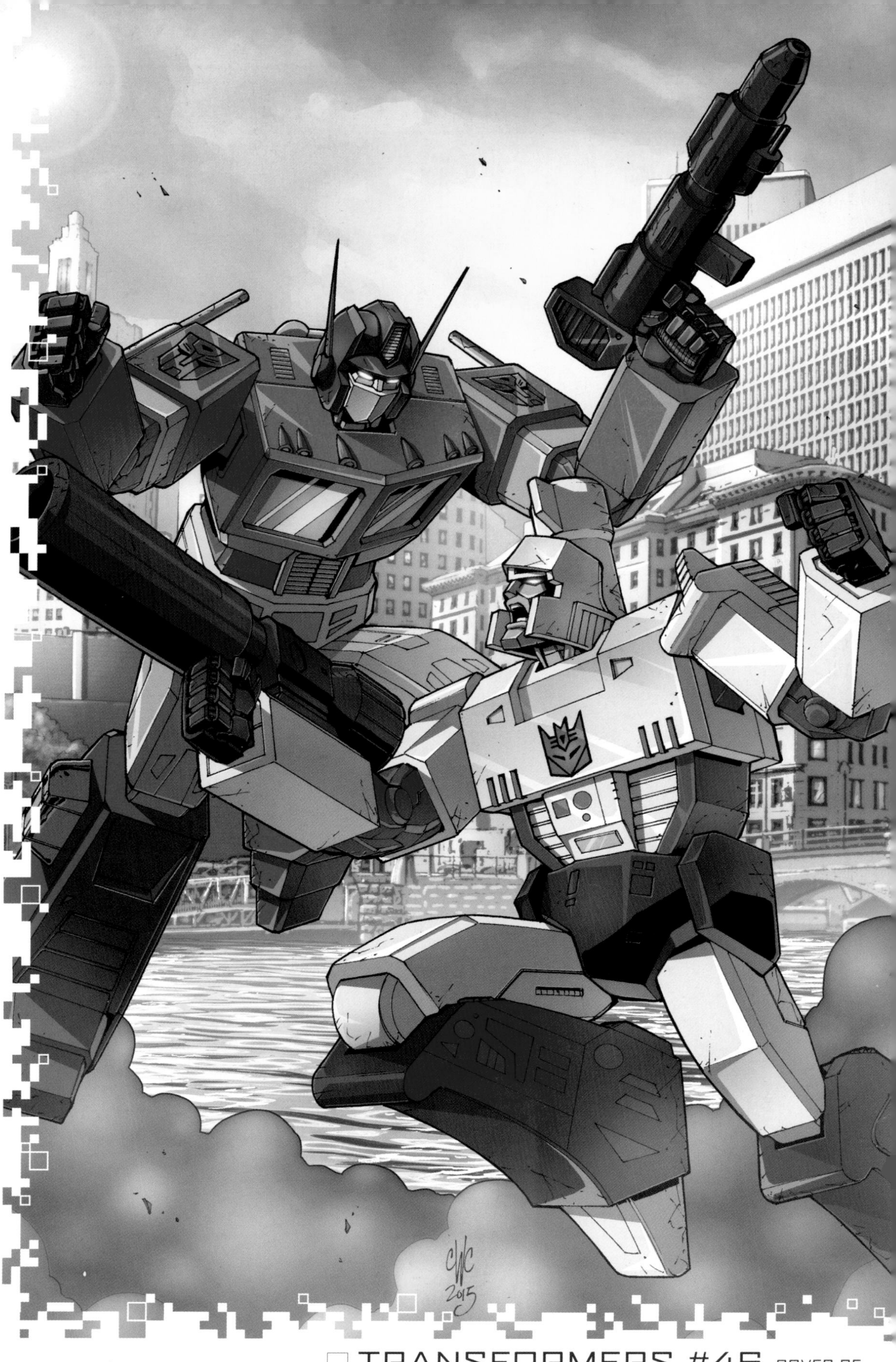

TRANSFORMERS #46 COVER RE

by **CASEY W. COLLER** Colors by **JOHN-PAUL BOVE**

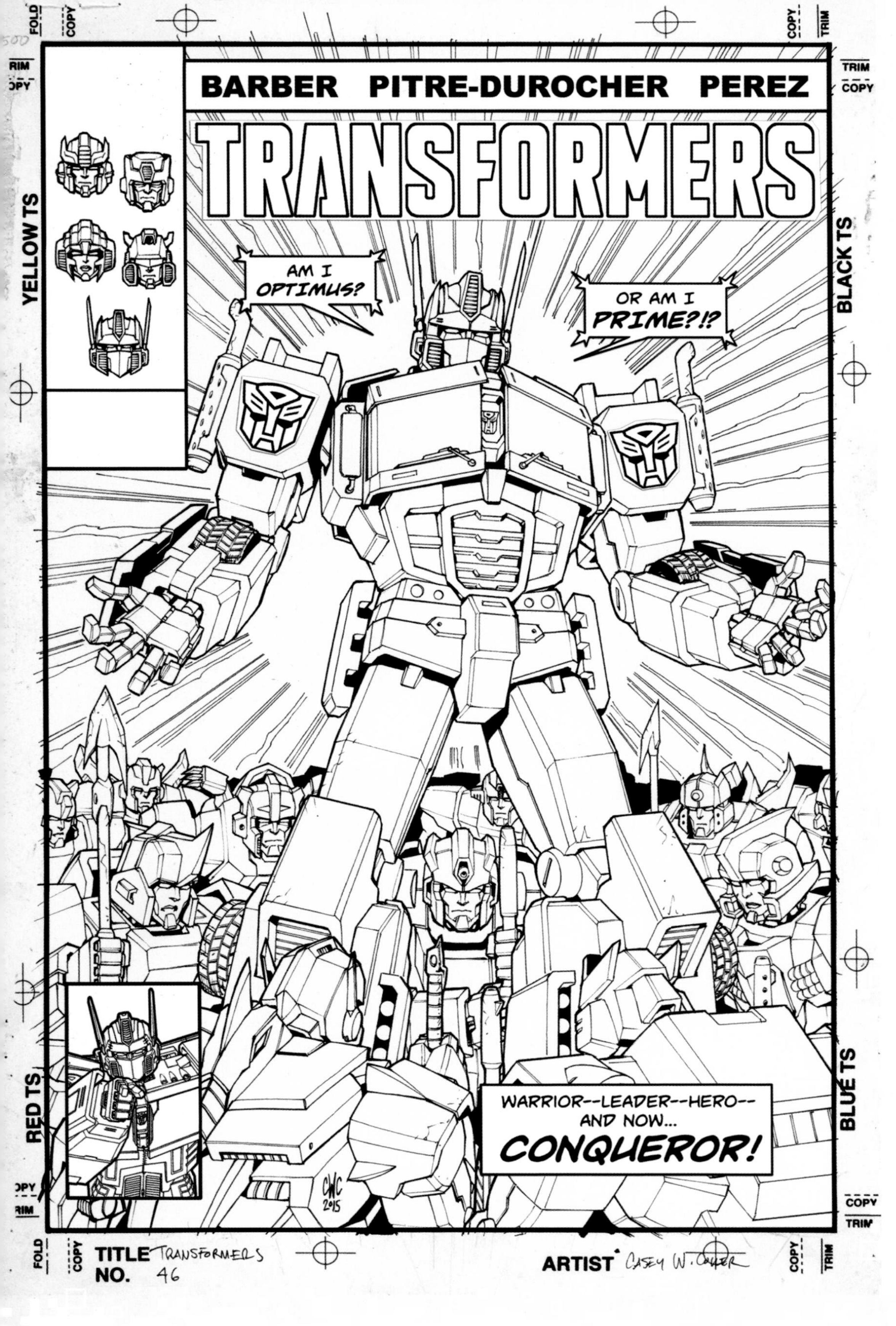
BARBER PITRE-DUROCHER PEREZ
TRANSFORMERS
AM I OPTIMUS?
OR AM I PRIME?!?
WARRIOR--LEADER--HERO-- AND NOW... CONQUEROR!
CWC 2015
YELLOW TS
BLACK TS
RED TS
BLUE TS
TITLE TRANSFORMERS
NO. 46
ARTIST CASEY W. COLLER

TRANSFORMERS #46 COVER RI

by **CASEY W. COLLER**

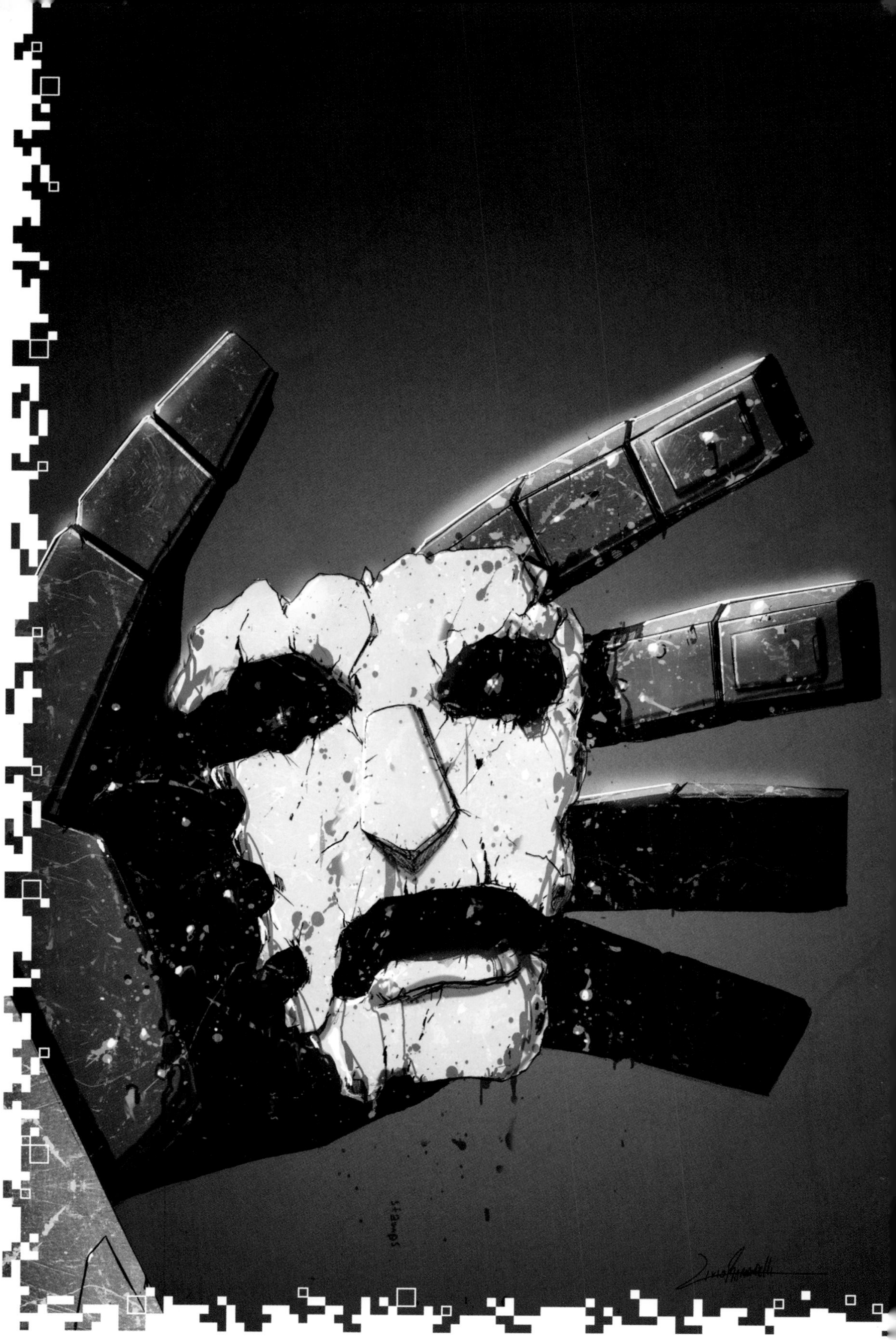

TRANSFORMERS #47 COVER RI

by **LIVIO RAMONDELLI**

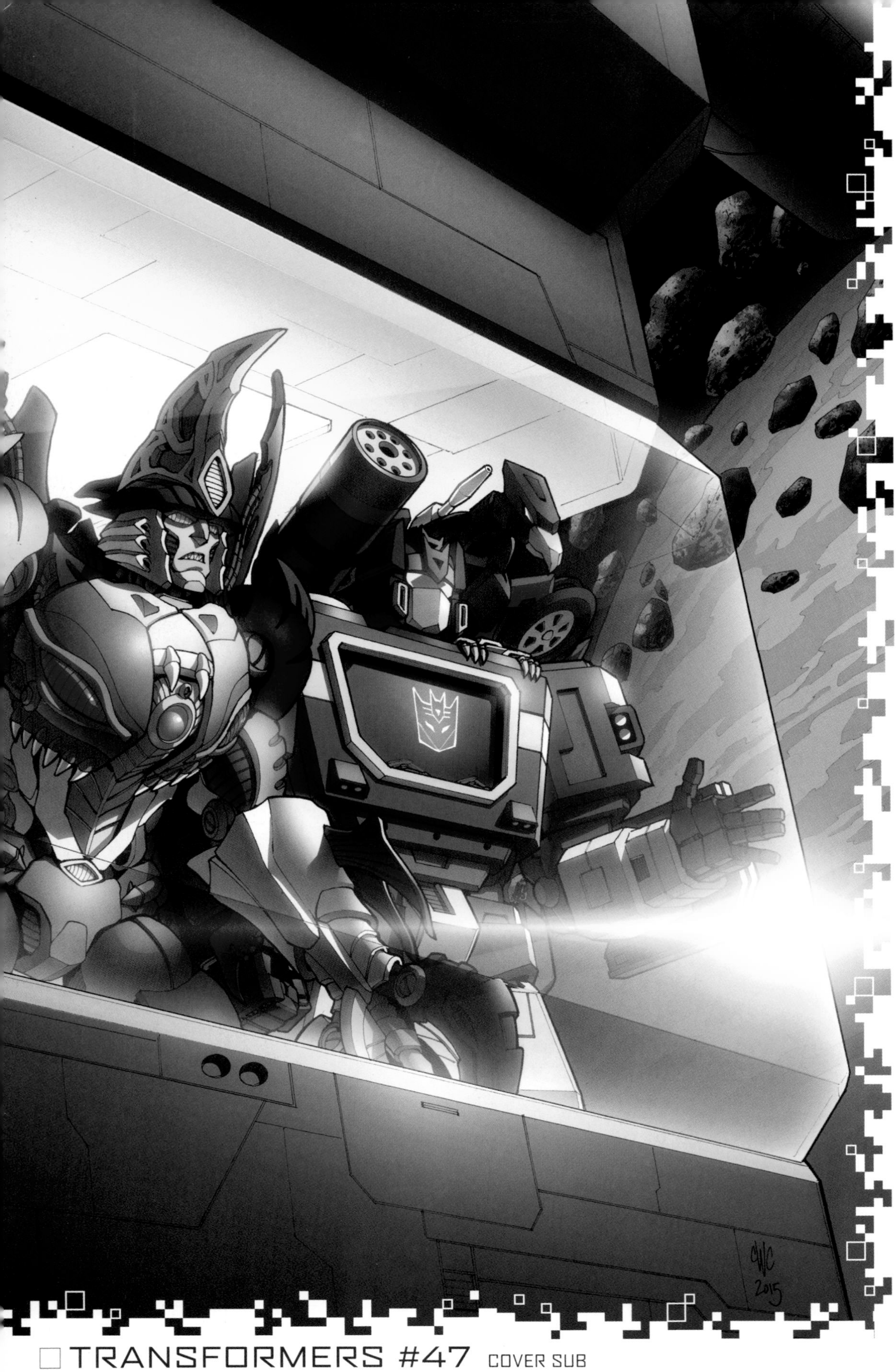
CWC
2015

TRANSFORMERS #47 COVER SUB

by **CASEY W. COLLER** Colors by **JOANA LAFUENTE**

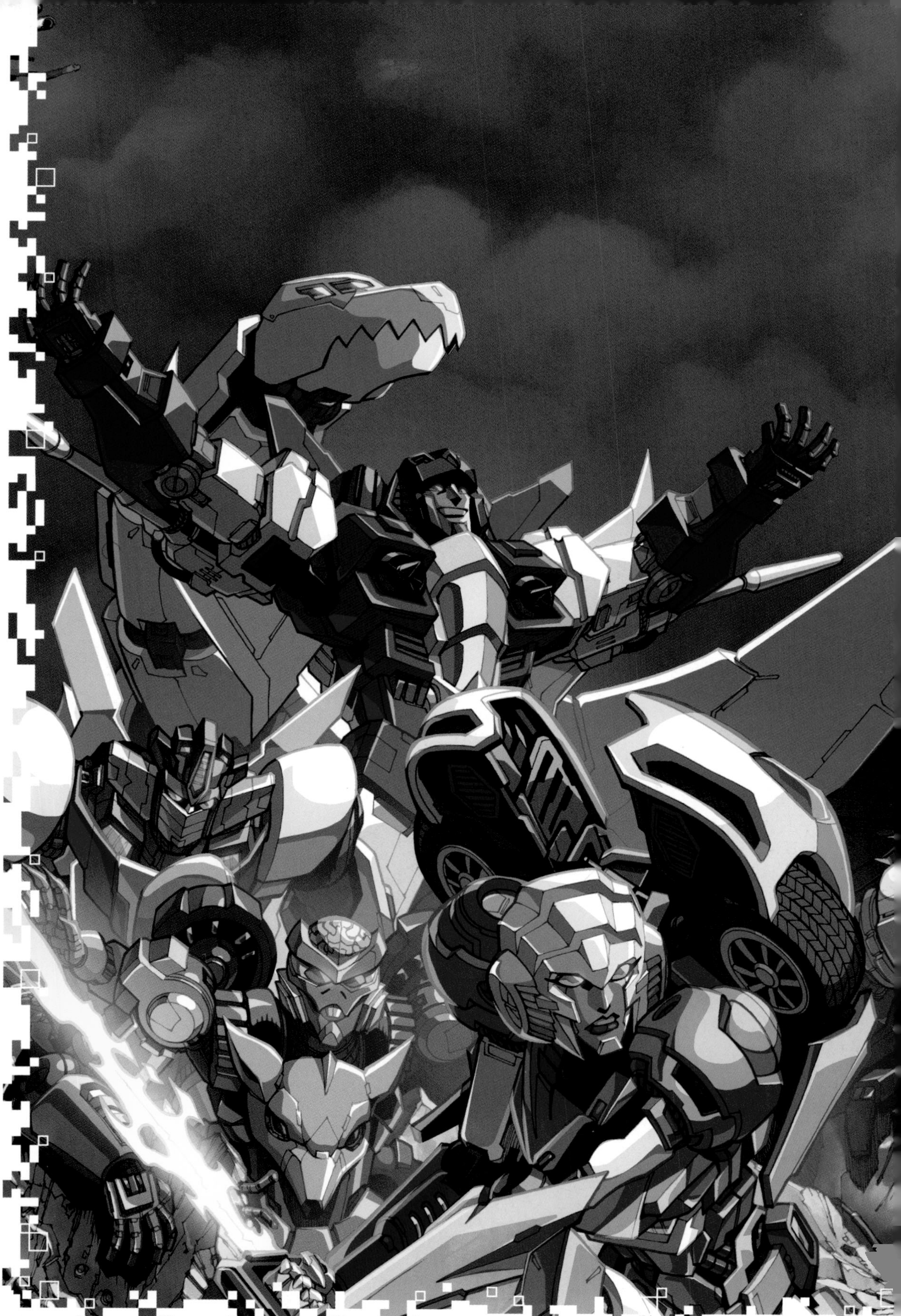

TRANSFORMERS #48 COVER RI

by **ALEX MILNE** Colors by **JOSH PEREZ**

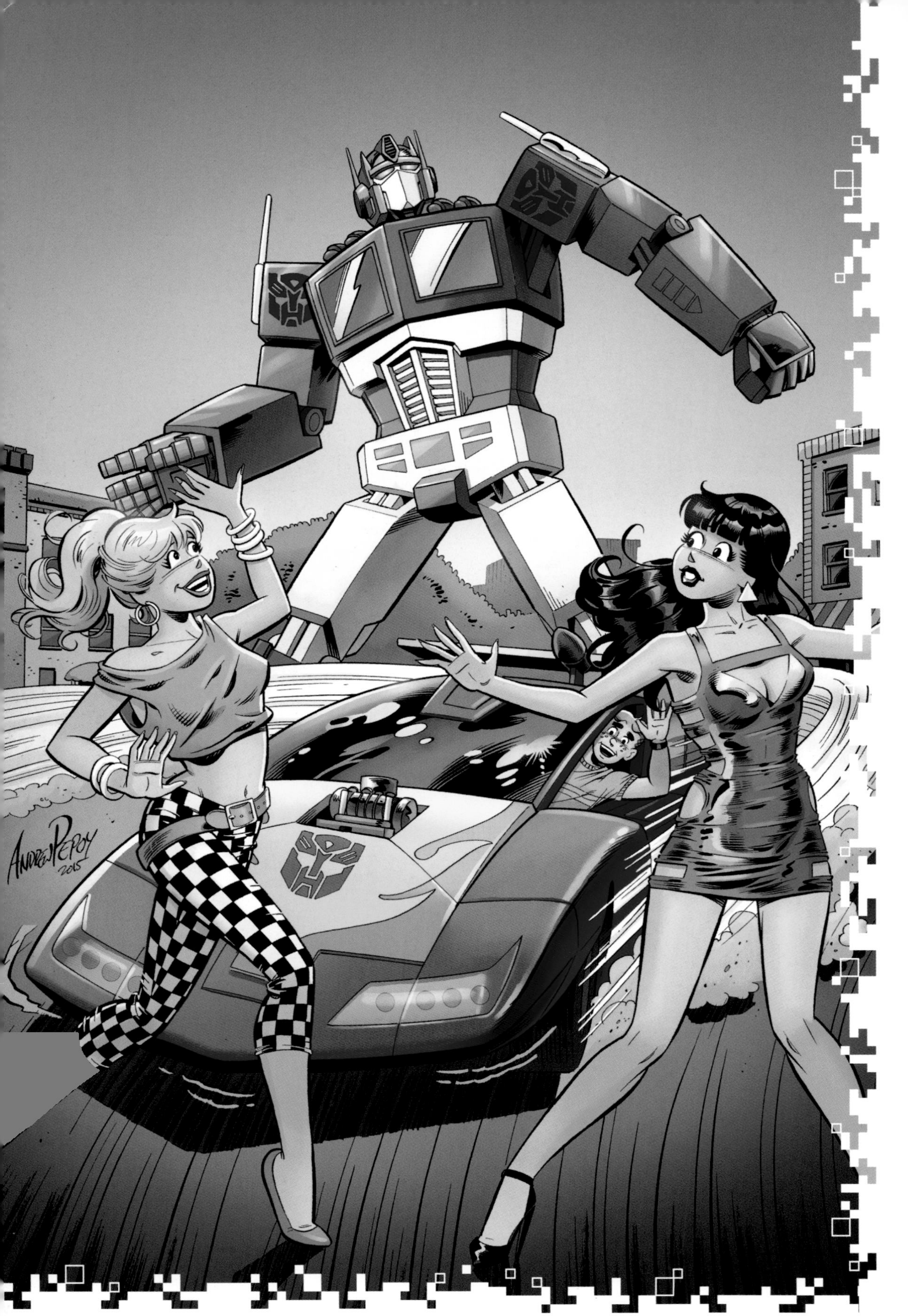
ANDREW PEPOY 2015

TRANSFORMERS #48 COVER SUB

by **ANDREW PEPOY** Colors by **JASON MILLET**

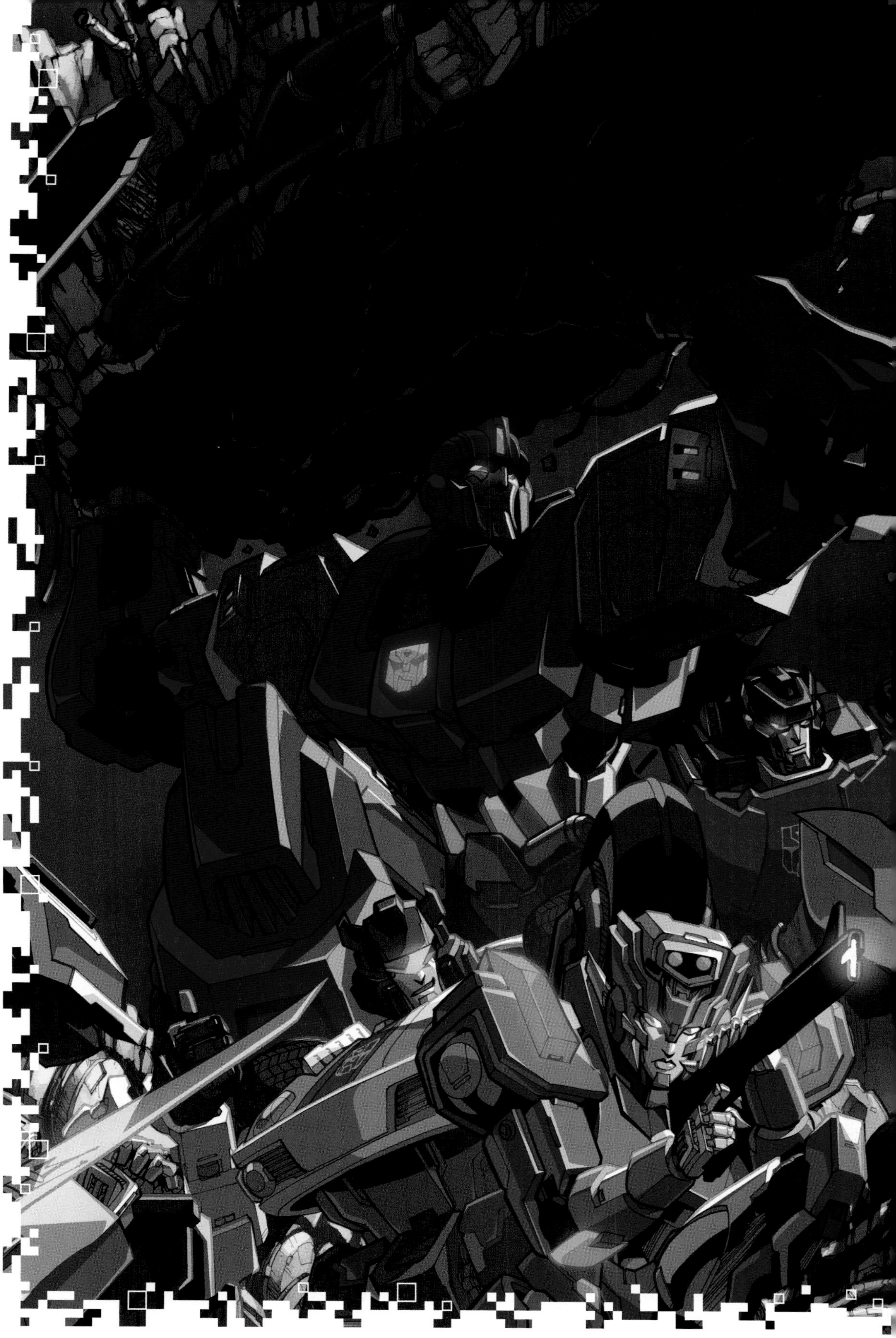

□ TRANSFORMERS #49 COVER RI

by **ALEX MILNE** Colors by **JOSH PEREZ**

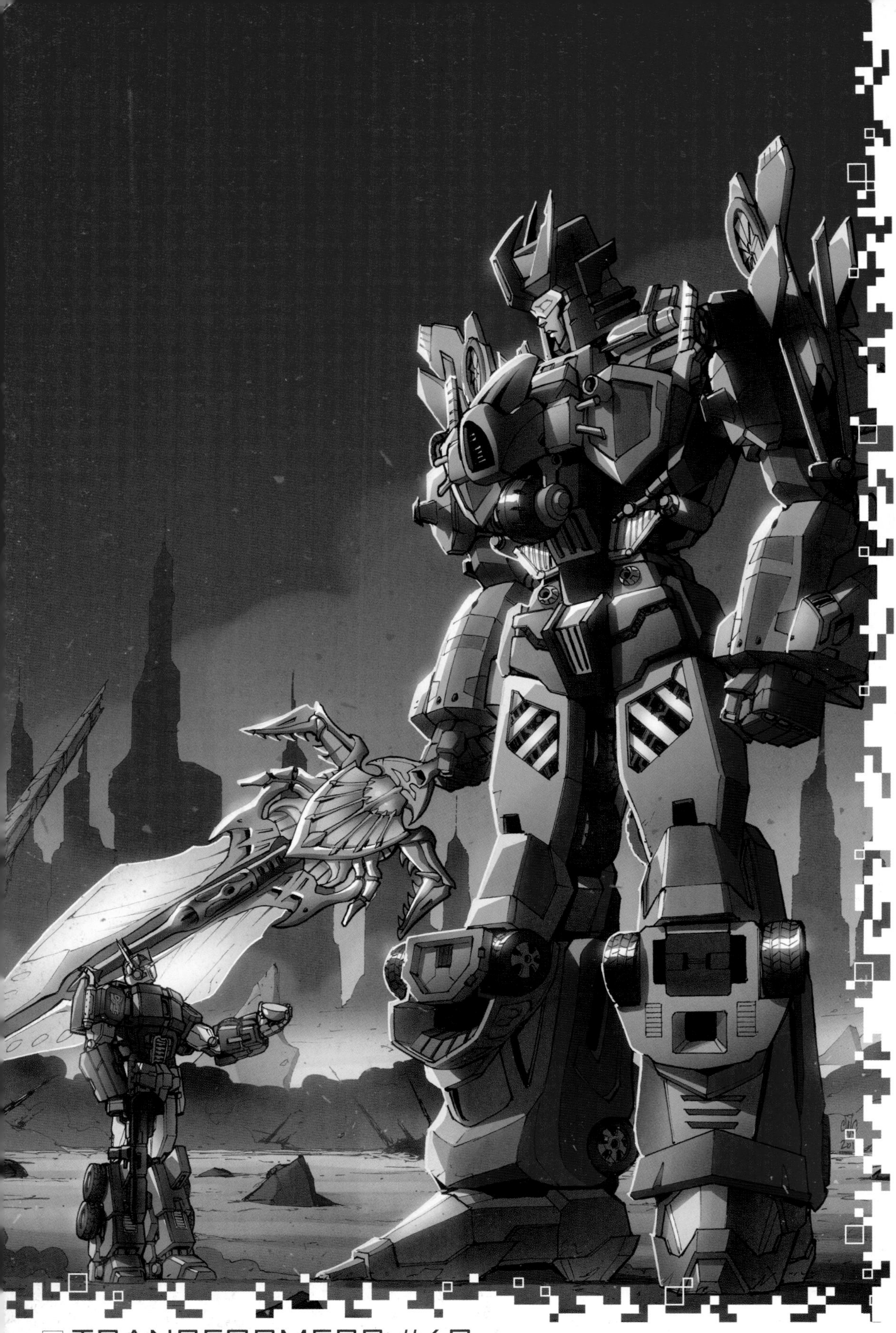

TRANSFORMERS #49 COVER SUB

by **CASEY W. COLLER** Colors by **JOANA LAFUENTE**